The Way of the Pipe

The Way of the Pipe

The Way of the Pipe

*Aboriginal Spirituality
and Symbolic Healing
in Canadian Prisons*

JAMES B. WALDRAM

broadview press

CANADIAN CATALOGUING IN PUBLICATION DATA

Waldram, James B. (James Burgess), 1955–
   The way of the pipe: aboriginal spirituality and symbolic healing in
   Canadian prisons.

Includes bibliographical references and index.
ISBN 1-55111-159-4

   1. Native peoples – Canada.
   2. Prisoners – Mental Health Services – Canada
   1. Title

E78.C2W34 1997   155.9'62'0971   C97-930279-X

broadview press
Post Office Box 1243, Peterborough, Ontario, Canada K9J 7H5

in the United States of America:
3576 California Road, Orchard Park, NY 14127

in the United Kingdom:
B.R.A.D. Book Representation & Distribution Ltd., 244A, London Road,
Hadleigh, Essex SS7 2DE

Broadview Press gratefully acknowledges the support of the Canada Council,
the Ontario Arts Council, and the Ministry of Canadian Heritage.

Cover design: Zack Taylor / Photograph: Tyrone Tootoosis.
The pipe on the back cover formerly belonged to Cree Chief Poundmaker.
The pipe is presently imprisoned in a Scottish Museum.

PRINTED IN CANADA

10 9 8 7 6 5 4 3 2 1

This book is dedicated to the memory of
my parents, Bill and Dorothy Waldram

Contents

It was foretold a long time ago, if the Aboriginal peoples should ever throw down the pipe and take up something different, that the Aboriginal peoples would have a hard time. They not only throw down the pipe, they throw down the family, the relatives and the tribe. For nothing shall ever sit above the pipe. The pipe meaning truth; the pipe meaning the old way; the pipe, a way of life that works.

— ELDER CAMPBELL PAPEQUASH

Preface Aboriginal peoples are over-represented in Canadian prisons, both federally and provincially. This is a well-known fact. Since the early 1980s, many Aboriginal offenders have been demanding recognition of their rights to religious freedom, to practise their spirituality while incarcerated, and in so doing to heal themselves in their own way. A profoundly intimate and intense process, this is the subject of this book.

Aboriginal spirituality is more than "religion," however; it is a way of healing and a mode of therapy. It is these components that I have chosen to examine since they are not well understood by the correctional system and seem to offer the greatest hope for Aboriginal inmates to find meaning in their lives. Although there are limits to the depth of descriptive analysis that is compatible with the world-view of many of the Elders involved in this study, to those with knowledge of Aboriginal spirituality, these limits will be self-evident.

In deciding to write this book, I was torn between my commitments to my academic discipline and to the many Aboriginal men in prison who had worked with me in the study. How could I write a book that would satisfy many different constituent groups? Science requires the adoption of a certain style of prose and presentation which, while accessible to other scientists, would quickly discourage all but the most interested lay person. The use of a more narrative style would frustrate some scientists, who might accuse me of unscientific reporting and therefore devalue the usefulness the work. But the book would likely then be read by more Aboriginal offenders, prison officials, therapists, and interested members of the public. Over the course of the research and writing, I encountered active support, even lobbying, for one or the other approach.

As an *applied* medical anthropologist, my first concern is to contribute constructively to change through knowledge and understanding, and this was the deciding factor. The Canadian correctional system is in need of change, and I believe a wider, more influential audience will be reached through the use of narrative than through a strictly scientific presentation. However, I was also influenced by a *Globe and Mail* article, appearing 20 July 1995. A prison warden, a believer in the therapeutic efficacy of Aboriginal spirituality, found it difficult to explain to his superiors why he needed more resources for his Aboriginal programming. He asked, "How do I justify in writing what he [the Elder] does? I know what he does, but I can't explain it."

Therefore, the purpose of this book, in the first instance, is threefold: to provide the Aboriginal offenders and Elders with a readable report on my research findings, to offer a reading source accessible to inmates, and to explain to the correctional authorities how, and why, Aboriginal spirituality operates as a form of therapy. To achieve these diverse goals, I have had to compromise. I refer to specific literature and the scientific and academic views on healing in various parts of the text, hopefully in a way intelligible to most readers. I also provide extensive narratives taken from interviews with Elders and inmates (and set out from the text). The latter have been edited, but in a way that retains the original language and meaning while rendering them a little easier to read. I attempt here to bring together two very different intellectual traditions, that of science and that of Aboriginal peoples, while privileging neither.

Another important goal, I hope, has also been achieved. In this book, I seek to provide insight into a unique form of therapy and treatment known as "symbolic healing," and in so doing to further our general understanding of this important human endeavour.

This study is based upon interviews with male Aboriginal inmates at federal and provincial correctional facilities in Manitoba and Saskatchewan, and upon interviews with many Elders and Native liaison personnel. As the primary researcher, I was also able to participate in many spiritual ceremonies undertaken behind the walls and to spend countless hours in informal discussion with inmates, Elders, and prison officials alike. A variety of research techniques were used, including participant-observation, survey instruments, and open-ended, ethnographic-style interviews. Initial research commenced in 1990 at the Regional Psychiatric Centre (Prairies) (hereafter RPC) in Saskatoon, with participant-observation and ethnographic interviewing of thirty inmates. The research continued through to January of 1994 when a new phase was implemented. This phase involved the interviewing of 249 Aboriginal inmates at Saskatchewan Penitentiary and Riverbend Institution (Prince Albert), Stony Mountain Penitentiary and Rockwood Institution (Winnipeg), and at the RPC. A parallel research project was also undertaken at this time at the Saskatoon Correctional Centre, a provincial correctional facility, by Randy Belon, one of my graduate students. In total, the research has solicited the views of over 300 Aboriginal inmates in two provinces.

Most of the individuals interviewed for this study were inmates of these institutions, and some remain there. For a variety of reasons, it is not possible to identify them by name. All were guaranteed confidentiality and anonymity, attributes essential to any effective work within the prison environment. Similarly, with one notable exception, Elders and spiritual leaders who were interviewed must also remain anonymous.

At each institution, a meeting was always sought with the resident Elder and the Native Brotherhood organization to explain the research and to seek permission. This was a somewhat unusual process since "permission" to undertake research had already been granted by correctional officials, some of whom clearly felt there was no need to discuss the work with the inmates. However, that is not how I, and most other anthropologists, work. I could have undertaken some research while bypassing the Elders and brotherhoods, but the quality of the data presented here speaks volumes for the need to secure the cooperation and assistance of researched populations. In each instance, I offered the Elders and brotherhoods what was, in effect, a veto over the research. If they did not approve, I would go no further. In each instance, approval was offered, but not routinely and not without a great deal of discussion.

In approaching each institution, and the Elders and Native Brotherhood organizations, I exposed myself to the toughest question any applied researcher faces: "How will your research be of benefit?" (in this case, to the Elders and inmates). It is not always easy to explain the complex relationship between research and public policy. I tried to impress upon these individuals that the execution of the research itself did not guarantee positive change and that, even where the correctional system might see merit in the work, actual change could be years away. For many, the research would be of little direct benefit, since they would likely be out of prison by the time any policy changes were enacted. The Elders and Aboriginal inmates, however, did recognize the need for change which could enhance the opportunities for healing for those unfortunate men who would take up their cells behind the walls. I promised them that I would produce something "useful," and this book is a partial execution of that promise. It is designed to be readable by the men who participated in this study and who are actively involved in spirituality, or who are considering it as a new lifeway.

Securing the permission of the Elders and Native brotherhood organizations was one step, but convincing individual offenders to participate in an interview was quite another task. One must remember that prisons are characterized by secrecy and paranoia; there is a perceived need to control knowledge and information about oneself. While confidentiality was offered, some inmates were not easily convinced that no matter how honest and sincere we were, "information" would not find its way to the administration and ultimately be harmful to them. Nevertheless, over the five institutions very few men refused outright to work with us.

Many Aboriginal offenders, when first approached to participate in various aspects of this research, questioned (quite rightly) what was in it for "them." Perhaps surprisingly, they thought not so much in terms of their own interests ("Will this help me get parole?"), but rather in terms of how Aboriginal inmates collectively would benefit from the study. Coming on the heels of the Aboriginal Justice Inquiry of Manitoba, whose recommendations were quickly consigned to the dustbin, I found myself walking into an environment in which "research" was a dirty, exploitative concept. Particularly difficult was my attempt to explain my understanding of how policy change ensues and how my role as a researcher is largely marginal to this process, since I did not work for the correctional system. But, as a researcher and university professor, what I lacked in inside clout, I perhaps made up in my role as a "scientist" who could "objectively" research and "tell it like it is." Some inmates clearly saw me as an advocate, a few as a typist ("we'll tell you what to say, and you put it down"), and thankfully only a few as part of the correctional establishment. Nevertheless, I had to be absolutely honest with them, explaining that change to the correctional system would not automatically follow my research. My work would be added to that of others, who also are calling for an overhaul of the system, and perhaps ultimately change would ensue.

Working with correctional staff was, in some respects, more difficult than working with the inmates. We encountered a small degree of open hostility, but for the most part staff was passively cooperative, especially after it was emphasized that we had "authorization." Most institutions were fairly easy to work in. Riverbend, Rockwood, and RPC, in particular, greatly facilitated access to the men. The first two are minimum security facilities where the men have a great deal of mobility. RPC is a multilevel secure psychiatric facility that operates on a hospital model. We were required to work around institutional schedules and inmate programs in accessing inmates, although in some cases inmates were given permission to be absent from a program in order to meet with us. The work was not so easy at Saskatchewan Institution. This is a true dinosaur of a facility whose aging and decrepit walls, and the attitudes of senior prison staff, seem to be from another era. This institution, classified as medium security, operated like a maximum security prison, at least to us outsiders (although many other prison staff intimated that the warden simply could not deal with the reality of a medium institution after it was reclassified from maximum). Despite clearance to undertake the research, each day we were confronted with the same old excuse that our temporary passes were "on the warden's desk," and that there were no day passes ready at the gate that would allow us in. We lost some interviews this way, as men arrived at our research location only to discover us absent. We were harassed in other ways as well, and what cooperation we received was given grudgingly by all but a few staff members. I came away with the distinct feeling that the cooperation, such as it was, fulfilled the responsibility of the institution to its superiors, but that within the walls where the warden and his staff ruled, efforts at passive resistance were coordinated.[1]

At each institution we worked closely with the Native liaison staff, who were instrumental in orienting us to each facility, helping us make contact with inmates, promoting the research, and providing us with space to work or relax.

I issued several basic promises to those who participated in the study as a way of ensuring accountability. Where possible, transcripts of interviews were returned to Elders and inmates. All Elders and Native liaison personnel were given the absolute right of control over their interviews, and interview transcripts were provided to them for additions or deletions. Where possible, draft copies of the manuscript were returned to the Elders for their perusal. In many instances, Elders returned their copies with valuable suggestions and criticisms, and I gave serious consideration to their ideas when preparing the final manuscript. I have also endeavoured to have many people who are knowledgeable about prisons or Aboriginal spirituality review this manuscript, and their responses have also influenced what you will read here. Some of the research money was used to purchase Native Studies books for the RPC library, since individual gift giving was prohibited. I also guaranteed that royalties from the sale of this book would be paid to the Native Brotherhood at the Regional Psychiatric Centre in Saskatoon. This forensic treatment facility was central to my research, and it is the one institution where individuals from the others may be temporarily incarcerated while undergoing special-ized treatment. Since treatment programs for offenders at RPC last from six to eight months, the inmate population is fairly transient. The Native Brotherhood there is constantly being reconstituted, with the result that it is difficult for them to raise funds for their cultural activities. The royalties from this book will help them in this regard.

A brief comment about the title of this book is also in order here. Throughout the research with Elders and inmates, I often heard indi-viduals speak reverently about the importance of Aboriginal spiritu-ality in their lives. Each saw Aboriginal spirituality as a process, one that had no logical end point, but one that could provide a blueprint for the living of one's life in a more fulfilling, rewarding, and altruis-tic way. Some referred to this as the "Red Road," others as the "Sweetgrass Trail" or the "Aboriginal way," and others more simply as "the way" or "the path." When deciding on the title, I solicited the views of many of the Elders, and a few others, only to discover that there was no consensus about what this process of spiritual re-birth and recovery should be called (and whether it was even neces-sary to call it anything at all). As a result, I tend to use all these expressions, though in the title I refer to the "Way of the Pipe," a way open to all who seek it. There are many teachings in the pipe. Learning and understanding these teachings, however, is an extremely indi-vidualistic process. The name is immaterial, of course; it is just a label. If it impedes understanding, it should be ignored; if it enlightens, so be it. What spirituality means to the Elders and men is far more important.

There are many people whose efforts were required to execute the research as successfully as we did. Again, for reasons of confidentiality, I cannot mention many of them. I wish to single out one individual whose work within institutions has been inspiring for myself, members of the research team, and many inmates: Campbell Papequash, whose vision and words are reflected throughout this text. I wish also to emphasize that, while I undertook much of the research alone, in the latter stages I was ably assisted by a fine research team consisting of Randy Belon, Audrey Hobman, James Taylor, and Vince Vandale. Working within the prison context was difficult and challenging; these individuals were able to adapt to changing institutional contexts, to deal with harassment from officials, and to engender trust from inmates while maintaining their sense of humour and dedication to the project.

Other individuals also assisted me at various stages of the research. In particular, I wish to thank Stan Guenther, Michael Jackson, Phyllis Iverson, Tyrone Tootoosis, Dan Stifle, Art Gordon, and Steve Wong.

The manuscript has been read by many individuals, and I have tried to respond faithfully to their comments and criticisms. These individuals include Campbell Papequash, Bea Medicine, Audrey Hobman, Noel Knockwood, Tyrone Tootoosis, Joe Couture, and Irene Fraser.

I am particularly indebted to my partner, Pamela Downe, a medical anthropologist with whom I was able to share ideas about this book, and who provided me with some important feedback as the project took shape.

Research funds were provided, in a variety of ways, from the Correctional Service of Canada, the University of Saskatchewan, and the Saskatchewan Health Research and Utilization Commission. I am grateful for this financial support. I am also grateful to the research staff at RPC for their continued interest in my research.

The first part of Chapter Four is an extensively rewritten version of ideas that first appeared in *Culture, Medicine and Psychiatry* (1993, Volume 17). A portion of Chapter Eight previously appeared in the *American Indian Quarterly* (1994, Volume 18, No.2), published by the University of Nebraska Press.

Of course, this book as a text is the product of my construction and therefore represents my views only. It cannot be construed as representing the views of those individuals who participated in the research, Aboriginal offenders in general, those who provided funding, or any others I have named above. I have learned much from working with the Elders and inmates, and their words have guided and informed my own perspective on the issues raised in this book. I quote extensively from the participants and have highlighted these quotations by setting them out from the text. Their words are every bit as important and, in some ways, more important, than those of the social scientist. Yet no text can be truly "objective," and I do not pretend to have "truth." What I offer here is my interpretation of a little-known, but immensely profound, spiritual and healing movement.

NOTE

1   I must stress that there has been some turnover in senior management within
the Correctional Service of Canada, including the warden at Saskatchewan
Institution, since this research was conducted.

A Story of Trauma, Healing and Transformation[I]

I talked to an Elder one time and it kind of blew my mind. He gave me a story about the eagle. I don't know if you've ever heard it. The story goes like this, and I think it's really my story too.

This eagle is flying around and all of a sudden, something happened. He got shot. He was wounded and he fell inside a ditch. A farmer saw this eagle and picked it up, but the eagle was fighting the farmer, still trying to get away. But being wounded and very defenceless, the farmer took the eagle to his farm and put him in the chicken coop with the chickens. So after a period of time, through feeding and through mimicking the actions of the chickens, the eagle started going through a change. And the eagle looked around and figured, "Well geez, if that's how they feed, I guess that's how I'll have to feed. If that's how they sleep, that's how I'll have to sleep. And if they hang around like that, well I guess I'll have to do the same thing." So there was an identity change, and the eagle started becoming a chicken.

So this went on for a period of time, and one day an Indian came along. He was walking down the road and asked the farmer for a drink of water. He looked over in the chicken coop and saw the eagle acting like a chicken. So he said, "What's that eagle doing there in the chicken coop?"

The farmer said, "Well, I found it in the ditch, mended its wing and put him in there. He just needed to heal up. The eagle can fly out any time. Its wing is healed. There's no cage over him. There's a fence around to keep the chickens in, but the eagle doesn't want to go. He just thinks he's a chicken I guess."

So the Indian told the farmer that the eagle was a proud bird and explained that it stood for courage, power, might. Anyway, the Indian guy said, "Can I take that eagle?"

The farmer said, "You can do what you want to do with it. Take him out of there. It's just one less I have to feed."

So the Indian took the eagle, but the eagle was very docile. He thought he was a chicken. He kept bobbing his head. He had lost his complete identity.

The Indian started talking to the eagle and telling him what the eagle represents. He said, "You shouldn't be there. You should be flying high in the sky, people looking up at you and seeing you spreading your wings and giving courage." The eagle didn't have a clue about what he was hearing.

So the Indian took the bird to the mountain and said, "I'm going to let you go. I'm going to drop you off here where you can fly and soar." So the Indian let the eagle go and the eagle just flopped back down to the earth just like a chicken. He just stayed on the ground. And the Indian went down and picked the eagle up, brought him back up again and again he explained what he represented and everything else about it. He explained that the eagle was not a chicken and that he's different from anybody else. "You have to know who you are and what you stand for." And he threw him off the mountain, and the same thing happened *again. The Indian went down and picked him up again and took him back up. He explained again and again and again about it. The eagle started to flex his wings. His keen eyesight started to return, and the strength in him started to come back. So he let the eagle go again, and this time the eagle soared with the wind before he fell back down. He was hopping on the ground this time. He was shaking his wings and looking around. Again the Indian went down and picked him up and took him to the mountain. Again, he explained who he was and what he represented. When he threw the eagle off this time, the eagle flew and soared and everything came back to him, who he was and that he wasn't a chicken. He wasn't like anybody else, he was completely different. He gained everything he'd lost because of where he was placed and put.*

I guess the bottom line is you have to know who you are, what you stand for, and that you can gain back whatever you've lost through perseverance and understanding. And you've got to have someone that's willing to take the time to share and to care and to teach.

NOTE

1. This story was told to me by an Aboriginal inmate, who in turn had heard it from an Elder who had spoken at the prison. In response to my request, the story was offered to me for use in this research. For reasons of confidentiality, I cannot disclose the inmate's name, and he cannot recall the name of the Elder who first shared the story. My thanks to both of them for the powerful teachings that this story contains.

"Religious freedom in the land?"—
Then leave us to our peaceful ways,
What boots it that we should depart
From ancient rites of bygone days?
— EDWARD AHENAKEW[1]

1
Rediscovering the Pipe

On the 30th of March 1983, two Aboriginal inmates at Kent Institution in Agassiz, British Columbia, began a spiritual fast to protest the denial of their right to practise their spirituality. While this decision led ultimately to the introduction of spiritual services for Aboriginal offenders in federal institutions in Canada, the road was long and difficult for all those who would become involved. To understand what happened at Kent, and its consequences, it is first necessary to understand why it happened.

The Repression of Aboriginal Spirituality and Healing

Historically, when indigenous peoples have been colonized, the colonizers have accurately identified religion as central to human cultural existence. They have often attempted to destroy or alter religion as part of a plan for alienating indigenous peoples' land, labour, and resources. In the societies of indigenous peoples, what westerners call "religion" and "healing" are an integrated and inseparable part of the cultural whole. Therefore, attacks on religion have often had negative consequences for traditional healing systems; the repression of one invariably included the repression of the other. The colonization of Aboriginal North America, primarily by the English and French, is a good example of the dynamics of this process.

In the early years of contact, Aboriginal religion and healing in Canada were threatened mostly by the activities of Christian missionaries, who sought to convert the peoples they encountered to the ways of Christianity. Their effectiveness in the first few centuries of contact can be debated; they made some progress, converted some "souls," and eliminated some traditional healing practices. But many aspects of spirituality and healing continued to be practised openly, and the ceremonies were often public affairs. With the formation of Canada in 1867, however, both religion and healing were targeted by the federal government and churches as part of formal policies designed to assimilate and "civilize" the Aboriginal inhabitants. Katherine Pettipas (1994) has documented much of this story.

In 1884 and 1885, the Canadian government passed legislation outlawing the ceremonial activities associated with the potlatch, or feast, among Northwest Coast cultures. Potlatches were highly public feasts at which clan stories were rendered, claims to territory reasserted, and marriages celebrated. One aspect of the potlatch involved the redistribution of wealth, either as foods and material goods or, in later years, cash, to the guests of the host clan. Occasionally involving the destruction of goods, this practice was viewed by missionaries as wasteful and primitive, and therefore as an obstacle to Christianity. Their campaigns to have the government render the potlatch illegal were ultimately successful.

The first federal proclamation banning the potlatch appeared in 1883, and in 1884 the *Indian Act* was amended to include the ban. This clause became known as the "Potlatch Law." But more than just the potlatch was involved because the legislation also banned the "tamanawas," the Salish healing ceremony known today as "spirit dancing." This was the first legislative attempt to outlaw an Aboriginal religious and healing ceremony in Canada.

The first arrest under the Potlatch Law was made in 1889, but the judge ruled that the law was too vague and that the whole ceremony could not be rendered illegal. In response, the government revised the legislation in 1895 to better define the illegal components and to be more inclusive. It now made aspects of the Prairie Indian "Grass Dance," in particular the "giveaways," illegal, as well as the "Sun Dance" practice of piercing.

The Sun Dance was an important annual ceremony celebrated by many different Plains Indian groups. Beyond its religious significance as a means of offering sacrifice and thanks to the Creator, the Sun Dance was also an important social occasion where many different bands came together for weeks at a time. The practice of "piercing" involved pushing wooden or bone skewers through the flesh on the chest or back, which in turn were tied to a central Sun Dance pole; the participants danced for four days and eventually attempted to tear away from the skewers as part of their sacrifice to the Creator. Christian missionaries found the practice to be heathen, and the government believed that such ceremonies wasted the time of participants and that unspecified "evils" occurred. A jail sentence of two to six months was mandated.

Under the 1895 *Indian Act* amendment, Indian agents were expected to use their influence, coercive if necessary, to discourage illegal activities and, in a broader sense, cultural practices that inhibited the goals of assimilation. However, their legal powers were ill-defined, and they were discouraged against using force to prevent or disrupt ceremonies. Similarly, the North-West Mounted Police were hesitant to act since their legal position was not clear either. Nevertheless, there were many instances of disturbances of ceremonies, often while in progress, and threats by Indian agents and police to discourage such activities. Sun Dances, for instance, were occasionally broken up, and Sun Dance lodges were destroyed. Even sweat lodge ceremonies were interrupted, despite the fact that these were not covered by the *Indian Act* ban.

The government continued to fiddle with the *Indian Act* legislation, amending it in 1914, 1918 and 1933, all in an effort to secure a legally enforceable ban on Aboriginal religious activity. Parallel policies were also developed by the government from time to time to facilitate the assimilation of the Aboriginal population. What became known as the "pass system" in the prairies was an ad hoc, likely illegal, attempt to confine individuals to reserves, in part to inhibit them from participating in various ceremonial activities. The residential school system was also developed, in which Aboriginal children were targeted for the purposes of assimilation, removed from their families, and educated for most of the year under the auspices of various religious denominations. Residential schools, in particular, had serious negative consequences for the health and wellbeing of generations of Aboriginal people, as we shall see in this book.

The Aboriginal people did not simply accept these limitations of their ceremonial life, and they often protested vigorously. Traditional religion and healing became politicized within the context of colonial relations. The reactions of the Indians to these legal and extralegal efforts to suppress their spirituality parallel the story of spirituality within the prisons being told in this book. Protests began with the use of petitions and appeals, and eventually lawyers were consulted and used to threaten the police and keep them away from ceremonies. Arguments were made that the treaties protected religious freedoms. Some groups defied the law, and held dances and ceremonies anyway, often in more remote areas. Adjacent Indian bands often held ceremonies on their joint boundaries so that participants could attend without technically leaving their reserves. There was also accommodation to the law: some ceremonies were shortened to one or two days, and certain components, such as piercing in the Sun Dance, eliminated.

It is not at all clear how many Aboriginal people were prosecuted or incarcerated for practising traditional spiritual or healing ceremonies. Murray Sinclair, co-chair of the Aboriginal Justice Inquiry in Manitoba, has written that "[t]he statistical evidence available (such that it is) for Stony Mountain Penitentiary in Manitoba at the turn of the century shows that most of the Indian people who were incarcerated at that time were sentenced simply for practising their traditional religions" (Sinclair 1990:5). Many Aboriginal peoples today relate oral histories that suggest that incarceration for "dancing," with or without formal charges or convictions, was common.

The Indian rights political movement began to accelerate after World War One, and rights to religious freedom were included in the demands. Edward Ahenakew, whose poetry opened this chapter, was a Cree leader with this movement. Between 1914 and 1945, political efforts to have the *Indian Act* ban repealed were unsuccessful, and the government actively worked to undermine any political mobilization by Indian peoples. It was not until 1951 that the repressive measures of the *Indian Act* were deleted, but by this time much damage had been done.

The results of the criminalization of Aboriginal spirituality and ceremony, combined with the effects of residential schools and other government programs to assimilate Aboriginal peoples, were profound. Many Aboriginal people today have grown up as Christians, with no knowledge of traditional spirituality, language, and in some instances, culture. The Elders, those who harboured traditional knowledge, have dwindled in number, and fewer young people have been inclined to pick up their mantle. Those spiritual activities that have persisted to this day did so primarily by going underground, away from the prying eyes of the non-Aboriginal law. Therefore, the view that such ceremonies are "secret," to be shielded from those who might oppose or exploit the traditional ways, has become more common.

By early 1980, with Aboriginal people disproportionately represented in federal prisons, it was as if traditional spirituality were still against the law. Aboriginal inmates were not afforded the same rights as non-Aboriginal inmates to celebrate their faith. Their ways were still viewed as primitive, as not really "religion" as Christians understood it. Many Aboriginal people, including Elders, believed that prison was an inappropriate place for sacred objects and ceremonies, and that the inmates were pariahs; they had no interest in facilitating any spiritual revival inside the walls. It would be up to the inmates themselves to undertake the political action to secure their spiritual freedoms.

The Incident at Kent Institution[2]

Kent Institution was a maximum security federal penitentiary in the early 1980s. Located in Agassiz, British Columbia, Kent would not have seemed to be the place where a new Aboriginal political and spiritual movement would arise. Yet the Correctional Service of Canada (hereafter csc), which had a penchant for moving inmates about the country to reduce institutional tensions and problems, inadvertently brought together a disparate collection of strong-willed men who were beginning to articulate their own vision of freedom and rehabilitation through spirituality.

At the centre of the movement were two cousins, Darelle (Dino) and Gary Butler. They were Americans, members of the Siletz Nation in Oregon. Dino Butler had been a co-defendent at the Wounded Knee trial in 1976, which followed a tragic shootout with the FBI and the deaths of two federal agents and one Indian. While Leonard Peltier was found guilty and remains in prison to this day, Dino Butler was found not guilty and released.

Butler's path to Wounded Knee had been a winding one, and from his youth he had experienced discrimination at the hands of the US justice system. Alcohol and drugs took on an increased importance in his life. That is, until he discovered the American Indian Movement, AIM, the radical "Red power" group of Native Americans that was beginning to shake the foundations of American society in the 1970s. Butler took up with AIM activists Russell Means, Dennis Banks, and Leonard Peltier, eventually ending up at the Pine Ridge Lakota reservation in South Dakota. In June of 1975, Dino Butler was at the Pine Ridge community of Wounded Knee when the shootout occurred. Though acquitted of murder, Butler remained scarred from the experience (Matthiessen 1983).

The experience in South Dakota was significant in other ways, for it was here that the Butlers became immersed in the spirituality of the Lakota. They experienced their first sweat lodge ceremony and took their initial steps on the Red Road, learning more about Aboriginal spirituality as a way of life and as an alternative to a lifestyle of alcohol and criminal behaviour. "Hate had a really strong hold on me in the 60s," Dino Butler is quoted as saying in 1983. "I hated myself, and it was easy to extend that hate to everyone around me. It came pretty close to destroying me. I have never drunk liquor since then. I have no need for chemicals in my body to get relief from reality. I've been in jail a couple of times since then, but it's lots different for me now."

Dino Butler crossed into Canada in 1981 to help organize a rally in support of Leonard Peltier, a man who many today believe was unjustly convicted of murder. Butler decided to stay, temporarily, in Canada, in part because he feared for his life in the US. As a friend of Butler's stated, "They'll be gunning for Dino the rest of his life because they think he killed two pigs and walked away" (Matthiessen 1983:534).

Dino Butler, now accompanied by his cousin, Gary, moved about, and the two eventually found their way to Vancouver. The cousins had the "Red Power" look about them; they were marked men even on this side of the border. One day, when they were signalled by the Vancouver police to pull over, they took flight, engaging the police in a high speed chase that ended with shots fired and their car being demolished. They may have thought of the kinds of police brutality directed towards Indians they had seen and experienced in the United States. They may also have thought of the illegal weapons they were carrying.

Life at Oakalla Regional Correctional Centre, where they were held in remand for the trial, was difficult for the Butlers. Dino wrote of this period: "All of a sudden we have been declared a high security risk... We are up on death row where Peltier was held, our doors are not only locked in the conventional way but have chains welded on and padlocked... We are not allowed our religious ceremonies, and everywhere we go, we have to wear shackles on our hands and on our legs, if not both... We have refused to walk into their courts with their shackles of hate and racism, so they choose to drag us in and out." Butler then concluded, dryly, "So that's how it goes nowadays for me, nothing out of the ordinary" (cited in Matthiessen 1983:540).

While awaiting trial at Oakalla, the cousins successfully went to the British Columbia Supreme Court to temporarily obtain their sacred items from the Royal Canadian Mounted Police. At their trial, they requested the return of their sacred eagle feathers, pipe, and medicine bundle but were refused by the judge.[3] During the trial, without their sacred objects, they became intransigent. They protested by dismissing their lawyer, refused to speak at the trial, and were convicted. To reinforce their demands for religious freedom inside Oakalla, they subsequently embarked on a fast that lasted twenty-two days. The strategy was successful; their sacred items were returned, and Oakalla allowed Aboriginal services to be developed. The cousins, however, received five years and were sent to Kent Institution to serve their sentences.

In June of 1982, the Native Brotherhood at Kent requested permission to hold a pipe ceremony and a sweat lodge ceremony. The proposal was a modest one, a request that selected inmates be allowed to possess sacred items, and that outside Elders and spiritual advisors be allowed to assist in ceremonies. They also raised the question of the frequency with which the pipe ceremonies would be undertaken.

The warden, a religious man himself (but in the Christian sense), had difficulty understanding how Aboriginal spirituality was "religion," and he turned down the request. Prison authorities suggested that a sweat lodge ceremony was not possible for security reasons. They did allow Dino Butler to have possession of his eagle feathers, but Butler was offended that a "permit" was required (in part, because of statutes protecting eagles). The sacred pipe bundle remained with prison officials; they viewed the pipe as a potential weapon. A proposal tendered by the Brotherhood, which outlined how their spirituality could be practised inside the prison, was met with a counterproposal by the warden which was so restrictive that it was deemed unacceptable. This counterproposal included conditions stating that the administration be informed when, where, and how the pipe was being moved. Further, inmates would not be allowed to keep sweetgrass and sage in their cells. The Brotherhood's response was poignant: "We ask you: Can a Catholic priest perform a ritual mass without an altar stone? Must a Christian fundamentalist notify the administration when he wants to carry his Bible to the prison yard or the prison chapel? We think not."

Months passed without satisfactory action, and the Aboriginal Brothers decided to take their case beyond the walls. They contacted a Vancouver lawyer, Stan Guenther, to provide legal advice on the issue of religious freedoms. Guenther met with the Brotherhood once, in July of 1982, and began to prepare a legal argument. However, he was subsequently prevented from entering the prison to meet with the Brotherhood. The warden advised the Brotherhood that Guenther would only be allowed inside after completion of a normal application for "visiting privileges," as if his purposes were only social. While Guenther completed the application, he also protested, arguing that the Brotherhood had the right to obtain legal representation. It took three months for the warden to finally approve Guenther as legal counsel!

The Brotherhood also contacted the Canadian Human Rights Commission in August of 1982, arguing that the Kent administration viewed their spiritual needs "as a program much as recreation and education are deemed programs." They outlined several legal conventions that guaranteed their religious freedoms.

By March of 1983, University of British Columbia law professor Michael Jackson had also been brought into the issue, and a community-based "Indigenous People's Defence Committee" had developed. The lawyers argued that freedom of religion was protected under the new Charter of Rights and Freedoms, and that Aboriginal spirituality could also be seen as an "aboriginal" right under Section 35 of the Constitution. They also pointed out that the CSC Commissioner's Directive dictated that religious programs would be available in all prisons, and that staff should encourage inmates to participate. But matters moved too slowly for Dino and Gary Butler.

On the 30th of March 1983, the Butlers began a spiritual fast. Dino Butler, a man who was described by Leonard Peltier as quiet, sincere, and dedicated (Matthiessen 1983:563), wrote at the time, "I want my Pipe, and if I can't have it in this world, I'll have it in the next... To deny me possession of it was to deny me of my human right to worship according to my belief." In a subsequent communique, Butler developed his ideas further:

> Because you are the way you are, I will begin a prayer Fast to pray that our Creator will have pity upon you in your ignorance and disrespect towards humanity and the values the Supreme Being blessed all life with... I will pray real hard that Tunkashila, Grandfather — the Creator, will bless you with wisdom to understand that we, too, are His children, so that you can accept in your mind and heart, our credibility that will allow you to let me have my Sacred Pipe Bundle and our Sacred Sweat Lodge to

worship in accordance to our beliefs as Native people and not
as criminals of your society under your dictatorship... Until my
spiritual hunger is satisfied, I cannot and will not eat the prison
food of hypocrites and oppressors of my spiritual being... I will
only accept water during this fast because that is from which
life came, and life is what I seek to enhance.

One week later, another inmate joined the fast. He was soon followed by another, and another. Then the movement began to spread.
Supporters outside the walls of Kent also began to fast. Other prisoners at Oakalla prison joined in, as did those at the Regina Correctional Centre. Many inmates in Kent lent support in a variety of
ways, including short fasts and work stoppages. Supporters on the
outside began to raise money for the bills that would accompany a
legal action as well as to fund an emerging public relations machine.
The national media began to notice, and the issue was raised in the
House of Commons by Svend Robinson, NDP Member of Parliament
for the Burnaby area. Solicitor General Robert Kaplan, in charge of
the CSC, rose to state that he had "no sympathy for Indians on a
hunger strike at the Kent penitentiary, especially since they spent several weeks fattening up before beginning the fast."

Kent officials insisted that the Aboriginal inmates were free to
practise their religion. One official of the CSC's British Columbia office
was reported in the media as arguing that guidelines were in place
that allowed spiritual ceremonies to take place. These included a
requirement that one inmate be designated the pipe carrier, charged
with the responsibility to look after the pipe, and that all spiritual
materials could be searched at any time for security reasons. He also
suggested that the Native Brotherhood had not made a formal request to build a sweat lodge (*Vancouver Sun*, 27 April 1983). The
Native Brotherhood rejected these guidelines, which they described
as "a warden's whim dictating... how to pray."

Frustrated, the Native Brotherhood continued to pursue their legal action, in the hopes that it could force the warden to reverse his
decision. UBC law professor Michael Jackson was an advocate of
prisoners' rights (see Jackson 1989), and he was certain that, under
the new Charter of Rights and Freedoms, which protected religious
expression, the Brotherhood would win the case. He nevertheless
felt that they should pursue negotiations first. Asking that they keep
in mind the kinds of concerns a warden of a maximum security prison
might have, he suggested that they moderate their position and develop another proposal for the warden's consideration. A small group

of Elders was also brought into the institution to help resolve the conflict. The Elders, Aboriginal brothers, their lawyer, and prison staff spent a day sitting in the circle trying to resolve the impasse.

Instrumental in this process was the work of Joe Couture, a psychologist with a Ph.D. who also happens to be Metis and who has had extensive experience apprenticing with an Aboriginal healer in Alberta. Couture was brought in to talk to both the Brotherhood and the warden. Sitting in the circle for a full day, Couture listened to the concerns of the Brotherhood and, at one point, brought the warden in to hear for himself. As a result, the warden was convinced that Aboriginal spirituality was indeed a legitimate "religion." He issued a directive to allow spiritual ceremonies on a limited basis and to exempt spiritual materials from all but visual inspection. Couture subsequently went on to develop a set of guidelines on the practice of Aboriginal spirituality in prison.

On May 2, 1983, Dino Butler ended his fast after 34 days. Despite assurances that spiritual ceremonies would be allowed, the Kent administration moved slowly, and the first sweat lodge ceremony was not held for another seven months. But this would be the first such ceremony inside the walls of a Canadian penitentiary.

The movement had started. Slowly other institutions began to seriously consider inmate requests for spiritual ceremonies, and Joe Couture's guidelines began to take hold. In 1984 Warkworth and Joyceville inmates were given permission to hold sweat lodge ceremonies, as were inmates at Edmonton Max. In 1985, the CSC adopted Couture's guidelines as policy,[4] and the movement continued to spread. There were still battles to be fought, however, as the policy was resisted by staff at many institutions. The CSC, seeking to break up the "ring leaders" at Kent, transferred most of them within a year of the fast. But like seeds scattering in the wind, taking root and growing into new plants, these inmates took the new spiritual and political activism with them. Gary Butler was transferred to Edmonton, and then Millhaven. One leader was shipped to Archambault, and another to Dorchester. In reference to these transfers, one of these men commented to me, "The way he [Dino Butler] explained it to me was pretty neat. He says they are not breaking up our circle, they are only making it bigger. He says where you are going, they probably need you down there to do some work... Truer words couldn't have been spoken. They didn't have anything down there. So when I got there, I got some Elders involved in coming into the place and we built our first drum and we got our first sweat lodge happening. So that was the purpose of me going down there." But there is usually a price to political activism, and those involved in the Kent movement were branded as troublemakers. They were often accused of conduct threatening to the institutions and were transferred regularly.

The Current Policy Context

While the constitutional protection of Aboriginal spirituality as a form of religious practice has been necessary, it has had the negative effect of obscuring this spirituality's inherently therapeutic aspects. In general, the correctional system in Canada views Aboriginal spiritual programs as "religion," especially as Euro-Canadian Christians would understand this concept, services being made available because of constitutional and legislative exigency. Recent studies done for the correctional service would bear this out: they emphasize the struggle of Aboriginal people to have their spirituality, and Elders, recognized in a fashion analogous to Christianity and the chaplains.

A report done in 1988 for the Solicitor General's office stated: "Many Native offenders have special social, cultural and spiritual needs. These include the observation of such traditional group ceremonies and rituals as pipe ceremonies and the sweat lodge. For Native offenders who have not had much prior contact with traditional culture and spirituality, the opportunity for instruction and participation in these areas can become an important part of their incarceration experience" (Canada 1988a:5). The report then erroneously suggested that "spiritual and related cultural needs" were well understood. It recommended that "Aboriginal spirituality shall be accorded the same status, protection and privileges as other religions," and that Elders be "recognized as having the same status, protection and privileges as religious officials of other religions" (Canada 1988a:34). Although suggesting that these programs appeared to be having positive effects on inmates, the report failed to raise the issue of the therapeutic aspects of Aboriginal spirituality.

On the heels of this report, the report of the "Task Force on Aboriginal Peoples in Federal Corrections" recognized the "traditional Indian view" of health and that services for Aboriginal offenders "must take their spiritual and cultural background into account" (Canada 1988b:13-14). But the report stopped short of recognizing the explicit therapeutic value of the spirituality programs, recommending only that Elders and spiritual programs be recognized with the same status as chaplains and other religions. Only when the report suggested that "exposure to Aboriginal spirituality and culture can make a major contribution to rehabilitation" (69) of alcohol and substance abusers was the issue of healing raised. Unfortunately, the discussion went no further.

Recently, the three prairie provinces have held inquiries into the process of justice for Aboriginal peoples (Hamilton and Sinclair 1991; Cawsey 1992; Linn 1992). The report of the Aboriginal Justice Inquiry of Manitoba (Hamilton and Sinclair 1991) was typical of all three on the issue of Aboriginal spirituality programs and the employment of Elders. Like previous reports, it called for the recognition of Aboriginal Elders on par with chaplains and for a policy guaranteeing Aboriginal offenders the right to spiritual services "appropriate to their culture" (1991:447).

Correctional policy with respect to Aboriginal offenders is now guided by federal legislation, the *Corrections and Conditional Release Act*. Passed in 1992, this act contains several sections that pertain specifically to Aboriginal offenders, underscoring the CSC's grudging acceptance of the view of Aboriginal spirituality as *religion* as opposed to *therapy*. Of particular significance here would be Section 83 (1), which states, "[f]or greater certainty, aboriginal [sic] spirituality and aboriginal spiritual leaders and elders have the same status as other religions and other religious leaders." Section 83 (2) makes specific reference to the CSC's responsibility to "take all *reasonable* steps to make available to aboriginal inmates the services of an aboriginal spiritual leader or elder..." after consultation with the National Aboriginal Advisory Committee, a group constituted to provide advice on Aboriginal offenders (italics mine).

The problem does not rest solely with the CSC, however. It is not uncommon for Aboriginal spokespersons to reinforce the analogy between Aboriginal spirituality and the prison chaplaincies. For instance, the report of the Aboriginal Justice Inquiry of Manitoba (Hamilton and Sinclair 1991), co-chaired by Aboriginal judge Murray Sinclair, noted that Aboriginal ceremonies "can contribute to the rectification of psychological and other problems that may be disturbing an inmate" (444). Further, the authors insisted that "[s]imply making identical provisions for elders as is made for chaplains, however, is not enough. The forms of religious observance are different. Participating in natural, outdoor surroundings is integral to Aboriginal spirituality and correctional institutions must adapt to that..." (445). Their conclusion was hard-hitting: "Our concern is not only that Aboriginal spirituality is not being encouraged. We believe these practices are being actively discouraged." But when it came time to make a recommendation, Hamilton and Sinclair reverted to the chaplain analogy! They stated that "[c]orrectional institutions [should] develop a policy whereby Elders recognized by provincial Aboriginal organizations as capable of providing traditional assistance or spiritual advice and counselling to Aboriginal inmates in a culturally appropriate manner *be granted status equivalent to chaplains* under the Chaplaincy program of the Corrections Branch" (477; italics mine).

Presently, all regions of Canada, except Quebec, have councils of Elders that serve to advise the CSC on Aboriginal policy. A Mic Mac Elder, Noel Knockwood, served as a special advisor to the Commissioner of the CSC while this research was being undertaken. The extent to which Elders have real input at the policy level is questionable, however. In the Prairie region, for instance, the Elders council meets infrequently due to cost limitations. One session I attended, which may or may not be typical, consisted mostly of the Elders detailing the difficulties they still experienced entering prisons and working with the inmates. They have, however, been able to educate CSC staff regarding the nature of Aboriginal spirituality, and identify the proper use of spiritual and ceremonial articles.

Notwithstanding the Constitution, legislation, and correctional policy, Aboriginal spirituality has continued to have problems even being recognized as equivalent in status to other religions. Many Elders still feel that they are subjected to discriminatory treatment at the hands of guards. The searching of medicine bundles and sacred pipes continues to be an issue. This is in contrast to the accepted practice of allowing priests, for instance, to enter prisons without being subjected to searches or inspection of religious items.

Conceptually, equating Aboriginal spirituality with Christian faiths is Eurocentric. It implies that these faiths are the standard to which Aboriginal spirituality, and presumably any other non-Christian religion, is to be compared. Such an approach, in addition to being culturally and morally repugnant, necessarily limits the availability of the Aboriginal services to those that have Christian parallels. Hence, "equality" is, in effect, inequality. Aboriginal spirituality cannot be practised for an hour on Sundays and Wednesdays, in one specific room within the prison. Its practice requires significant outdoor activity, the preparation of foods and sweat lodges, fasting, and ceremonies that may last from a few hours to several days. Further, as noted above, the idea that involvement in spirituality is therapeutic, that it can lead to a "healing" of the individual in a different but equally valid way as other prison rehabilitation programs, is still not widely accepted. The CSC's own policy for the delivery of "mental health" services to Aboriginal inmates recognizes that these "shall respect the individual's religious or cultural values" but that such services be provided only by "professionals/practitioners currently registered/licensed... in Canada and preferably in the province of practice." This would, of course, preclude the utilization of Aboriginal healers *as healers*. These issues will be discussed in more detail in subsequent chapters.

Although Dino Butler argued that his spiritual fast at Kent was not "political" because it was not a secular hunger strike within the framework of prison-inmate relations, it was still a political act. Like those spiritual leaders of the late 19th century who fought against the government repression of their spirituality, using whatever tactics that were available to them, so too did Butler and the members of the Kent movement. And like their precursors, their demands were not acted upon immediately. It has taken many years for Aboriginal spirituality to be even minimally accepted as a legitimate form of religious expression, and the correctional system still does not recognize its inherent therapeutic nature. This, then, is the task to which this book sets itself: to demonstrate that Aboriginal spirituality, as a form of what anthropologists and others call "symbolic healing," is inherently therapeutic and, indeed, tailor-made for helping many Aboriginal inmates deal with their problems both within and beyond the prison walls.

NOTES

1   This untitled poem by the Reverend Edward Ahenakew, a tireless advocate for Indian rights in the first part of this century, was found by Katherine Pettipas in Rev. Ahenakew's personal papers housed in the Saskatchewan Archives Board, Regina. The entire poem is reprinted in Pettipas (1994:233-236).

2   The information in this and subsequent sections of this chapter is derived from a variety of sources, most of which are not readily accessible to the public. The Native Brotherhood at Kent produced materials documenting their struggles, and these were provided to me by members of the public who supported the activities on the inside. I have also had the opportunity to interview some individuals who were incarcerated at Kent during this time. Information has also been derived through discussions with lawyers and Elders involved in the early years of the spiritual movement and from court documents. It is necessary to keep confidential the identities of many of these individuals.

3   The judge was Justice Allan McEachern. He subsequently went on to infamy in presiding over the Gitksan-Wet'suwet'en land claim trial, in which he described these people's lives before the arrival of Europeans in Hobbesian terms, as "nasty, brutish and short."

4   Many Elders today feel that these guidelines are now dated and in need of renovation. However, they acknowledge the important role the guidelines played in allowing Aboriginal spirituality to gain a foothold in the correctional system.

*What the Creator gave us, this is what I learned
in the pen. It took me in prison to learn this,
and that's sad. If I would have learned all this
years ago, I wouldn't be sitting here.*

— ABORIGINAL INMATE

2
Incarceration
and Aboriginal
Inmates

Aboriginal men are over-represented in the Canadian correctional system. Over the years, there have been many inquiries into how corrections can be adapted to what are perceived to be the unique needs of Aboriginal inmates. The purpose of this chapter is to provide a background to those incarceration issues that are particularly important to an understanding of the therapeutic nature of Aboriginal spirituality in prison.

The Incarceration of Aboriginal Peoples

Nationally, Aboriginal peoples appear disproportionately involved in crime, either as perpetrators or victims. Data from a 1991 report of the Department of Indian Affairs indicated that whereas the national crime rate in Canada was 92.7 per 1000, the crime rate for Indian bands was 165.6 per 1000, almost twice as high. In terms of violent crime, the Indian band rate of 33.1 per 1000 was almost four times the national rate of 9.0 per 1000 (Hamilton and Sinclair 1991:87). These numbers do not tell the complete story, however, since criminalization is a product of many factors other than simply the commission of a criminal act. For instance, the Aboriginal Justice Inquiry of Manitoba argued that "[c]ultural oppression, social inequality, the loss of self-government and systematic discrimination, which are the legacies of the Canadian government's treatment of Aboriginal people, are intertwined and interdependent factors." However the report acknowledged that "in very few cases is it possible to draw a simple and direct correlation between any one of them and the events which lead an individual Aboriginal person to commit a crime or to become incarcerated" (Hamilton and Sinclair 1991:86).

Discrimination operates in many ways and at many levels. Most critical analysts believe that Aboriginal peoples attract more police attention than non-Aboriginals. They are more likely to be stopped and questioned, for instance. They are less likely to be able to talk their way out of a problem with the police. Urban neighbourhoods with higher concentrations of Aboriginal residents may be patrolled more frequently. And once an Aboriginal person is stopped by the police, the judicial system that kicks in operates to systematically increase the likelihood of incarceration. The Manitoba justice inquiry noted that Aboriginal accused are more likely to be denied bail, spend more time in pretrial detention, and spend less trial preparation time with lawyers. They are more likely to be charged with multiple offences than non-Aboriginal accused and, therefore, are more likely to be sentenced to incarceration.

The Correctional Service of Canada operates on a regional basis, and there are discrepancies in terms of Aboriginal inmates. The Prairie region, where the research for this book was undertaken, has the highest proportion of Aboriginal inmates. Of a total inmate population of 2231 in 1987, 730 inmates, or 32.7% identified themselves as Aboriginal. This is in contrast to 13.5% for the Pacific region, 4.3% for Ontario, 3.2% for the Atlantic, and 0.75% for Quebec. Of the total national Aboriginal inmate population of 1143, 64% are found in Prairie region institutions. Clearly, the Prairies are an inhospitable environment for Aboriginal peoples.

Aboriginal justice inquiries undertaken in all three prairie provinces are revealing. In Manitoba, it was determined that of all the inmates admitted to both federal and provincial correctional facilities in 1989, 56% were Aboriginal (a total of 4772 individuals). At two federal institutions where aspects of this research were undertaken, Stony Mountain and Rockwood, data for 1990 show that the percentages of Aboriginal inmates incarcerated were 46% and 37% respectively (Hamilton and Sinclair 1991:393). In Saskatchewan, data for 1991 indicated that 44% of the 746 federally incarcerated offenders were Aboriginal; of the 343 federal offenders who were under community supervision, 45% were Aboriginal (Linn 1992:11). For Alberta, the picture is similarly troublesome. Data for 1989 indicate that 31% of the inmates, in federal and provincial institutions combined, were Aboriginal, even though Alberta's Aboriginal population constitutes only 4% to 5% of the provincial total (Cawsey 1991:6-4).

A 1988 Solicitor General's report (Canada 1988b) revealed that Aboriginal inmates are disproportionately represented in higher security institutions, where access to rehabilitative programming is more problematic. For instance, while 8.1% of Aboriginal inmates were in minimum security level institutions, so too were 15.6% of the non-Aboriginal inmates. In medium security institutions, we find almost 32% of the Aboriginal inmates, compared to 38% of the non-Aboriginal inmates. Most significantly, at the maximum security level, we find 39% of the Aboriginal inmates, in contrast to only 30% of the non-Aboriginal inmates. The data also show that 25% of the Aboriginal inmates could be found in multilevel security institutions, compared to only 12.6% of the non-Aboriginal inmates (Canada 1988b:25).

There are no comprehensive data that identify Aboriginal inmates specifically in terms of cultures, such as Cree, Ojibwa, Blackfoot, and so on. Since inmates are normally institutionalized within their region, certain patterns are evident. So, for instance, we are most likely to find Blackfoot, Blood, and Piegan inmates in southern Alberta institutions, such as Drumheller, and Plains Cree and Northern Cree at Saskatchewan Institution in Prince Albert. Stony Mountain likely has a higher proportion of Ojibwa or Anicinabe peoples, due to its proximity to Northwestern Ontario. The 1988 Solicitor General's report did identify Aboriginal inmates according to the broad categories of "North American Indian," "Metis," and "Inuit," and found, for instance, that within the Prairie region 69% of the Aboriginal inmates were Indian, 29% Metis, and only 2% Inuit.

Complexities of Culture and Experience

Aboriginal Canada is a complex country both culturally and linguistically. The 1991 census identified more than one million Canadians who were "Aboriginal." At about 4% of the total Canadian population, this is likely an underestimation, as the census is known to under-count Aboriginal and other minority groups. Whatever the numbers, we must resist the temptation to assume that "Aboriginal" is a culturally meaningful category. Within Canada there remain eleven different Aboriginal language families, representing languages that are much more different than they are similar; for instance, the cultural and linguistic differences between Cree and Mohawk, languages both found in Quebec, are much greater than those between English and French!

Of course Aboriginal cultures do not look the same as they did when Europeans first arrived in northern North America (and neither do the European cultures). Many changes have taken place. Particularly important in the analysis here are those changes that have followed as a result of acculturation (a process of cultural change when two cultures meet and coexist) and through assimilation (a more directed process of cultural change in which one culture effectively absorbs another).

In Canada, after 1867, the federal government launched a variety of campaigns to assimilate Aboriginal peoples and cultures. This was done, in part, on the assumption that these peoples would otherwise disappear, but also because of Eurocentric beliefs in the superiority of European culture. Assimilation took many forms. Aboriginal children were removed from their families and forced into residential schools where their culture was denied and they were punished for speaking their languages. Legislation made certain aspects of Aboriginal spirituality illegal. Individual registered Indians who became "educated" or fought in wars were removed from the Indian registry. Indian women who married non-Indian men also lost their Indian status. Aboriginal individuals, families, and whole communities were relocated to urban areas for education and upgrading. Northern megaprojects, such as hydro dams, seriously damaged the environments from which Aboriginal peoples made a living, and upon which their cultures were based. Christian churches, especially the Anglican and Roman Catholic denominations, were given considerable power by the federal government to effect cultural change through religious indoctrination. Aboriginal children were removed from homes thought (often erroneously) by child welfare agencies to be unstable. This period of Canadian history, which is only now ending (and some would say it has not yet ended), resulted in profound cultural changes for Aboriginal peoples.

The cultural facts today are clear, if complex. There are many Aboriginal peoples with little or no knowledge of their heritage cultures or languages. For instance, the 1991 census indicated that slightly more than 10% of Aboriginal peoples still spoke their language. Only three languages, Inuktitut, Cree, and Ojibwa are considered safe. Not surprisingly, these three are northern languages, generally further away from southern, Euro-Canadian dominated areas. An untold number of Aboriginal people lost their languages through residential schools, or through placement with non-Aboriginal foster or adoptive homes. Many are no longer Aboriginal in a cultural sense: they neither speak an Aboriginal language nor have an Aboriginal cultural background. In effect, some may be culturally Euro-Canadian.

The correctional system in Canada has been unable to come to grips with the cultural diversity of Aboriginal peoples, and there still exists a tendency to assume cultural homogeneity. Although there have been some studies of Aboriginal offenders in Canada since the 1970s, very few have paid any attention to the cultural variability that exists, both in terms of orientation to Aboriginal cultures, on one hand, and Euro-Canadian cultures on the other. Consequently, very little is known about the manner in which these differences in cultural orientation affect such issues as offender evaluations, parole deliberations, conduct in prison, and rehabilitation or psychological treatment.

In a report on "Native Offenders and Correctional Policy," Reasons (1975) noted that consideration must be made of the "specific habilitation needs of native offenders in terms of the culture they will return to upon release." Reasons is quite critical of "traditional" correctional approaches, in particular the "order/assimilationist" approach which emphasizes changing members of racial or ethnic minorities so that they fit within the institutional structures and, I would add, within the larger, Euro-Canadian culture. As Reasons (1975:27) states, "[t]he goal of rehabilitation has been to strip the convict of his previous identity and help produce a new person who would make it in society." Of course, such an approach assumes that "society" is meaningful in the same ways to all offenders, and this simply is not so. In my view, any attempt at assimilation within the prison context will encounter a reaction from Aboriginal inmates no different from the reaction of Aboriginal peoples to over a century of federal assimilationist policies: they will resist. But, for the offender, crucial questions regarding issues like treatment outcomes and parole seem to hinge on the degree to which they have allowed the prison-based assimilationist programs to be effective.

Don McCaskill's (1985) comprehensive study of Aboriginal offenders in Manitoba demonstrated the very high degree of instability and pathology that existed within the homes and families of Aboriginal offenders. Nearly two-thirds of his respondents reported having some foster home experience or having been raised by a non-parent. He also noted an increase in the proportion of offenders born in urban areas between 1970 and 1984, from 11% to 20%. Furthermore, in 1984 some 67% of offenders were residing in a city at the time of their incarceration, regardless of place of birth. Therefore, McCaskill seemed to be documenting a significant increase in the proportion of Aboriginal offenders with extensive Euro-Canadian cultural experience. Furthermore, he noted that while 40% of the inmates he interviewed were living in Winnipeg at the time of incarceration, 80% were paroled to that city. Thus the correctional system acts as a mechanism to increase the urbanization, and possible assimilation, of Aboriginal peoples.

Perhaps the most important aspect of McCaskill's study, for my purposes, is his assertion that "Native offenders cannot be viewed as a homogeneous group with easily generalizable patterns of criminality" (1985:39). In particular, he notes that some Native communities are starting to view offenders as "deviants or members of a particular subgroup" (1985:53). Furthermore, he states: "The contention that Native offenders are more alienated from the Native community would appear to be particularly true of the urban Native offender. It can be argued that this group has even fewer ties of support to a stable Native community" (1985:54). While not expressly stating it, McCaskill implies that the lack of a cultural connection with the rural and reserve communities and the process of "cultural revitalization" that is occurring explains, to a great degree, this discordance. As he notes, however, "[f]or some Native offenders, being Native may be almost irrelevant to their criminal activity" (1985:62). In particular, Aboriginal offenders who are second-generation urbanites with no knowledge of their culture may be viewed in this manner.

McCaskill also warns that it is not appropriate to lump all Aboriginal offenders together as if they represented a homogeneous group. He states that "[t]hey will differ significantly in their backgrounds, identities, personalities, attitudes, interests and behaviour" (1985:72). Some, he notes, are not as shy or passive as in the past; they are aggressive and antisocial just like some Euro-Canadian inmates. For some, their identity as "Natives" remains important, while for others integration into the broader prison population is unproblematic. Somewhat different correctional and therapeutic programs are needed.

More recently, Manitoba Aboriginal judge Murray Sinclair has emphasized the importance of understanding an Aboriginal individual's cultural orientation. "Probably one of the trickiest issues arises however when considering those accused for whom traditional aboriginal culture is no longer as great an influence," states Sinclair. "This is generally reflective of a decline in traditional aboriginal cultures resulting from assimilationist pressures and what some writers have termed a breakdown of societal bonds. When confronted with an aboriginal accused who has no identity with his aboriginal identity, what does one do?" (Sinclair 1990:15).

In examining the courtroom context and sentencing, Sinclair writes: "Simply put... the point appears to be that if the accused has no connection to his aboriginal culture, then it is no longer a factor to take into consideration." But he also warned "that the appearance of a lack of connection to past cultural practices may be deceiving." Like many commentators, he supports the view that there are certain common features of Aboriginal cultures that characterize them no matter the region. This theme also runs throughout the final report of the Aboriginal Justice Inquiry of Manitoba, alongside an explicit acknowledgement of cultural heterogeneity. "Aboriginal people are many peoples, cultures and languages in many regions," the report states. "Aboriginal people, it is important to stress, are not all the same" (Hamilton and Sinclair 1991:29). Nevertheless, the authors support the work of many researchers over the years who have identified common Aboriginal "ethics" or "rules of behaviour." Important to a correctional setting are ethics that emphasize harmony in interpersonal relationships and emotional restraint; these preclude bragging and the criticism of others. Ceremonies, such as the sweat lodge, are the vehicles for the "controlled release of emotions in an appropriate manner" (Hamilton and Sinclair 1991:35). "The concepts of adversarialism, accusation, confrontation, guilt, argument, criticism and retribution," they write, "are alien to the Aboriginal value system, although perhaps not totally unknown to Aboriginal peoples. In the context of Aboriginal value systems, adversarialism and confrontation are antagonistic to the high value placed on harmony and the peaceful coexistence of all living beings, both human and nonhuman, with one another and nature. Criticism of others is at odds with the principles of non-interference and individual autonomy and freedom" (Hamilton and Sinclair 1991:37). Nevertheless, as Sinclair noted before, not all Aboriginal peoples have knowledge of or accept these ethics and rules of behaviour, in part because so many have been raised within a Euro-Canadian cultural environment.

Aboriginal Cultural Orientations in Prison

From a cultural perspective, prison populations are, in many ways, microcosms of the national society. Therefore, we find many Aboriginal inmates with little or no knowledge of their Aboriginal cultures and languages. In the Prairie region, where this study was undertaken, we find a higher proportion of culturally grounded Aboriginal men, perhaps because many northern people in the west still maintain their cultural roots. Nevertheless, of the 249 men interviewed as part of this study in 1994, 17% indicated that they spoke only English or French, and of the 60% who stated that they spoke an Aboriginal language, only half suggested that they were fluent. Familial disruption was also fairly common: 30% indicated that they had spent some time in residential schools, 35% in foster homes, and 5% in adoptive homes. Only 45% of the men interviewed had spent all or most of their lives living in an Indian reserve community.

In addition to different degrees of orientation to Aboriginal and Euro-Canadian cultures, Aboriginal inmates also exhibit a broad range of heritage cultures. In this study, Northern Cree (22%), Plains Cree (22%), Saulteaux (14%), Metis (14%), and Ojibwa (7%) were most commonly represented, reflecting the cultural composition of Saskatchewan, Manitoba, and Northwestern Ontario. However, also found in the prisons were Chipewyan, Inuit, Blackfoot, Dakota, Stoney, Slavey, Loucheaux, Gitksan, and men from complex or blended cultural heritages (e.g., Metis-Cree, Cree-Saulteaux).

Cultural orientation, therefore, can be thought of as operating on at least two dimensions.[1] One dimension pertains to the differing Aboriginal cultural orientations, and the other to the degree of orientation to those Aboriginal cultures relative to the broader Euro-Canadian culture. Only a few individuals interviewed during this research were so uniculturally Aboriginal as to preclude any meaningful involvement in the research. All of the individuals we encountered spoke English to varying degrees. This is the legacy of colonialism and assimilation.

Nevertheless, the Aboriginal cultural context of Canadian prisons, especially in the Prairies, is complex. There are some very traditional men, who often come from small, isolated reserve communities and who have little direct experience with the outside world. A number of men we interviewed had never been to a city until they were imprisoned. Some had spent their life primarily on traplines, hunting and fishing. In contrast, others were born and/or raised in urban areas, had never been to a reserve, and knew nothing of their heritage culture. Still others had spent their lives in Aboriginal communities or reserves in more southerly areas where there was easy access to larger Euro-Canadian communities.

The report of the "Task Force on Aboriginal Peoples in Federal Corrections," released in 1988, recognized four categories of Aboriginal offenders. These were:

1   "Traditional persons" – No definition is offered.
2   "Persons-in-Transition" – These are persons "whose culture is Aboriginal who are moving towards non-Aboriginal culture but as yet have limited functional experience with non-Aboriginal society."
3   "Bicultural" persons – These are persons "who are experienced in both Aboriginal and non-Aboriginal societies."
4   "Assimilated" persons – Those persons who function more easily in non-Aboriginal environments." (1988b:39)

In this research, I did not find category two, "persons-in-transition" to be identifiable in an empirical sense; otherwise, the three remaining categories in the Task Force report bear similarity to the analytic categories used here. However, this research progresses from simply delineating the existence of categories to examining the implications of their existence. An effort was made to understand these differing degrees of cultural orientation in the belief that they were meaningful for understanding forensic programming and Aboriginal spirituality. Three broad cultural orientations were empirically identified to serve as a guideline in this analysis: traditional, bicultural, and Euro-Canadian.[2] What follows is a sketch of these orientations, derived from the statistical analysis of the 249 inmates interviewed in 1994. An analysis of the cultural orientations of these men suggested that 39% could be thought of as Euro-Canadian, 28% as traditional, and 33% as bicultural.

THE EURO-CANADIAN ORIENTED

These individuals are characterized by their relative lack of exposure to Aboriginal culture as children. Their cultural orientation is primarily Euro-Canadian. Some of these individuals would be indistinguishable from non-Aboriginal (specifically, English speaking, Caucasian, Canadian-born) individuals in cultural and linguistic terms. Most cannot speak any Aboriginal language. This is not to deny the consequences of their Aboriginality, however. Issues pertaining to their self-identity and experiences interacting with the non-Aboriginal world (including prison) are still defined to some extent by their heritage and appearance.

Those with a Euro-Canadian orientation are more likely to have personal knowledge of only one or neither of their birth parents, and to have more experience in non-Aboriginal foster homes. They are more likely to associate with non-Aboriginal peoples, romantically, in friendships and through employment. They find it easier to communicate in predominantly Euro-Canadian social contexts, including those found in the prison (especially various treatment programs). Their education levels are the highest, and they are most likely to have had some employment where the majority of other employees were non-Aboriginal. These men are likely to have been fairly mobile over their lives and to have significant urban experience. Within prison, these individuals may occupy more leadership roles, including those within the Native Brotherhoods. Use of the English language is unproblematic.

Issues of identity are important for Euro-Canadian oriented individuals. In particular, it is noteworthy that they are most likely to view their identities problematically, to think of themselves as only "partly Native," and to suggest that they are still trying to understand their Native identity. They admit to a poor understanding of Native history. Perhaps most importantly, they are most likely to admit to having been embarrassed or ashamed of their Nativeness at some time in their life.

THE TRADITIONALLY ORIENTED

These individuals are characterized by their full enculturation into an Aboriginal society. This enculturation can be seen in the learning of an Aboriginal language as their first language and continued used of this language throughout their life. Often, these individuals began to learn English only when they started school, a fact that explains in part their lower educational levels. A small segment of this group, generally older individuals, will continue to have extreme difficulties understanding and expressing themselves in English. They will have had relatively little firsthand exposure to non-Aboriginal cultural contexts, spending much of their lives in their Aboriginal communities (and often in rural or remote areas).

These individuals are most likely to come from relatively stable family structures (in the sense that individuals are surrounded by family), and where both parents were Aboriginal (and of the same culture). Furthermore, where they have experienced foster homes, their foster parents were more likely to be Aboriginal.

Traditional individuals do not appear to experience significant problems with their identities as Aboriginal peoples. Of the three groups, they are most likely to describe themselves as "completely Native," and the least likely to suggest that they have ever felt ashamed or embarrassed at being Native. They believe strongly that their children should be brought up as "Native." Traditional men are most likely to say that they have a good knowledge of Native history and spirituality.

In many contexts, traditional men demonstrate a greater propensity to associate with other Aboriginal peoples than with non-Aboriginal peoples. For instance, they are more likely to suggest that they are most comfortable with other Aboriginal inmates and that their friends, both before prison and while in prison, were/are all or mostly Aboriginal. They are least likely to have been employed in predominantly non-Aboriginal contexts.

Communication problems are evident among traditional men, due largely to their relatively poorer English abilities and cultural differences. They experience difficulty speaking English and often state that they prefer to use their Aboriginal language (in which they are fluent) when speaking. They are least likely of the three groups to offer feedback to other inmates or talk extensively in group contexts. They tend to view criticism of others as inappropriate. Not surprisingly, these individuals are least likely to serve in Native Brotherhood or other prison organizations. In many ways, their voices are the most silent of all the Aboriginal inmates.

THE BICULTURAL

As a middle category, bicultural men are the most difficult to define. Obviously, they are not as Euro-Canadian in orientation as the first group, and they are not as traditional as the second. They represent individuals who seem to operate within both the Aboriginal and non-Aboriginal worlds, a product of their exposure to both.

Bicultural men are likely to have knowledge of their birth parents; they fall between the other two groups in terms of residential school and foster home experiences. They are more mobile than traditional men, and have significant experience in Euro-Canadian communities.

These individuals express comfort with their Native identity. They are more likely than Euro-Canadian men, and less likely than traditional men, to describe their identity as "completely Native," and less likely than Euro-Canadian men, but more likely than traditional men, to suggest that they have felt embarrassed or ashamed of being Native at some time in their life. They also place in the middle with respect to their knowledge of Native history and spirituality.

These individuals are characterized by their bilinguality. However, in comparison to traditional men, bicultural men are more likely to suggest that they have no preference about which language they use or that they prefer English. They are also less likely than traditional men to say that their Indian language is their "best" spoken language (the majority stating that it is English) or that they speak it fluently.

Personal interaction patterns also bear out the biculturality of these men. They demonstrate a greater balance between Aboriginal and non-Aboriginal friends, both outside and within prison. Of the three groups, they are most likely to have been employed where most of the workers were non-Aboriginal.

These individuals can communicate fairly effectively in mixed settings. Most find it easy to communicate in English, to offer feedback to others, and to speak in front of groups, although in these areas they are less comfortable than Euro-Canadian oriented men. Similarly, they are more likely than traditional men and less likely than Euro-Canadian men to have served on the executive of a prison organization.

Throughout the remainder of the book, the cultural orientations of individuals quoted will be identified (e.g. "Traditional"). Similarly, I will also identify the speaker's Aboriginal cultural heritage (e.g., Cree). In a few instances, where the individual does not know his cultural heritage, I will note that it is "unknown," and where the disclosure of cultural heritage could possibly identify the speaker, I will note that it is "anonymous."

Correctional Perspectives on Aboriginal Cultures and Inmates

When it comes to identifying Aboriginal offenders in cultural, legal, "tribal," or linguistic terms, correctional officials demonstrate a great deal of confusion. It is quite possible that this confusion stems simply from an attitude that Aboriginal heterogeneity is not an issue, and therefore it is not necessary to take care to describe Aboriginal offenders accurately. However, reference to an offender's ethnic or cultural status, even if inaccurate, would not be made unless there was some intrinsic meaning to the use of these terms by the writer. Detailed examination of correctional files for a sub-sample of thirty Aboriginal respondents in this research did shed some light on this area. Some examples follow.

One Euro-Canadian oriented inmate was described by a psychiatrist as a "Caucasian." A report subsequently referred to him being of "Metis background," and a psychiatric assessment simply stated he was "Metis." His security profile and identity card also referred to his "race" as "Metis." Elsewhere in his file, there was considerable confusion regarding his Aboriginal status. Apparently he was administered the General Statistical Information on Recidivism scale. This instrument was designed to assess the risk to re-offend, but it has been deemed invalid for Aboriginal offenders. In this instance, the instrument suggested that he was at high risk to re-offend; however, someone had handwritten on the bottom of this document the comment, "Native Indian N/A" [not applicable]. Earlier entries in the file mention his "native mother," some involvement in a Native Brotherhood, and participation in a Native Awareness program. When I interviewed him, he unhesitatingly declared he was "Native," describing his heritage as "Ojibway." He was a fair skinned individual with light brown hair and brown eyes; in my view, based on physical appearance, he could pass as "Caucasian." Physical appearance can be misleading, however, and even a superficial examination of his file or a detailed personal interview would have prevented him from being mislabelled.

Another Euro-Canadian oriented offender was referred to as "Native," "Indian," "Reg[istered or status] Indian," "Blackfoot," "Metis" and "Aboriginal." A psychiatric report stated he was "of native extraction" and "of native origin" (two possibly different concepts). This latter report suggested that he was suffering "some identity confusion." Certainly, the CSC seemed to have problems identifying him!

Aboriginal identity confusion does not occur only for the more Euro-Canadian oriented offenders. Traditional men, those firmly rooted in an Aboriginal culture, have also experienced the same problem at the hands of corrections personnel. For instance, one individual was identified as a "Reg[istered] Ind[ian]" and a "Treaty Indian," complete with a band name. Yet, three subsequent reports referred to him as "Metis," while a more recent report again restored his "native Indian" status. Perhaps the most perplexing comment of all came from a report that referred to him as a "Metis offender from the [deleted] Reserve in Alberta." Metis, by definition, do not have "reserves."

Another traditional man, an Inuk from the north whose facility in the English language was limited, was accurately referred to as "Inuit" throughout the Case Management files (with some use of the archaic term, "Eskimo"). Then, when he arrived at one institution, a psychiatric report transformed him into a "native indian" [sic].

These are some of the more extreme cases of confused labelling. There are some instances in which the problem is relatively benign, such as alternately referring to an individual as "Native" or "Indian." Perhaps more significantly, in many reports, no mention is made at all of an offender's Aboriginal status.

Clearly, the correctional system needs to come to grips with the varying terminology applied to Aboriginal offenders. In many cases, the files are essentially useless in accurately identifying an individual due to shifting and contradictory labels. Physical appearance, biological heritage, parental ancestry, and self-identification appear as criteria applied haphazardly by some staff. Accurate labelling may be essential to gathering statistics on Aboriginal offenders for research purposes. More important, accuracy is necessary if these individuals are to be treated as cultural beings. There is a need to determine the contexts in which labelling is useful and to establish guidelines to do it properly. It can be argued that the lack of care and coherence in identifying Aboriginal offenders simply reflects current views regarding Aboriginal cultural matters.

The files also contain a variety of information on the personality and life experiences of each offender. It is not possible to state unequivocally when an assessment is in error due to a misunderstanding of cultural traits. Nevertheless, the files demonstrate that some potential exists for assessing Aboriginal offenders inappropriately. Observations found in psychological or psychiatric assessments are particularly important. Since the greatest potential for cultural misassessment exists for those Aboriginal offenders with the strongest adherence to their own cultures, I will examine those cases primarily.

There were a few examples of traditional Aboriginal offenders whose personalities were viewed as prohibiting assessment and program participation. A Cree man from a northern reserve was initially described as "not ready for large group therapy due to his shyness and lack of communication skills." He was "not very well endowed with verbal communications... [Which]... could lead to the false impression that he is not concerned about treatment.... As he very clearly indicated... he was not willing to speak in groups." This theme seemed to run throughout his files. Another assessment referred to him somewhat contradictorily "as being aggressive, withdrawn and introverted." Presumably the aggressiveness related only to his behaviour while intoxicated. The possibility that his shyness and reluctance to speak in groups were cultural in origin was recognized by one psychiatrist, who wrote: "He was somewhat shy and took a while to organize his thoughts when answering questions. This could very well be a cultural factor and can be due to his educational background." This view was in contrast to an earlier assessment that stated that he "appears to have some form of brain dysfunction and appears to be mentally slow... Subject's mental stability is questionable." There is quite a striking difference between a diagnosis of brain dysfunction on the one hand, and a "cultural factor" on the other. It is possible that other Aboriginal men may likewise be assessed as "slow" for erroneous reasons.

In my interview with this individual, he displayed certain behaviour patterns common to Northern Cree people, in particular quietness or shyness around strangers (especially "White" strangers), which he attributed to his predominantly bush upbringing. He also demonstrated some difficulties expressing himself in the English language, saying that Cree was his first language and that he never really learned how to speak English until going to prison. The correctional staff who interviewed him and who labelled him "slow" were blind to the influence that his culture and language exerted upon him in the alien prison setting.

Another traditional Aboriginal inmate was described in terms similar to the above. A psychiatrist wrote that "he presented as a rather shy and reserved individual who initially found it quite difficult to speak in therapy. In earlier sessions, he was only comfortable in talking with me for 10-15 minutes at a time. He reports that such behaviour is not unfamiliar with him, and that he often hesitates for lengthy periods of time before initiating a contact with someone." This report then continued to assess the root of the problem. "My opinion," wrote the psychiatrist, "is that some of this difficulty is related to [his] generally high anxiety level, and his difficulty in establishing a trusting relationship and that it is also related to the remoteness of his Native community, and his general lack of contact with whites outside the penal system." After suggesting that this offender would feel more comfortable relating to a "Native Counsellor," the analyst insightfully offered that "in general, due to his shyness, and his tendency to misunderstand our culture, it seems that [he] tends to present himself in a manner which does not serve his best interest in dealing with the penal system. He reports considerable anxiety in dealing with questions in formal settings, and that he tends to remain silent and withdrawn on such occasions."

This inmate's consistent refusal to sign documents or meet with other psychologists made him appear "indifferent or somewhat uncooperative." A subsequent psychological assessment corroborated these views; it was noted that "he did not engage in any spontaneous speech, had poor eye contact, and spoke at a low volume." The report recommended that "support and encouragement may be best provided by Native counsellors and Native Elders, since [he] indicated that his level of comfort is higher with other Native Canadians." Despite these accounts, with their clear links to cultural factors, a subsequent psychiatric report referred only to his lack of "spontaneity in speech" and his "soft voice," without reference to cultural background.

My interview with this individual corroborated the above assessments regarding his quietness and deferential demeanour in group settings. These traits were identified by prison staff during a group therapy session, but it was suggested that they were part of his "problem." Yet such traits are commonly characteristic of northern Aboriginal individuals from traditional backgrounds. Indeed, the reluctance to make eye contact is seen as a sign of respect in some Aboriginal cultures!

There were a few instances in which an inmate's personality and behaviour were viewed as part of a ploy to avoid certain circumstances. For instance, a report on one individual stated that "one of his 'reasons' for poor participation in groups was his poor grasp of the English language. Yet for his claim of not understanding he is able to accomplish much in areas he is interested in and in subsequent conversations/interviews it is apparent he comprehends more than he lets on." This inmate suggested that there was some conflict between what he was learning in treatment and his "native ways." According to the report, "[he] has also avoided doing homework assignments for groups and being an active participant in group by hiding behind his native ways as an excuse. He has never been able to identify in what way what we are teaching him as skills or information runs contrary to his beliefs or would be detrimental to him." It is interesting that, according to this staff member, the onus was on the inmate to explain why the treatment program was culturally inappropriate. Ironically, for a traditional person, openly criticizing the program and staff would be culturally inappropriate!

My interview with this man led me to believe that he had a good command of English and that, in this case, the reports of his language abilities may have been correct. However, he may have found some cultural incompatibilities in what he was learning; although he was fully bilingual, he had learned his Aboriginal language first, as a child, and had lived most of his life on a reserve. Nonetheless, it seems dangerous to suppose that an inmate is deliberately avoiding participation, and that he is using cultural or linguistic differences as the excuse. Such cases require more thorough investigation. In this instance, both my interview and the files suggested that this man had personal animosities toward "White" people in general, and "White" staff in particular, which were related to negative past experiences.

Another offender, a very traditional man from the north, was also suspected of hiding behind language and cultural difficulties. His files contained many references to his poor grasp of English. Yet, one late 1980s report indicated that staff were exasperated with their efforts to deal with him: "This subject has been given numerous breaks by this writer in the past," wrote one official. "I have not been by the book' with him because I felt it necessary to take into account his cultural differences and his poor communication skills. However, my attitude toward [him] has changed. When I talk to other staff on the unit the feeling appears to be mutual. All patience has been exhausted. [He] exemplifies the word belligerent in his behaviour towards anyone in a position of authority. He neither benefits from positive reinforcement nor does he learn from negative reinforcement." A contradictory psychiatric report stated that he "presented as a cooperative, friendly and plausible young man who was greatly handicapped with spoken English and sometimes it became very difficult for the writer to make him understand the abstract and conceptual meaning of a question." Subsequently, while at another institution, this individual was seen by a psychologist who spoke his language, and who reported that "his difficulty speaking and understanding English is related to speed rather than content. In other words, if the time is taken to speak more slowly, and to ask [him] to clarify what he said, workable communication can take place. When this happens... [he] appears to be more cooperative and motivated."

By 1990, suspicion of the true nature of his language capabilities surfaced. A report stated: "This man has language difficulties... although it appears he sometimes uses this to his advantage... The writer feels [he] may be a good candidate [for a treatment program] although his cultural barriers may make things difficult for him."

During my interview with this individual, he seemed to find English exceedingly difficult to understand, no matter what the pace. He frequently misunderstood even slowly delivered, simple questions despite his obvious attempts to be cooperative and helpful. My view of the inmate at the time was that he could not easily grasp the concepts of his rehabilitation program.

In these two latter cases, it is extremely difficult to unravel the Aboriginal cultural aspects from aspects of prison culture. Were these individuals truly experiencing linguistic and cultural difficulties? Quite likely. But it is also possible that they did manipulate these to their advantage as part of their resistance to imprisonment. What is needed is a more concerted and informed effort to determine the possible influences cultural and linguistic phenomena may have on the effectiveness of treatment programs. A "cultural assessment" as part of the overall preliminary assessment of new inmates would be helpful.

This section has detailed the profound difficulties that the correctional system has in accurately identifying Aboriginal inmates in cultural terms and in understanding the influence that culture has on their prison behaviour. How likely is it, then, that the correctional system will understand the essence of Aboriginal spirituality as a form of therapy, and the role it can play in the healing of Aboriginal men?

Correctional Perspectives on Aboriginal Spirituality

The correctional system has at best a minimal understanding of Aboriginal inmates' involvement with Elders and spirituality. Anecdotal information to this effect can be found within offenders' case management files, if the correctional officers responsible for writing assessments and progress reports make relevant notations. However, there is no consistency of any kind in the reporting and no indication of the purpose that such notation is to serve.

Most comments found in the files simply note that an individual is involved with the Elders and Aboriginal programs in addition to other prison programs. Staff occasionally make referrals to the Elders for specific offenders. However, perhaps most indicative of the institutional views of Aboriginal spirituality, some files contain suggestions that an inmate's allegiance to the Elders and the spiritual path is an interference with mainstream correctional programming. This is especially true when an individual makes a decision to direct his rehabilitation efforts primarily towards the Aboriginal way. The following passages are indicative of this attitude:

He has been actively involved with the Native Elder and in Native Spirituality programming. [He] feels that his involvement in the AA program is no longer beneficial to him and he feels he is benefitting more by being involved in the Native Awareness program. The AA Counsellor feels there is room for both.

[He] attended most group sessions and was frequently late. Was heavily involved in Native Awareness groups, which conflicted with Thursday afternoon Anger Management program sessions.

In the following passage, a case management officer with little understanding of Aboriginal spirituality nevertheless felt qualified to pass judgement on an inmate who was opting for the Aboriginal over other correctional programming:

He was reluctant to attend AA, stating that it didn't address his problem in his cultural terms. While he says living his Native ways will prevent him from reoffending, he really doesn't adhere to the traditional teachings. He has been confronted about his lack of respect for women and children, his judgementalness, and air of superiority over non-Natives... Unfortunately to date he's been unable to work a compromise between his ways and the treatment programs goals.

Only rarely did a passage in the case management files refer to a positive outcome with respect to involvement with Aboriginal spirituality. This inmate received an uncharacteristically glowing report:

[He] informed me that he has been actively involved for the past six months in the Native Alcoholics Anonymous and Sacred Circle Group. He stated he has received a lot of help from both groups but especially from talking out his problems with the Native Elders in the Sacred Circle Group. He feels these talks have better prepared him to bear the pressures he initially felt upon entering prison and cope with institutional life generally. During the last quarter, I personally have noticed a vast improvement in [his] self-confidence and general well-being. He is displaying a much more positive attitude lately.

It is not easy to make sense of the occasionally laudatory, sometimes critical, and often conflicting views of Aboriginal spirituality as it is documented in the inmates' files. There appears to be an acceptance of Aboriginal spirituality as an adjunct program if it does not conflict with or interfere with other correctional programs. Aboriginal spirituality is tolerated in many instances but not embraced, and it is always seen as subordinate to mainstream correctional programming. As individuals, clearly some case management officers are more receptive than others to the therapeutic benefits of working with Elders; at the institutional level, however, one gets the feeling that Aboriginal spirituality is a thorn in the administration's side.

In this research I did not examine how Aboriginal spirituality and work with Elders played out in the parole process. This is obviously an important issue since an inmate's institutional record is presented and discussed during parole hearings. Failure to complete any institutionally recommended programs makes parole highly unlikely. Inmates are allowed to have witnesses speak on their behalf, and some Aboriginal men elect to have Elders present. In the Prairie region, the parole board hearing may include an Elder who assists the board, although this Elder is not normally one who has been working with the offender. Some change in the perspective of the parole board is evident. For example, in a 1992 report, the National Parole Board's (NPB) Irene Fraser (1992:4-5) argues that "equal weight in the decision process is not given to Aboriginal programming, such as sweats, longhouse ceremonies, and meetings with an Elder, as would be given to conventional programs such as AA or life skills." Instead, Fraser argues that the extent to which involvement in Aboriginal programs was considered was dependent on chance, that is, on the attitudes of the particular individual chairing the meeting and on comments contained within case management reports. Her report is insightful. While she argues that this inequity was not likely intentional, she suggests that "there is not sufficient awareness on the part of many members to be able to ask the kind of questions that would be helpful in determining the amount of healing gained through the Aboriginal programming." By 1996, however, this situation had changed: new policy guidelines indicated that equal weight must be given to offenders' involvement with Aboriginal programming. To this end, Board members have received extensive Aboriginal cultural education.[3] However, my previous discussion suggests that case management officers, who prepare documentation for parole hearings, lag somewhat behind the NPB in their recognition of the significance of Aboriginal spirituality.

It should be clear by now that the task of the Elders and spiritual leaders in prison is difficult and challenging. They must find a way to reconcile broad Aboriginal cultural differences, differing linguistic abilities, and differing degrees of orientation to or familiarity with Aboriginal and Euro-Canadian cultures. Yet they must do so within institutions that demonstrate a profound lack of understanding of Aboriginal cultures and spirituality. A process of cultural and spiritual education for most Aboriginal inmates is absolutely crucial for the establishment of the cultural foundation needed for Aboriginal spirituality to be effective as a form of therapy. It cannot be assumed that inmates are equal in their knowledge of spirituality or that they understand the symbols and ceremonial procedures. It is apparent that, at the outset of their prison terms, very few understand Aboriginal spirituality. Hence, the process of education begins. The Elders and spiritual leaders must engage in therapeutic relationships with men who have often lived profoundly difficult lives. It is to this issue that we now turn.

NOTES

1   From an anthropological perspective, cultural and personal identities are immensely complex, considerably more so than what I am presenting here.

2   We nevertheless must not lose sight of the fact that "culture" is amorphic and defies boundaries, and that individuals can exhibit a multiplicity of orientations and identities. These three categories must be seen in this light. Furthermore, the reader should not get caught up in the labels but should focus on the implications of cultural diversity.

3   I am grateful to Irene Fraser for updating me on developments concerning the National Parole Board in the Prairie region.

The only thing I can't do is say I'm White,
because everybody will look at my skin.
Maybe in my next life I'll be a White Man.
— ABORIGINAL INMATE

3
Trauma, Racism, and Identity

In recent years, psychologists and other mental health professionals have developed new ideas regarding the effects of traumatic experiences on individuals. It is proposed here that many Aboriginal peoples and societies have experienced a kind of trauma, in some cases for generations, which has had profound consequences for both individual and collective behaviour. This is a trauma that flows from colonialism and oppression. It is one that the Elders have not only experienced but with which they must continually deal in their work with Aboriginal inmates.

Trauma

Post-traumatic stress disorder (PTSD) is recognized by the American Psychiatric Association (APA) as a legitimate diagnosis for a constellation of psychological and physical symptoms related to traumatic life events.[1] The diagnosis was originally developed to deal with individuals who had encountered very sudden traumas, such as natural disasters and personal violence, or who had experienced prolonged, acute trauma, such as combat or situations of terrorism and kidnapping. Witnessing traumatic events, for instance the injury or death of another person, can also lead to this condition.

It is now recognized that childhood sexual abuse and extensive family violence may also result in PTSD. Key to the diagnosis, according to the APA's *Diagnostic and Statistical Manual of Mental Disorders* (DSM-IV) (1994:424) is that there must be exposure to an "extreme traumatic stressor," which revisits the individual through traumatic memory, such as flashbacks and nightmares. Symptoms can include irrational fears, insomnia, nightmares, digestive complaints, depression, anxiety or nervousness, irritability, and outbursts of anger. Also experienced are feelings of guilt, shame, fear, and hopelessness. Self-destructive and impulsive behaviour has also been noticed. As a result, victims of post-traumatic stress disorder often find it difficult to establish meaningful relationships or maintain jobs because of their occasionally erratic behaviour.[2]

Sociologist Kai Erikson (1976) took this general concept and applied it to the aftermath of a disaster in Buffalo Creek, West Virginia, where, in a matter of a few minutes, a flash flood wiped out an entire valley full of small, close-knit Appalachian communities. But Erikson moved beyond the application of the syndrome to individuals, describing a "collective trauma" resulting from the loss of "communality." He argued that this loss of community was every bit as devastating as the loss of homes and family members that these people experienced in those few moments of terror. While individuals experienced many symptoms of post-traumatic stress disorder, according to Erikson, it was their sense of loss with respect to their community and way of life that seemed to be most traumatizing. In effect, the flood washed away the culture of the valley. With it went the ability of the people to deal with the disaster as a collective and, therefore, their ability to cope with the trauma as individuals.

Psychologist Judith Lewis Herman (1992) has also attempted to redefine the concept of post-traumatic stress disorder. She has examined not only disasters and acute events such as combat, but also more prolonged forms of trauma and terror, like that experienced by battered wives and abused children. She has focused on what she sees as the "commonalities... between rape survivors and combat veterans, between battered women and political prisoners, between the survivors of vast concentration camps created by tyrants who rule nations and the survivors of small, hidden concentration camps created by tyrants who rule their homes" (1992:3). "Traumatic events," she writes, "destroy the victim's fundamental assumptions about the safety of the world, the positive value of the self, and the meaningful order of creation" (51), and that "[t]he damage to the survivor's faith and sense of community is particularly severe when the traumatic events themselves involve the betrayal of important relationships" (55). Such trauma can be both experienced and witnessed, two different forms of victimization. In her examination of child abuse, for instance, she notes that "repeated trauma in childhood forms and deforms the personality." "The child trapped in an abusive environment ... must find a way to preserve a sense of trust in people who are untrustworthy, safety in a situation that is unsafe, control in a situation that is terrifyingly unpredictable, power in a situation of helplessness" (96).

In her work, Herman describes the "pervasive terror" of physical or sexual abuse experienced by children, including the deprivation of the necessities of life, such as food. Abused children are survivors. But to survive they must go to extraordinary lengths, such as physically hiding and running away, internalizing the abuse and blaming themselves for being bad, or even cooperating in the abuse to avoid even more severe punishment. Anger, resentment, and hate are engendered. Trust is sacrificed. Fantasies of murderous revenge intrude on young minds, and they may act out their feelings on other children, adults, even family pets. The development of positive self-identities is compromised. While arguing that most victims do not become perpetrators of violence, Herman also notes that "men with histories of childhood abuse are more likely to take out their aggressions on others" (113).

Herman argues persuasively that victims of trauma, terror and abuse are often misdiagnosed by the mental health professions as having personality disorders (a diagnosis which is also frequently made for prison inmates). She proposes a variant of post-traumatic stress disorder, "complex post-traumatic stress disorder," which is designed to facilitate the proper diagnosis of the problem and treatment for individuals suffering the effects of long-term, sustained trauma.[3]

Psychologist Joe Couture has also been thinking about these issues with respect to Aboriginal peoples. Having worked for many years with Aboriginal people, including inmates, and being Aboriginal himself, his insights are significant. He has written that "[t]he concept of a damaged communal self challenges current constructs. Its operationalization through therapies poses a definition problem. Because of acculturation pressures, Aboriginal communities present, in many cases, a damaged collective self, reverberating through community and its component families" (Couture 1994:15).

Many, though not all, Aboriginal inmates have experienced such long-term trauma. Although it was not typical of all Aboriginal offenders, this research uncovered a considerable degree of violence, physical and sexual abuse, and alcoholism in the various individual life-histories documented. In the survey of 249 men, 66% admitted that there was physical violence in their families when they were growing up, and 80% suggested that at least one parent (or foster/adoptive parent) had a problem with alcohol or drugs. Familial disruption was also very common. Some 35% of the men interviewed had spent some time in foster homes, 30% in residential schools, and 5% had been adopted. Many had also spent considerable time in various group homes and youth correctional facilities. These experiences, occurring frequently or repeatedly, are significant enough in some instances to lead to a form of complex post-traumatic stress disorder of the type described by Herman. It is therefore essential for the Elders and spiritual leaders to deal with the pain and hatred engendered by these experiences.

If the concept of PTSD is to be useful to us here, it needs to be reconceptualized. In particular, PTSD needs to be understood as not simply traumatic memory, but also as lived experience. The DSM-IV fails to comprehend the manner in which long-term exposure to traumatic events shapes personalities, attitudes, values, and behaviours. It would seem that an individual who is exposed to prolonged terror, especially from a young age, is likely to develop into an anti-social being. A whole community or society which is victimized by trauma is likely to develop aberrant moral reference points for its citizens, leading to the intergenerational transmission of pathological behaviours. The experience of trauma then becomes the lived experience of a whole culture.

I believe we can add to Erikson's notion of community trauma, Couture's notion of a damaged communal self, and Herman's notion of long-term, cumulative trauma, by introducing an understanding of colonialism and historic policies of assimilation, and the effects these had on Aboriginal peoples. Programs of assimilation, in particular, can be seen as forms of prolonged terror perpetrated on Aboriginal peoples for generations. "Residential school syndrome" is one example of the effects of such trauma. In this sense, Aboriginal men in prison are survivors of a historic cultural trauma. Some will have experienced community trauma, perhaps as the result of the relocation or abandonment of their community, or perhaps because of the terror brought to the community by widespread substance abuse and violence. And of course many men have experienced personal trauma in the form of violence, sexual abuse, alcoholism, and, to paraphrase one inmate, having their culture literally beaten out of them. It is because all these forms of trauma can be linked to cultural oppression that Aboriginal spirituality, as a form of symbolic healing, has taken on such a profound meaning to many men. Indeed, as Duran and Duran (1995:52) have written, "[m]any Native American people are diagnosed based on erroneous criteria; the diagnostic process never takes a historical perspective in the placing of a diagnosis on the client." In their treatment of what they call "postcolonial psychology" for Native Americans, they "fantasize that one day the DSM... will have diagnostic criteria such as 'acute or chronic reaction to genocide and colonialism.'" It is to these reactions that we now turn.

Trauma Narratives

Trauma was a part of the home life of many Aboriginal men. The intensity of the violent acts witnessed by and perpetrated on these men when they were young is clear from the following passages. Themes of fear, terror, and betrayal weave throughout the texts.

> Even my Dad, my real Dad, I used to be scared of him. One time I wanted to go visit him when I was really small. He put me on a table like this and I was crying. He was trying to make me look at him and I'd look away. He was drunk and he got mad and he slapped me and scared me... One of his buddies come to get him to go to the room and I ran out... went back down the hill where we were living. So I didn't like my parents. [Traditional – Ojibwa]

> I didn't have it easy. There's not very many people that believe what I went through. I used to be beat with a bridle over my head and I got proof of evidence and marks on my back, on my head. If I had a hairless scalp right now, you would see dents that you would never believe to see. I was gone. I did not think good up here [points to head]. I was crazy up there by the beatings and mistreatment. When I got older, I was violent. I hated him, I despised him. But today I could not despise him... He had the same problem as me, this evilness inside. I could not do nothing when I seen my mother getting pounded. All the kids ran outside and I was left over in the corner in the porchroom. She let me see what was going on. I bet you if I had a gun in my hand when I was that age, I could have pulled that trigger. [Traditional – Plains Cree]

Violence between spouses or against other family members was witnessed on many occasions. Taking refuge was the only answer for many young people. They would run to a relative's house or hide under a bed or table. They were often witness to violent acts, frequently against their mothers.

> They [parents] used to fight a lot. When he [father] was sober, he was always angry about something. We were scared to walk by him... we'd get punished or something. That's the lifestyle we lived, fear of getting hit for nothing. And scared if you moved the wrong way while we're watching TV. When they drank, that's when we all hid. Wherever we'd find a good hiding spot, we spent the night there. [Bicultural – Plains Cree]

> A couple of times I would see them and they were drunk. But one time they were really drunk, and my Dad beat up my Mom. I woke up. And he was really mad and throw my Mom on the floor and start beating her up. And I went back to my room and watched them. And my Dad was kicking my Mom around, punching her. And other time my Mom stay on the floor all the time, and my Dad grab a chair and used the chair to beat her up. I was scared and the tears [flowed]. [Traditional – Cultural heritage anonymous]

> I was the one that told my Mom about the sexual assault [by father] on my sister. I witnessed it. So I was the one that was picked on more. Like I was the last to eat. I had to sleep on the floor... Like my brothers were beat, but I was the one that had to find a good hiding spot. [Bicultural – Plains Cree]

Some men were raised by extended family members, sometimes because their own parents were not able to adequately care for them. But this was no guarantee of freedom from witnessing and experiencing abuse.

> My granny raised me up ever since I was a little kid... I remember there used to be a lot of parties in my granny's house. My granny used to drink a lot, mostly every day. And I seen people getting beat up and getting cut up. Like I used to sit under the table and watch the fight. I seen people's blood all over the place. [Traditional – Chipewyan]

I was put into my grandfather's [home] and I guess I had to grow up. There was no more crying. I had to learn to do things like a grownup is supposed to do. I had to learn how to cut wood, haul water, lift traps, do ice fishing in the winter time. In the summertime I'd go out in the boat and do fishing. I had to learn all these and there was no crying... if I was to cry, my grandfather would give me a reason to cry and that would be with a stick. I lived this life until I was twelve years old. And then [one day] we came into the reservation for supplies. I made my mind up I didn't want to go back with my grandfather, because I couldn't live with the abuse anymore. Like I'd been burned. My bottom was burned so many times. I had been beaten up for something that I didn't do or if I didn't set the traps right, I was beaten. If I ate too much, I got a licking. So I couldn't live with that anymore. I took off. I got the idea that I was going to kill my grandfather. My intention was to kill the old man for the abuse that he put me through. Eventually I was sent away to a home for boys. I don't know how to describe it. I think I was real happy to get away from my grandfather. I had decent food, I had clothes I could wear that are decent, you know, and there was such things as water where you could wash up and take a shower. You know, things like that. So I made up my mind that I would never go back to this old man again. [Traditional – Northern Cree]

Abuse takes many forms, of course, and as the previous inmate suggests, physical violence is just one aspect. Sometimes the basic necessities of life were rationed or simply not provided.

Well my Dad never did hit us, but we never had anything to eat in our place. My Aunt used to bring us food all the time, 'cause my parents drank day and night. They were never home at all. [Bicultural – Northern Cree]

Family disruption was common for many of the men who would ultimately end up in jail. Abuse by step-parents sometimes created the same type of fear in blended families as did violence by biological parents.

Yeah, the old man [stepfather] was pretty violent. Like physical violence on me and my brothers. Except for his own [children]. My real father was murdered when I was too young to even remember. My stepfather... was pretty violent, you know, kicks,

punches, and the odd stick, board or something. [Euro-Canadian
– Cree/Metis]

Like I was getting beat up and I was getting punished and
everything. I had my skull cracked open. I have a scar right
there from my skull being cracked open. I've got a scar right
there where I got hit with a baseball bat. By my step-dad. I got
scars on my back where I have been hit by boards with rusty
nails from my step-dad... [One day] I walked in the back door,
walked into a forty-four magnum rifle, and my [step-] dad said,
"leave or die." And I left. [Euro-Canadian – heritage unknown]

Defiance in the face of violence often led to even more violence.

I was so used to being abused. Like my Mom, every time she
wanted to give me a licking, she had to count about ten times as
longer. Like normally she'd give me a couple of whacks and I'd
start crying, right. But then she had to give me ten more, or
thirteen more or maybe fifteen more whacks before I'd start
crying. I started resenting her. [Traditional – Saulteaux]

Criminal activity was seen by some as a form of escape from desperate home and community situations such as these.

There was a lot of alcoholism in my family, lots of fights, lots of
arguments, lots of abuse. That's why I started to get into trouble.
I just wanted to get out of there, so I did some B & E's. The cops
didn't find nobody who had done them, so I just phoned there
and I said, "I did it." [Traditional – Northern Cree]

The removal of Aboriginal children from their parental homes
and communities was a cornerstone of governmental policies of assimilation until very recently. Even though there was often abuse and
violence in these homes, within their families, Aboriginal children
were not forced to deny their cultural heritage and language. They
were not made to feel inferior to members of the larger society. This
cannot be said of the many non-Aboriginal foster homes and residential schools where these children were often placed.

Foster homes were sometimes abusive places. Interviewees believed
that foster parents were often interested primarily in the money that
was generated from agencies for their care, and they came to resent
their second-class treatment and exploitation.

An Indian couple took us in. Basically, they got paid in order to take care of us. But as we were growing up, they had other kids older than us in the family, but still we had to haul water and get wood. That was our job. When it comes to feeding time, like to feed the family, we'd sit on the floor waiting for our turn, while the rest of the family ate. That's how we were treated. We were like the work horses in that family. I hated going there [foster home] in the summertime, because we used to get beaten up by the older kids there, their kids. I think that the only reason we were taken in was they got money off us from the Family Services. As soon as there weren't no more money coming in, they didn't need us. They used to tell us to take off, or "you're no damn good for nothing." [Traditional – Ojibwa]

Our foster father, he was sexually assaulting my sister all the time. I was seven years old and I didn't really know what to do, out of fear. So I tried to fight him a few times and that, so I'd get beaten up so bad I couldn't even go to school. I had black eyes and everything. So I promised myself when I grow up, I'll beat him up. You know, here's my sister crying. When I turned twelve years old I beat him up with a baseball bat and I took my sister and ran away. And we grew up on the streets. [Euro-Canadian – Saulteaux]

The denial of Aboriginal culture was also a feature of some foster homes.

I remember when I was first going into the foster homes and what not, like they'd cut our hair and they'd tell us or accuse us of being culturally deprived and stuff like that. That was a common thing, they were there to teach us. If you didn't listen, well, you'd get a strap or you'd get this or that. [Bicultural – Plains Cree]

I was seven years old and put into the system and I haven't been out since. My first foster home, I didn't know how to speak English or understand it. I was put into my first foster home and it was... let's see, how would I put that... my language was beaten out of me, right? You know, me and my brother, we weren't allowed to speak our Native tongue, and every time we did, we'd get a licking. [Euro-Canadian – Saulteaux]

This last individual, later in the interview, made the connection between the abuse he had experienced and his prison rehabilitation:

> It was bad, the beatings. [A] conveyor belt strap was what was used on me. When you're beaten like that, you learn fast... The tears were also beaten off. [I] took the beatings without tears. From those days, I haven't cried yet. Even at my mother's funeral a few years ago, my cousin's funeral, my brother's, I couldn't cry. I don't know how the system wants people. They mess people up and then they try and straighten them out later. That's psychology, you know. Mess things up and now they try to fix them.

The physical and sexual abuse experienced in some foster homes often left an indelible mark.

> To me, they [foster parents] were psychotic. They didn't give a shit. They needed some workers. They needed somebody to control, somebody to take their aggression out on, and I was one of them. They wanted us as a go boy, and when I didn't do what they said, they beat me really badly, really badly. In that four years I learned not only to resent but to hate. I used to drown cats in the bathtub just because I hated, because I had so much hate. Because I hated them so much I used to kill their animals. It took me four years to run away. I was giving blow jobs by the time I was ten years old. [Euro-Canadian – Cultural heritage anonymous]

This same individual then articulated the effects this had on his life:

> The Indian guy that did that to me in the foster home, he got me real confused. Taught me how to manipulate. Taught me how to coerce. Taught me how to keep a secret. Nobody knew until I was late in my teens that I was molested there. You know, he taught me how to take advantage of somebody when they are hurting. I was hurting. I was lonely. He was going to be my friend. All I had to do was give him blow jobs and hand jobs and keep him happy. I was happy, but it taught me a lot of negative stuff. Basically the whole foster home was the most negative experience [in] that I held on for so long to the hate, the resentment, the judgemental attitude. [I] judged everybody.

Residential schools were also places where intense physical and sexual abuse, and cultural denial were often perpetrated on the young Aboriginal wards.

At a very early age, my parents put us in a residential school. We went through a lot of problems at the residential school. English was the only language that we were allowed to speak, and if we did speak our own language, we were severely reprimanded. So basically, there was a lot of hatred, fear, and a lot of negative things that I hated against the people in authority or people with power. I also felt that I was just dumped there, with promises from my mother that she'd be back in a week to pick us up. So I had a tendency to run away and rebel at a very early age, more out of fear of living in the residential school because I was physically abused and sexually abused. [Euro-Canadian – Ojibwa]

In the school – there was a lot of physical violence. A lot of people got homesick and they decided they wanted to run away and the search teams would go out and the guy would be brought back. And they used to have this big common day room and all the small boys, the intermediate boys and senior boys were seated right around this entire thing. And the principal of the school at that time would come in, in the middle of the room. He had about a half-inch thick strap, about four inches wide and about two feet long. And he'd make the guy kneel down. He'd tell the guy to lean his head forward, he would put the guy's head in a leglock and he would take the guy's arms and hold them behind his back and he would strap him in front of everybody to make a spectacle of him and an example for the rest of the people, to deter any running away because we were homesick, because we wanted to go home. It [physical abuse] was common. At one point in time, I pissed off the Master. He cuffed me up side the head. And he used to wear these steel-toed boots. Like I was an eight, nine year old kid, you know. He literally kicked me around on the floor. I was in a little ball and he clunked me up in the ribs and I would go rolling down and I tried telling him I was sorry and he kicked me again, you know. This was in front of everybody. I had bruises. Maybe I had broken ribs. I was scared, scared to say anything. [Bicultural – Plains Cree]

Trust of parents and foster parents, when violated, can be traumatic. Young people trust authority figures, so when the abuse came from priests and nuns, the trauma seemed even more incomprehensible.

> Residential schools are a lot worse than where I am now [in prison]. Especially when people, the highly talked about priests and nuns... that kind of treatment coming from them, you know you look at it, you don't know who to trust. You try to be good. The more you try to be good, the more it seems you are getting thrown around. "Go sit in the corner!" "Go lie in bed!" Then you know you are out there lying, and the tears, if you cry, it seems like it gives them that reason to punish you more, when they see tears in your eyes. [Bicultural – Plains Cree]

Trauma also operates on the community level, and some inmates characterized their entire communities as pathological.

> Drinking in my home town is a lot, like a lot of Native people drink. People burn in the fire, freeze, die of alcohol when they are sleeping. Where I am from, a lot of Native people drink and they are dying off and nobody is doing a damn thing about it. [Traditional – Slavey]

> They [the people] were always getting into fights or look for fights and I think it was kind of affecting the whole community. A lot of fights. People go run away to other places, I mean to same community, they ran away from their house because of the drinking there. [Traditional – Cultural heritage anonymous]

> So, throughout my growing up years, a lot of my relatives, close relatives, they all died mostly alcohol-related deaths. And a vast proportion of my people spent time in jail for one thing or another. So it was more or less something that was expected because everybody was drinking. People were killing each other, people were dying alcohol-related deaths. Maybe freezing to death. They were getting hit by cars. And it was devastating in this sense, and I grew up seeing it happen. So as we were growing up, we had to live in a violent atmosphere. It was pretty hard and devastating. I can't recall too many happy incidents in my life because I never really experienced childhood or growing up as a normal child. As I was growing up, all I saw was violence, I experienced violence. And I live in a world where my people

were looked down upon because of the lifestyle we were living...
So even the basic necessity of food and clothing was very hard
to acquire. [Bicultural – Chipewyan]

Familiarity with violence and death was widespread to the point
where some became almost oblivious to the carnage.

People would injure themselves left and right. They would shoot
at each other and axe each other, stab each other. It was amazing.
I would see dead bodies. And when they're frozen out in the
winter time, or when they're drowned... Old bodies stink... So
you got really used to that. [Bicultural – Northern Cree]

The effect of trauma on these individuals contributed to an ongoing cycle of abuse and violence that, for some men, was difficult to
break.

I am a product of my environment. I learned violence and
everything at home, and I just carried it on when I got older. I
drank, getting high, and the cycle continues. I end up in jail,
you know, and if I didn't stop and realize what I was doing,
then my kids would end up like me. Drinking and stuff like
that. See I thought when my step-dad used to be with my mom,
[then] when I got older and I was with my old lady, I thought it
was normal for me to slap my old lady. But then I realized that
I didn't like that when my mom got a licking, so I wouldn't
want that to happen to my daughter. A lot of Native people
don't realize that, they just keep continuing the cycle and it just
keeps going on and on, and it has to stop some place. And that
is why I figure I ended up in jail, because of that cycle. And I fell
right into it. And now that I'm in jail, I realized, okay, I've got
to stop. [Bicultural – Saulteaux]

There were a number of ways in which individuals reacted to or
dealt with physical and sexual abuse, and alcoholism. Not all adap-
tations were successful, obviously, since each individual ultimately
ended up in prison. Some sought to escape their situation, and prison
was sometimes seen as a better alternative. Escape was also sought in
alcohol and drugs. Violence, too, was a reaction; a common theme
throughout the previous narratives is that of the offender seeking to
protect siblings and friends from trauma. Some men adapted not by
resisting but by cooperating with the perpetrators, at least superficially.

This is especially true in cases of sexual abuse. Many men remained scarred by their experiences as youngsters, and these shaped their behaviours and attitudes as they reached adulthood.

Racism

Racism is an undeniable social fact of life in Canada, and therefore it should not be surprising that the Aboriginal offenders express views, and detail experiences, similar to those of other Aboriginals and members of racial minority groups. Their lives, both on "the street" and in prison, represent a microcosm of the experiences of minority groups in Canada. Violence and terror associated with racism seems to have been a common feature during their formative years, and many men responded by developing prejudices of their own. When seen within the context of the other aspects of their lives as previously discussed, it can be argued that racism as it is experienced by Aboriginal people is a key component of trauma.

In the survey of 249 men, 74% responded that they had experienced racism from non-Aboriginal people outside prison, and a surprising 45% stated they had experienced racism from other Aboriginal people. Inside prison, 52% said they had experienced racism from non-Aboriginals, and 33% said they had experienced it from other Aboriginal people.

The least problematic group in terms of racism was the traditional men. They were less likely than others to view Canada as a racist country, or prison as a racist place, and they were less likely to admit to having experienced racism personally at some point in their lives. Originating in predominantly Aboriginal communities, with relatively little experience in the Euro-Canadian cultural milieu, these individuals seem to have escaped the more overt forms of racism experienced by other Aboriginal offenders. Nevertheless they encountered racism whenever they were removed from their families or communities, for instance to foster homes and residential schools. One of the traditional offenders explained that his experiences with racism were related to a relatively brief period of schooling in an urban centre:

> I still am like that. I am still prejudiced sometimes towards certain people. I used to go to school [in a northern Saskatchewan community] and then for some reason I got shipped to P.A. [Prince Albert]. I was at the residence in the school at P.A. and I had to go to a White school in P.A. , but I did not last that long.

I fought all the time. I fought the White boys all the time. And finally I walked home [to the reserve]. I just couldn't take it anymore. [Traditional – Northern Cree]

Experiences of racism at school were considerably more profound for the bicultural and Euro-Canadian oriented offenders, most of whom were educated at predominantly Euro-Canadian institutions. Two bicultural offenders detailed their experiences as follows:

When we started going to the city schools, there were a lot of problems, because we were a bus load of Indians getting off. And that's what we were called sometimes. And I found myself fighting a lot of times because I was Indian. People used to say things. So I was beating up the White kids all the time. We just didn't like being called "Indian" or stuff like that, or "wagon burners" or stuff like that, so we would get into fights. [Bicultural – Plains Cree]

So in my teens, I remember being the only Indian person in twenty square blocks of the city. There was only three of us in one particular high school, so it [racism] was always an occurrence... A lot of fights, a lot of fights. Just the constant feeling that you had to protect yourself at all times, otherwise somebody would be taking a run at you for whatever reason. Even in sports, like the basketball team, you know, hockey or whatever, they were taking a run at you... for no other reason other than you were an Indian... I'd walk into a hamburger joint and I'd get served last. A lot of shit like that. [Bicultural — Plains Cree]

The effects of racism on the developing identities of young Aboriginal boys was profound, as this bicultural offender suggested:

When I was in school, I was always ashamed. My teacher would crack a racial joke, right in front of everybody and they'd laugh at me. This was a whole class. I used to run away from school and run home. [Bicultural – Plains Cree]

The problems with racism were perhaps even more compounded for the Euro-Canadian oriented men, many of whom were struggling to understand their own identity in the face of overwhelming cultural pressure from the dominant society.

When I was young... the school was basically all White, a few half-breeds, a couple of Indians. But there it was hard. We got beaten up and it was hard to get along with people 'cause they were basically prejudiced. And then when my mom died and we moved to the farm and then we went to school right into town, and there were a few more Indians, and they seemed to be a little more easier to get along with. But on the outskirts of town there was something there wasn't right, and we were getting beat up all the time because of our race. [Euro-Canadian – Cultural heritage anonymous]

I rebelled a lot. In elementary school, I was always a big scrapper and stuff like that and I had a bad reputation and it carried on in grade seven. I tried to be quiet for awhile, but being called "bush nigger," "jungle bunny" and stuff like this, it is sort of hard to swallow, so I started fighting. [Bicultural – Saulteaux]

It is not surprising that minority individuals experiencing racism would develop negative attitudes toward the majority group. Some of the respondents in this study openly contemplated their own racism toward "Whites," often rhetorically asking the question, "Am *I* prejudiced?" One Euro-Canadian oriented offender (whose cultural heritage must remain anonymous) admitted that racism "has made me resent White people. It has made me more untrustworthy. I don't trust like I know I should." A traditional Northern Cree inmate stated a similar view: "Because Natives have been put down since forever, and that's why I had a hard time accepting White people."

It might be a little more surprising that some Aboriginal inmates developed negative attitudes toward other Aboriginals as a result of racism when growing up. This is particularly the case for Euro-Canadian oriented men, many of whom were grappling with questions of their identity and finding that they didn't fit in with either the Euro-Canadians or the Aboriginals. They may have looked Aboriginal, but culturally they were Euro-Canadian, which created problems. One traditional man described how city-raised Aboriginals were viewed by the reserve people:

In the school that I went to [briefly; in a city], there was two other Native kids. Well, I thought they were. They were brown. I thought they were, but I never talked to them. They grew up in cities and I felt we had nothing in common. They were just like those other people [ie. "Whites"]. [Traditional – Northern Cree]

A bicultural inmate echoed these views:

> [There were] hardly any [Indian children in his city school] and
> if there was, they were "apples," you know, white on the inside
> but red on the outside. Some of us just didn't want to turn into
> that. [Bicultural – Plains Cree]

Of course, it was the Euro-Canadian oriented individuals who bore
the brunt of these negative views. Two common features of their
stories are ostracism and persecution by other Aboriginals; these experiences clearly affected their self-identity.

> The term "apple" is being used against me as a child or as an
> adolescent, which means red on the outside and white on the
> inside. Which is because I didn't speak the language or know a
> lot of the customs and stuff. And in a way it was true, because
> I was a little bit ashamed because I didn't know nothing about
> my past. [Euro-Canadian – Saulteaux]

Another offender, adopted at birth by a Euro-Canadian family,
related a long story of simultaneous persecution by Aboriginal and
Euro-Canadian peers in a prairie city. A small part of his story is as
follows:

> I was nine years old when we moved and when we first got
> there we were walking down the street, me and my mom and
> my dad. And I saw this old guy. And he had dark skin and I
> asked my mom, "is that an Indian?" And she said "yeah it is."
> And like he was all drunk, walking on the street... And I can
> remember my mom saying, "Oh, I hope that you don't turn out
> like that." I guess in my rebellious teenage years if anybody
> ever called me an Indian, I would lash out at them, because I
> didn't like that. My mom and dad would ask me what happened,
> but I never ever wanted to make my parents feel sorry that they
> had adopted me... [When] I was fifteen... I met this Native girl,
> and she talked funny. She has a Cree accent. And then I asked
> her one day to go to a movie, and at first she wasn't quite sure
> because her type, her friends, didn't hang around with my
> friends. It was still at a point where Native students don't really
> mix with Whites, and I had grown up in a White society and I
> was looked upon as a White person, in a sense... And her friends
> were sitting in the food fair area [in a shopping mall]... and I

was holding her hand while walking through the mall, and all of a sudden these girls and guys started yelling at her, "why are you hanging around with a White guy?" Like, I got mad, but I didn't know what to do, because they were calling me a White guy but yet like I was Native... [I started] getting back at the Native people. Like, they said something I didn't like, so I would beat them. A lot of Native people, if they saw myself or my friends coming, they would go on the other side and you know we would make racist jokes at them. [Euro-Canadian – cultural heritage anonymous]

Skin colour, of course, is an important signifier of race, and Aboriginal men sometimes experienced racism based on interpretations of their skin colour or "shade of brown." The discrimination they felt was often directed toward them by other Aboriginals. One offender stated:

Mostly why I never got involved with some things [was] 'cause I got a fair colour... I kind of felt left out because my brothers are dark and that kind of pulled me away from things, too. [Euro-Canadian – Plains Cree]

For some, being of fairer complexion was actually seen as an advantage because it allowed them to escape the more negative conceptions associated with Aboriginality. The following individual clearly experienced denial in his relationship with his family:

I was ashamed for a long time about my brothers and sisters, my Mom, sometimes how dark they were. Like I wish Mom and them would admit to it [being Native] now... Basically, I still consider myself White, but I know in the back of my mind that there's some Native in there. There's no denying it. I mean it's in the blood. I could pass for White. I mean I can fit in pretty easily. [Euro-Canadian – Cree-Metis]

His ability to pass for "White" was nevertheless a problem at times; it meant that when he tried to claim his Aboriginality, it was often denied him by other Aboriginal people. Again, we get the sense of a man who feels caught between two cultures:

I feel uncomfortable sometimes because I think they're [other Aboriginal people] thinking, "well this guy's White, why does he think he's Native?" That's a big part of my conflict I'm having with myself, because my family is dark, I'm White and I am part Native and it's a big problem... Personally, I would rather be labelled an Indian. It's hard; because of my outward appearance I am not really accepted... There was a time when I used to hate my skin colour.

Experiencing racism during the formative years has greatly affected many Aboriginal offenders. However, some respondents failed to acknowledge that they experienced racism to any degree during their life. Some offered contradictory statements, describing extensive conflict with Euro-Canadians but denying the existence of racism. How racism is perceived by individuals will, of course, vary. So too will the readiness of individuals to discuss or disclose racist feelings and experiences. Clearly, not all were willing or able to identify racism as a problem in their lives.

Racism shapes attitudes, blurs identities, and engenders hatred. This experience and these attitudes are brought into the correctional system where they are frequently reinforced by the social setting of the prisons. Many offenders related perceptions of racism in various prisons; 84% saw prison as a racist place, and 33% reported being called a racially derogatory name by staff. For the Elders and spiritual leaders, it is essential to break through the barriers created by racism in order to eliminate the hurt, the anger, and the hatred that racism has caused.

Identity

One of the central aspects of complex post-traumatic stress disorder as presented by Herman (1992) is that an individual's self-identity can be compromised as a result of long-term abuse. Earlier in this chapter we saw how this problem can be examined within the context of cultural denial which, for members of an oppressed minority group, can have devastating consequences. Not surprisingly, there was a varied response to the issue of self-identity, how it was expressed and problematized by the Aboriginal offenders in this study. In general, the more traditional the inmate, the less likely that identity appeared as problematic. The more traditional an Aboriginal inmate was, the more likely he would think of himself as "completely Native" (as opposed to "partially Native"), and that he would express comfort with his identity as a Native person. In contrast, the more Euro-Canadian in cultural orientation, the more likely an inmate would describe himself as "partially Native" and note that he was "still trying to understand" his identity. Significantly, these more Euro-Canadian oriented men were also more likely to admit to having been ashamed or embarrassed by their Aboriginality at some point in their life.

In general, traditional men tended to exhibit very little identity conflict with respect to their Aboriginality. For instance, they often simply declared themselves to be "Cree" or "Dene." Only secondarily did they refer to themselves in more general terms, such as "Indian," or "Native." Hence, they tended to identify quite strongly with a particular Aboriginal cultural group. As a product of their upbringing, these men are the most strongly rooted in their Aboriginal cultures. In many instances, their exposure to non-Aboriginal culture, especially during childhood, was minimal, and their Aboriginal language was the *lingua franca* in their families and communities.

Insofar as there was some identity conflict for traditional men, it tended to revolve around questions of legal status. One inmate in particular found himself in an anomalous position: he was, in his own terms, both a "half-breed" and a "treaty" Indian, the latter status being acquired as a result of the 1985 amendment to the *Indian Act* (Bill C-31). By his own admission, in his Dene community there were no apparent cultural differences between the "half-breeds" and the "treaty" or federally registered Indians: "it is just rights." In effect, his legal status allowed him to operate in three worlds if he were to so choose:

> I'm in between, a half-breed. I could go either on their side, the Native side. I could take both sides. I could go into the White man's side or I could go into the Native side. I am caught right in the middle. I don't know what side to pick. [Traditional – Slavey]

However, feelings of embarrassment and shame could still develop. Some traditional men were removed from their communities for short periods, for instance to residential schools or foster homes. One traditional man described these feelings with respect to his childhood:

> I didn't like being an Indian at first, I guess, when I was younger. I guess I was ashamed. [Traditional – Ojibwa]

Bicultural men demonstrated considerably more identity conflict. For these individuals, there has been some degree of struggle in their lives to maintain their Aboriginal identity in the face of a domineering Euro-Canadian culture. They were inclined to talk about their "people" and to view their own identity within the context of the history of contact between their "people" and the Euro-Canadians, as well as in the context of more recent government policy. Bicultural offenders, in particular, often articulated their view of identity within the context of the trials and tribulations of their "people":

> We are just an oppressed people right now. We are a depressed people right now. That is why you have all the alcohol on the reserve. People just don't have the determination anymore that they once had. And at one time we used to have braids and be proud of it. Now we are having just a hell of a time on the reserves and you know we are having this identity crisis on the reserves. People only seem to be looking after "number one." [Bicultural – Plains Cree]

Another offender related a very detailed history of his people, who had been severely traumatized when forced to relocate to a Euro-Canadian town. Many people died, often violently. This individual was raised in the context of the social pathology of the new community:

> My parents, their parents, my grandparents, they didn't know how to speak English and they were taken out of their environment and made to live in a foreign society, a different lifestyle altogether. So the ways of the people, the lifestyle, it changed. They could no longer have the freedom and the spirit to do what they are capable of doing so they lost all their self-esteem and self-respect... and eventually the people started drinking because they couldn't cope with the change. [Bicultural – Dene]

As a result of this social pathology, he was removed to a residential school at the age of twelve. By the time he was an adult and ready to return to the community, the people had relocated back to the bush. He had learned how to survive during the band's town years and how to survive in the Euro-Canadian residential school system, but he had no experience of his people's culture in the bush. The idea of being somehow caught between the two cultures, but not able to function effectively in either, was expressed:

> I was lost in two worlds. There was my people living [in the northern bush] and there was me trying to live in the White man's world. So for the longest time I was lost. I didn't have an identity, so to speak. I couldn't make it with my own people, and I can't make it with the rest of society.

As we have seen in this chapter, foster homes and residential schools are also responsible for blurring the identities of some offenders, as well as for introducing a considerable amount of cultural change. One man of mixed-ancestry raised in foster homes on land adjacent to a reserve explained why he thought of himself as "Metis":

> The reason that I would not say I'm an Indian is that I grew up in a White man's world but I still have the belief of what a Native stands for. [Bicultural – Metis]

Considerable conflict with non-Aboriginals characterized the early years of bicultural men, especially in schools where they were subjected to racist taunting. This often led them to question their own identities and to resent being Aboriginal. School-yard fighting usually began early in childhood, and for many men developed into a pattern for adult life.

> Like I said, we used to get into fights all the time. In a way I sort of regretted being an Indian, that I had to go through all of that. There was certain times that I didn't think I should have to fight for who I am. But I did and that sort of made me angry. [Bicultural – Plains Cree]

This individual also echoed the negative stereotypes of Aboriginal peoples often held by Euro-Canadians:

> I seen the Indian people drunk on the streets and stuff like that. And I have always had the stigma of being Indian, from the respect [perspective] of other people. And when you see a drunk person on the street, sitting on the street or slopped out on the street, you sort of feel shameful because that is your people there.

Euro-Canadian oriented offenders best typify those "caught between two worlds," unable to fit comfortably in either the Aboriginal or Euro-Canadian worlds. This is a well documented sociological phenomenon for Aboriginal peoples. Conflict with both Aboriginals and Euro-Canadians is a common feature of their lives.

A few such individuals, adopted at an early age by Euro-Canadian parents, were completely unaware of their Aboriginal ancestry until late childhood. The consequences of this were apparent in the early formation of self-identity.

> You know, I was pretty messed up when I was a kid. I used to get into fights all the time... I used to be called a lot of names and I would fight. but I would always go home and my mom would ask me what happened this time, and I would tell her. And I would put it on her. I would ask her, "Well, why are these guys calling me names and stuff?" That is when I was young, five or six. I asked her, you know, "am I Native, am I Indian, or what?" And she always told me "no". But later you know, a few years later, when I knew who I was then, she was still saying no. I felt that she was ashamed of me. So I never really felt close to my family because of that. [Euro-Canadian – heritage unknown]

> But like I didn't even realize that we came from a Native background until we came to Saskatchewan. I didn't even realize, even though my Dad, like he's got a dark brown complexion like the way of Natives, and my Mom had a lighter pigment of skin. And yet my Mom was a full-blooded Indian and my Dad was a half-breed. [Bicultural — Metis]

This next individual learned of his Indian heritage later in life, after he had internalized some of the more common negative stereotypes:

> It was also a shocker to find out that I was an Indian. I thought they were all extinct. Because [in] your books, they were all savages and killers... That's what the Indians were. But we weren't that! So we couldn't identify with them. [Bicultural – Northern Cree]

The early exposure to and adoption of negative Euro-Canadian stereotypes of Aboriginal peoples was a theme common to interviews with Euro-Canadian oriented men. For instance, one inmate stated:

> You know how White people look upon Natives. If they are Indian people, they are wild people. They drink, they use violence. That's how I was raised, to believe that. [Euro-Canadian – heritage unknown]

Another man echoed these views:

> I always saw Native people drunk, high. I heard a lot of Native
> people go to jail. I heard a lot of Native people are on welfare.
> When I was growing up, I heard nothing but bad things about
> Native people... and I guess I didn't want to be looked down
> upon as one of the Native people... I just didn't want to be a
> Native person. [Euro-Canadian – cultural heritage anonymous]

Racism and discrimination also affect identity. The following
individual was torn between defending his identity as an Indian, and
hating it:

> I knew I was an Indian, growing up and being teased, being
> called "chief." So there was a lot of fighting in my life, defending
> my identity and dignity. I grew up hating, I guess, myself and
> especially other Indian people. [Euro-Canadian – Ojibwa]

He laid much of the blame on the residential schools he attended
which, he argued, were very effective in assimilating him:

> Through the residential schools, I lost my language. I became
> White, even though I was "red" outside. I lost my identity. I
> lost my culture. I lost total respect for myself.

Perhaps the identity conflict experienced by the Euro-Canadian oriented individuals is best summarized by the following inmate:

> Well, I was raised Caucasian, you know. I was raised with the
> White people's beliefs and I never felt comfortable with that.
> Then on the other hand, my [birth] parents are Native. So I
> don't really think of myself as a Native and I don't really think
> of myself as Caucasian. [Euro-Canadian – heritage unknown]

Identity problems are pervasive. A few offenders interviewed for
this study went so far as to speculate out loud how much better their
life would be if they were "White." One traditional man, when asked
how he defined his identity, began by admitting, "I'm kind of mixed.
I don't know who I want to be." Then he added,

> I wish that I was White, you know. Like that was always one of
> my biggest wishes. White people, they get away with a lot of

things. They get the better end of the stick... They're treated
more fairly... They get what they ask for. Native people have to
fight for what they ask for. People don't listen to you because
you're Native. And I guess that's what I hate about me being an
Indian, 'cause nobody wants to listen to me. [Traditional –
Northern Cree]

Many Aboriginal offenders are currently experiencing an identity
conflict of one sort or another. Some are very seriously challenging
past understandings of who they are; others are only passively interested in exploring their Aboriginal roots. Bicultural and Euro-Canadian oriented offenders demonstrated the greatest conflict in this area.
For bicultural offenders, the problem has been to maintain their
Aboriginal identity in the face of fairly sustained pressure by Euro-
Canadian society on their communities, and on themselves as individuals. For Euro-Canadian oriented offenders, the problem has been
to sort through the various identities they have assumed over the
years, and those that have been ascribed to them, to determine if
being Aboriginal, in effect, means anything at all.

It has not been the purpose of this work to determine if self-identity is a factor which explains why an individual engages in criminal
activity. However, the data suggest that identity issues are fairly central to the overall rehabilitation process. Since identity issues are firmly
rooted within the colonial experience of oppression and policies of
assimilation, they are best handled within an Aboriginal framework.
Much of the work of Aboriginal Elders and spiritual leaders in prison
is directed toward resolving identity conflict and establishing a positive, proud Aboriginal identity within troubled inmates.

There are some basic themes which weave their way throughout the
narratives contained in this chapter. These themes both support and
expand our understanding of the effects of trauma on individuals,
communities, and cultures.

The links between Aboriginal inmates and their families and communities were disrupted. Abuse at the hands of parents, relatives,
and those in positions of trust was common. These inmates invariably experienced the grief of many deaths, including those of parents
and siblings. They witnessed violence on many occasions. The basic
necessities of life, such as food and shelter, were often denied them.
They were introduced to alcohol and substance abuse at a young
age, through which they sought escape. During the interviews, they

spoke of a lack of love and affection. They talked at length about how their lives and identities had been affected by racism, and not just from non-Aboriginal people. Emotionally, the scars are evident. Some men talked of hate and bitterness. Others expressed profound sadness. They spoke of an inability as adults to love their own families and to trust people. And they demonstrated profound difficulty establishing positive identities for themselves.

Trauma, it is argued here, also operates at community, societal, and cultural levels. Narratives presented in this chapter characterize some Aboriginal communities as pathological in a way that is clearly damaging to residents. Furthermore, we must also appreciate that some men interviewed looked considerably beyond the community level in describing the roots of their problems. They spoke of the profound effects of racism directed against them and their people, by both non-Aboriginal and Aboriginal people. In effect, they described what I would call a cultural memory, that is, the memory of a time when these types of trauma were uncharacteristic, and when the government and churches subsequently sought to eliminate the Aboriginality of their people. Aspects of this memory are apparent in what is often referred to as the oral tradition, but this represents only one element. Current psychopathology, and other problems experienced by Aboriginal inmates, must therefore be seen as the product of events and circumstances operating at four levels: the individual, the community, the society, and the culture. Rehabilitative programs which ignore this fact, for instance by focusing only on the individual, will not likely be successful. As we shall see, the Elders and spiritual leaders do, in fact, deal with each of these levels.

Not all Aboriginal offenders have been traumatized or suffer from identity conflict, or have alcohol or substance abuse problems. It would not be accurate to describe Aboriginal communities solely in terms of pathology, since they exhibit many positive features that have allowed the people to successfully resist assimilation and adapt to Euro-Canadian society. Nevertheless, the lives of many men were traumatic in some of the ways I have discussed here. Aboriginal spirituality, as a form of therapy, appears well suited to deal with these issues of trauma, abuse, racism, and identity confusion.

NOTES

1   Post-traumatic stress disorder is considered an "anxiety disorder" in DSM-IV, the most recent *Diagnostic and Statistical Manual of Mental Disorders* published by the American Psychiatric Association (1994).

2   In some circles, it has become fashionable to dismiss the concept of post-traumatic stress disorder simply as a fad diagnosis. While it always necessary to critically analyze new concepts and paradigms, we cannot lose sight of the fact that individuals are still experiencing distress. It is essential that we attempt to understand such idioms of distress, that is, the ways in which distress manifests itself physically, emotionally, and even spiritually in culturally meaningful and understandable ways. Allan Young's (1995) recent critical examination of PTSD, while challenging its universality, nevertheless notes that we must not trivialize "the acts of violence and the terrible personal losses that stand behind many traumatic memories. The suffering is real; PTSD is real" (10).

3   The American Psychiatric Association does not include Herman's notion of "complex" post-traumatic stress syndrome in DSM-IV.

We have to understand the symbolic meanings of our culture. Once you understand the symbolic meanings of Aboriginal spirituality, then it enhances your understanding about life.
— ELDER CAMPBELL PAPEQUASH

4
Aboriginal Spirituality and Symbolic Healing

The biomedical system is a culturally constructed system of symbols for healing. So too are the various Aboriginal medical systems in Canada. Although technology can rid one of disease, "healing" can only occur where the medical system is interpretable between the healer and patient. This is because "healing" and "illness," as opposed to "curing" and "disease," are cultural constructs. Biomedicine has tended to concentrate on developing an understanding of the body and mind as separate biological entities, and on how disease affects various body organs and systems. Aboriginal medical systems, in contrast, have focused more on developing an understanding of the body and mind as a whole, and on how illness is symptomatic of an imbalance between the individual, the society, and the spiritual realm.

In this chapter, I seek to describe Aboriginal spirituality as a form of symbolic healing. The use of the term "symbolic" is not meant to imply something intended but not real (as in a "symbolic gesture"). It refers to the fact that this form of healing is very dependent on the use, interpretation, negotiation, and manipulation of cultural symbols as central to the process of healing.

The Nature of Symbolic Healing

"A symbol is any *thing* which may function as the vehicle for a conception," writes Donald Sandner in *Navajo Symbols of Healing* (1979:12). Language represents a symbolic system in which individual words are employed to represent ideas or concepts. Sandner notes that "a mathematical notation, an act, a gesture, a ritual, a dream, a work of art, or anything else that can carry a concept" can be a symbol. Symbols pervade all aspects of human existence and can be found embedded in, for instance, a given culture's medical system. *All* medical systems employ symbols. "Symbolic healing," or the use and manipulation of culturally-constructed symbols in healing, is then a component of all healing traditions. Within biomedicine, it is most evident in "talk therapy," that is, psychotherapy, a treatment approach based on the use and manipulation of words and mental images as symbols. The importance of symbolic healing in the other sectors of biomedicine may appear less obvious but is nonetheless observable (Kleinman 1988).[1]

Thomas Csordas (1983), in his research into "religious healing," has suggested that its global prevalence argues persuasively for an examination of the "holy" as fundamental to our understanding of health. In his examination of Catholic Pentecostal healing, he has argued that "the locus of therapeutic efficacy is in the particular forms and meanings, i.e., the discourse," that are reified (or made real) in the healing encounter. Through the use of symbols, the interchange of language and other forms of communication between healer and patient is essential, leading to a transformation in the patient's understanding of the problem. Such a conception presupposes that the language and symbols used are meaningful for both the healer and the patient. The religious community plays a crucial role in this interchange. Both the definitions of the problem and the cure "conform to the agenda of the religious community," and "healing is understood to occur in terms of integration of the healed person into the religious community" (1983:347). Among religious groups such as the Catholic Pentecosts, healing is viewed not as a fixed phenomenon, but rather as a continuing process that requires ongoing support from, and in effect integration into, the religious group. Healing invokes lifelong subscription to the healing or religious order.

Csordas (1983) suggests that what he calls the "rhetoric of healing" must, in the first instance, convince the patient that healing is possible; the patient must be "predisposed" to being healed. By participating in the social and religious setting of the church, Catholic

Pentecosts are exposed to the relevant symbols that will ultimately allow healing to ensue. However, Csordas (1983:349) notes that individuals do not primarily become involved in the movement to seek healing; rather healing often follows a period of involvement. The implication is that some form of education, an introduction to the basic elements, principles, symbols, and rhetoric, is required first. Ultimately, the patient undergoes a transformation when he/she "is persuaded to change cognitive, affective, and behavioral patterns... in order to achieve the construction of a self that is healthy, whole and holy." This ensures acceptance into the wider community of reference (in this instance, the religious order) (Csordas 1983:356).

Csordas (1983) refers to this form of healing as "religious," but it is clearly also a form of symbolic healing. Building upon the earlier work of Daniel Moerman (1979), James Dow (1986a) has outlined what he believes to be the "universal aspects" of symbolic healing. According to Dow, symbolic healing involves the generalizing of social and cultural experiences through the use of symbols specific to the culture. These symbols are embedded in cultural "myth," which he defines as a "model of experiential reality" containing the "truths" of the culture as the people understand them (Dow 1986a:59). Laurence Kirmayer (1993:171), in explaining the meaning of "myth" within the context of symbolic healing, states: "I mean not false or foolish beliefs that are widely held, but those narratives that are embraced by a culture and by which a society structures and legitimates itself." This might be thought of as their world view, which explains the position of people in relation to other people, animals, the rest of the environment, and the cosmos. It is "truth" as a people understand it and would include notions of creation (and of a Creator) and define the responsibilities of such creation to the people, and the people to creation. Symbolic healing involves the healer convincing the patient that his problems can be defined in terms of this world view and treated through the manipulation of healing symbols.

Symbolic healing is more concerned with the social aspects of illness, and teaching people to cope with trauma and dysfunction, than it is with achieving a "cure" as the biomedical system would define this term. Kirmayer (1993:163) writes: "The healer aims not simply to convince people that they are better but to help them to understand, accept or transcend their predicaments — to show that afflictions make sense, even if they are terrible; to show how illness can be mastered, controlled, or transformed; or, when neither understanding nor control can be achieved, to demonstrate to the survivors that there is a way to continue with life, in this world or the next." But it is important to emphasize that what is considered an illness or a behavioural problem, and what is treatable within the domain of symbolic healing, are all culturally defined. One must not make the mistake of viewing symbolic healing in biomedical terms. Just as biomedicine defines pathology, what it is and how it is to be treated (even what constitutes "success" in treatment), so too do systems of symbolic healing.

Symbolic healing depends on the use of rhetoric, a form of language designed to invoke emotional or intellectual reactions, to "move" people. Through metaphor (thinking of one thing in terms of another, or crossing semantic domains), rhetorical language is used to connect the individual to the cultural myth so that his or her problem can be defined within the context of this reality. An important example of a metaphor in this study is the characterization of the sweat lodge as a woman's womb from which one can be "reborn." But metaphors are not only reified through words; images and gestures can likewise have meaning (Kirmayer 1993:172). Symbolic healing, through the use of metaphor, can result in behavioural transformation within individuals.

Symbolic healing employs a variety of techniques. "Suggestion" involves the healer's "ability to develop new patterns of thought and behaviour in the patient in a way that the patient could not achieve by himself in his normal environment" (Dow 1986b:138). "By manipulating symbols," states Dow, "shamans [and other healers] suggest to their patients new ways of viewing the world." But the patient's receptivity to the ideas suggested will depend, in part, on the authority and competence vested in the healer and in the healer's ability to "touch a chord" through empathy, thereby helping the patient to realize that the healer "has been there before" and has the knowledge of experience.

Catharsis, another important technique, essentially involves the release of emotions. This release may take many forms, such as yelling or crying, or simply talking out one's feelings. It may also be a silent, contemplative process, as in prayer. The context in which this occurs is important, however. Again, the healer must be vested with the power to hear, not as a simple human being, but as someone for whom the act of hearing defines the therapeutic encounter. The healer is himself a symbol of healing; talking to him is very different, from a therapeutic point of view, than talking to any other person.

Social restructuring may also occur through symbolic healing. This involves redefining the patient's problem in terms of broader issues, such as family or social problems, or for Aboriginal peoples, colonialism and oppression. In part, then, the responsibility for the patient's condition is shifted onto some other phenomenon, relieving the patient of any guilt that the condition may have engendered. It also provides a framework for understanding how a problem developed and, by extension, how it can be resolved.

Dow (1986b) suggests that psychochemical action, such as the release of endorphins through induced stress, may also contribute to the healing and the patient's sense that something positive has happened. Sometimes, the use of trance and the achievement of altered states of consciousness may facilitate this form of healing. These techniques are as common to western psychotherapy as they are to indigenous symbolic healing traditions (Kleinman 1988:123).

Symbolic healing may also work, in part, because of the "placebo effect," the idea that a patient may experience an improvement in symptoms without scientifically proven intervention. The placebo effect is often described in terms of the improvement in symptoms or medical condition that follows the administration of an inactive substance (such as a sugar pill). As Moerman (1979) and then Arthur Kleinman (1988) have stressed, the placebo effect is a much maligned component of all healing systems, and Moerman (1983:157) prefers to call this "general medical therapy." In biomedical research, efforts are made to distinguish changes brought about by the placebo effect from changes caused by the "real" medicine that is being tested. Indeed, biomedicine still operates on the faulty premise that mind and body are separate, that disease affects the body "whereas perception (of treatment) is an aspect of the mind" (Moerman 1983:157).

Biomedicine, according to Moerman, has generally ignored the role of the mind in treatment, in part because mind and body tend to be mediated by such unscientific concepts as the "soul." But even the scientific evidence demonstrates that the placebo effect results in an average 35% improvement rate for medical conditions, underscoring the simple and obvious fact that this is an integral part of healing. Clearly, the efficacy of the placebo is dependent upon the relationship between the healer and the patient, and the patient's willingness to attach himself or herself to the healing symbols employed (be they pills or a healing ceremony). The placebo effect speaks to the importance of the therapeutic relationship, of the faith in the abilities of the healer, through which the patient mobilizes internal forces (endorphins, thoughts, hopes, or whatever) to effect a positive change in his or her condition. Simply put, the placebo effect describes the ability of the patient to heal himself or herself under the right conditions. Kleinman (1988:112) argues that "[p]sychotherapy may very well be a way of maximizing placebo responses." The same can be said of symbolic healing systems.

Kleinman (1988:112) has defined a key controversy in regard to psychotherapy as "the question of whether the effects of psycho-therapy are due to specific or nonspecific agents of change." In other words, do specific techniques of psychotherapy invoke specific effects or are such effects the product of nonspecific or shared components of these techniques? He argues for the latter. Kleinman (1988:134) also argues that the patient may not fully understand the symbolic system that is at work and, by extension, may not be able to explain it to an observer. In a similar vein, Kirmayer (1993:176) suggests that symbolic healing does not result in "the grand sweep of healing transformation," but rather "the small turns of thought and feeling which metaphor engenders." "Even dramatic changes," he adds, "may, on closer examination, be found to be composed of these small turns." The problem for symbolic healing, when confronted with demands of "proof" by the biomedical sciences, is that these nonspecific agents of change, these "small turns," are not easily observable by the scientific method. Furthermore, the symbolic world is not easily explainable by the patient or healer (especially if this world has been constructed within an Aboriginal linguistic context; many concepts do not translate easily into English, the language of science). Often, Indigenous healers are reluctant to allow scientific investigation of their methods. This poses a problem for the recognition of symbolic healing within cultures dominated by the scientific intellectual tradition, an issue to which I will return later in this book.

Symbolic healing as it is currently constituted in the literature is culturally based and, in effect, healer-centred. According to Dow, "the experiences of healers and healed are generalized with culture-specific symbols" (1986a:56), and "the first requirement for symbolic healing is that the culture establishes a general model of the mythic world believed in by healers and potential patients" (1986a:60). Such a model presupposes that both patients and healers share more or less the same culture and world view in order for there to be a successful therapeutic outcome, a principle accepted by other authors as well. But John McCreery (1979:53) has challenged the idea that individuals necessarily experience rituals in the same way, arguing that "[t]ypically, rituals are ambiguous; they mean different things to different people. A ritual which is deeply moving to one individual may have only a superficial impact on another, while to still another it may be nonsensical or a mask for deceit." Similarly, Kaja Finkler's (1985:9) study of spiritualist healers in Mexico questioned whether "all members of a given culture respond equally to symbolic healing and whether all members in a given culture respond equally to the same therapeutic symbols." The existence of intra-cultural variability, as Finkler suggests, poses another question, "[do] all persons within a given sociocultural segment share the same healing symbols?" (1985:9). Deborah Glik (1988:1202), in a study of Christian and New Age healing movements, likewise stresses that "the degree to which a participant shares these myths and internalizes healing symbols may determine their therapeutic impacts." "Symbolic systems of healing are most effective," she argues, "if culturally relevant for adherents" (1988:1204).

It would be contradictory to suggest that symbolic healing could exist in situations where the cultures, and more specifically the symbols, metaphors, and "mythic world," are not shared between the healer and the patient. Nevertheless, being of the culture from which the healer and the particular form of symbolic healing both emanate is not a guarantee that the patient will successfully engage in the therapeutic encounter. Colonization and missionization, for instance, have turned many Indigenous peoples away from their traditional healing systems. Nor is it clear that a non-culture member is prohibited from learning the necessary symbols, their meanings, and how these relate to their life, therefore successfully experiencing symbolic healing. Furthermore, how a patient experiences and interprets symbolic healing is highly individualistic, confounding scientific studies of outcomes.

Dow's (1986a) analysis tends to place the onus on the healer to convince the patient that they share sufficient elements of culture and mythic reality to allow for symbolic healing to occur. Borrowing from Jan Ehrenwald (1966), Dow suggests that the patient must undergo an "existential shift." "As the patient believes in the therapist's power to help, he is able to change and find new opportunities for adaptation" (1986a:60). Kleinman (1988:119) adds that "[t]he practitioner must reconfigure the patient's illness narrative, within his therapeutic systems taxonomy, as a disease [or illness, or behavioural problem, etc.] with a particular cause, understandable pathophysiology, and expectable course." But current understandings of symbolic healing would have us believe that the patient adopts a passive role in this. As Kleinman (1988:133) writes, "[h]ealer affirms and patient accepts... ," and only then does the patient become active. This seems to express a biomedical view of the therapeutic encounter that does not hold in many systems of symbolic healing. It is likely true that the patient must respond to the therapist's world view in a positive way. Missing from this conceptualization is the possibility that the patient may need to adopt a more active role in helping the healer to construct this symbolic reality in the first instance. This construction involves a complex process of negotiation between healer and patient.

Of course it would be offensive to the Elders and Aboriginal inmates involved in prison spirituality programs to fail to mention their belief that healing occurs precisely because of the intervention of the Creator or other spiritual forces. The existence of such forces as *real,* as opposed to being elements of cultural "myth," is not considered by other scholars of symbolic healing. Regardless of the rhetoric they employ, in the end these scholars all approach the topic from an implicit scientific perspective that, I will argue in the conclusion of this book, is incapable of fully understanding Aboriginal spirituality as a form of symbolic healing. For the Elders and inmates involved, there is nothing puzzling about this form of symbolic healing: it works because the Creator, the Grandfathers, and other spiritual forces will it to be so. This notion is not fundamentally incompatible with the premise of symbolic healing since the symbols themselves are seen as gifts of the Creator. Science may have "discovered" endorphins, but their existence is unproblematic for Aboriginal healers. One Elder, when informed of these biochemical substances and how science believed they acted as part of the healing process, simply responded by noting the complexity of the Creator's work. Clearly, the existence of the Creator and of the spiritual forces involved in healing are integral parts of this form of symbolic healing. One should not waste time debating whether, from a scientific view, such things exist. Within the Aboriginal world view, they do, and this is all that matters.

Symbolic Healing in Prison

Canadian prison inmate populations reflect a very broad variety of cultures, a reflection of Canada itself. As we saw earlier in this book, in terms of Aboriginal inmates, the cultural picture is far from clear. A prairie penitentiary, for instance, is likely to house Metis individuals as well as those from Cree (both Plains and Northern), Ojibway, Saulteaux, Dakota, Chipewyan, Blackfoot, Blood, Piegan, Sarcee, and Stony First Nations. Individuals from the Northwest Coast, Northwest and Yukon Territories, and the high Arctic may also be encountered. There may also be some men from Eastern Canada. While the CSC attempts to keep inmates within their home region, as we saw earlier it is common for individuals to be transferred out of the region for security reasons. In addition to these varied Aboriginal cultural orientations, there are also many Aboriginal inmates who were raised in non-Aboriginal foster or adoptive homes, or who for other reasons have had virtually no exposure to Aboriginal culture. The prison will contain inmates from very remote areas of the country, who speak an Aboriginal language and very little English, alongside those who speak only English and have been raised in urban centres. This is a complex cultural situation. Most prisons employ only one or two Elders, and it is not possible for an Elder from each cultural tradition to be available. So which cultural tradition, and system of healing symbols, is employed, and how do all the other inmates react to this?

Given this cultural heterogeneity, symbolic healing in the prison is predicated on the ability of the Elders and inmates to negotiate meaning and ritual, to establish a common cultural ground and understanding of the symbols to be used. The Elders develop this through education, both formal and informal, and through dialogue and counselling. Indeed, this process parallels that described by Csordas (1983); recruitment into the Aboriginal awareness and spirituality programs precedes healing, and it is a precondition for healing to occur, but healing *per se* is not normally the reason an inmate initially becomes involved. Inmates are most likely to be interested in sorting out identity conflicts and learning more about Aboriginal cultures and histories. There is also a need to demonstrate solidarity with the other Aboriginal "brothers" within the institution; the Aboriginal programs in general, and the work of the Elders in specific, are among the best markers of this solidarity.

Once involved, the Elders work with the inmates to develop an understanding of the healing symbols and world view. The fact that the inmates are actively involved in this cultural construction suggests a new dimension to our understanding of symbolic healing, one that extends beyond Dow's (1986a) implicit assumption that it is the healers who are exclusively involved in this. It is not surprising, therefore, that a pan-Indian, heavily Plains-influenced culture is being promoted: it provides highly visible symbols that many offenders (like non-Aboriginal peoples in general) have come to view as being quintessentially "Indian." This is even more significant for Aboriginal offenders with no knowledge of their own cultural heritages: they are considerably more free to adopt a culture of their choice. Those with more knowledge of their traditional cultures, including very traditional people, strive to find the common cultural ground between themselves and the Elders so that they may then establish the therapeutic relationship. This process involves negotiating and redefining the symbolic meaning and procedural aspects of spiritual ceremonialism, and other cognitive manipulations regarding the meaning of various elements of spirituality, in a search for a more common cultural base.

The healing is not simply the product of the encounter between a healer and a patient. The group process as a whole becomes significant, as the "brothers" work together to negotiate and redefine their cultures and to support each other within the restrictive confines of prison. Effective healing entails abstinence from alcohol and drugs, resulting in a decrease in tension and stress; these are important cognitive, affective, and behavioural changes (Csordas 1983:356). Healing itself is viewed as an ongoing process, one that will continue to require disciplined adherence when the offenders are ultimately released from prison.

Of course, the discussion to be presented in subsequent chapters also demonstrates that symbolic healing in Canadian prisons is not without problems. Not all Aboriginal offenders are willing to engage the Elders in negotiating a world view in order to achieve a consensus concerning the relevant cultural phenomena. Some reject this process because they are too traditional and cannot accept that spirituality and healing belong in prison. Others are unable to objectively assess their own cultures in comparison to that of the Elders and cannot agree to certain common principles. Still others reject the healing because they fear the unknown, or because they are ideologically opposed to it, as in the case of fundamentalist Christians. Furthermore, each inmate interprets the symbols and defines the therapeutic relationship in a way that is appropriate for him. It is a highly individualistic process. Negotiating the common cultural framework within which Aboriginal spirituality will function is indeed difficult.

Symbolic Healing:
An Elder's Perspective

Aboriginal peoples from a variety of cultural backgrounds come together in prison to negotiate and construct a world view that allows for symbolic healing, through spirituality, to ensue. The symbols utilized in this process are not just cultural but are highly particularized to specific communities and adherents. Aboriginal spirituality is very individualistic, and Elders from the same culture and even the same community will likely have a somewhat different approach to various ceremonies or to explaining the nature of symbols.

Therefore, it is not possible to present a definitive explanation of the world view and healing symbols of Aboriginal spirituality. What follows are the various perspectives of one Saulteaux Elder, Campbell Papequash, who has worked extensively within prisons in Western Canada. The text is taken (with his permission) from presentation materials utilized in formal education sessions with inmates. In other contexts, such as in the sweat lodge, the education continues in an informal manner. The material is presented here only as an example of the spirituality being shared. It is not a comprehensive presentation of Campbell's views, and it is not necessarily representative of the views of any other Elder. Many prison Elders explain to inmates from other cultures that they should learn what they can in prison, do things the Elders' way, but when they are released they should return home and learn their own people's way. There is no "one way."

Campbell's text is set out; my observations are in regular font style. As one reads his words, it is pertinent to keep in mind the kinds of life experiences and problems described by the men in the previous chapter. Campbell is speaking directly to these experiences.

Campbell's philosophy toward learning is emphasized in the following passages; the onus for learning and behavioural change is placed squarely with the individual.

> LEARNING: You will learn whatever you decide that you want to learn. Learning can't be told. It has to be experienced
> - by Sight
> - by Listening (hearing)
> - by Smell
> - by Taste
> - by Touch
> - by Something You Do
> - and by How You Feel about What You Do

> CHANGE: As we learn we always change. So does our perceiving. If Man wishes to grow, he must become a seeker. Our first teacher is our own hearts. It is not enough to want to change. We have to take steps to change whatever we want to change: the Mind, eg the way we think; our character; our conduct; and our personality.

Campbell's world view, or what Dow would refer to as the "mythic base," begins with a prophecy that describes both the descent and ascendency of human beings.

> Our ancestors warned and predicted that for many generations the people would have a hard time. A dark black cloud would surround and plague all the peoples of the Earth. They foretold this dark black cloud would bring darkness into peoples lives. They foretold that for many generations this dark black cloud would cause great sorrow and suffering. That many would become sick at heart. And that the people would lose their way and powers. Their minds would become distorted and distracted. They would forget how to respect and survive in their own land. They would become filled with anger and gloom. They would begin to quarrel amongst themselves over worthless things. They would become unable to speak truthfully and to share honestly with each other. Slowly they would destroy and poison themselves and all they touched. It was foretold that the day would come when this dark cloud would weaken slowly at first and then diminish; and that the people would reawaken slowly as if from a long drugged sleep. It was also said these things would come to pass, and that the seventh generation would rise and become strong. They would do this by seeking out the ancient teachings of our forefathers.

On Creation:

> The Great Spirit beheld a vision. In this dream He saw a vast sky filled with Sun, Earth, Moon, and Stars. He saw an Earth made of mountains and valleys, islands and lakes, plains and forests. He saw flowers, grasses, fruits, and trees. He saw crawling, flying, swimming and walking beings. He saw and witnessed birth, life, growth, and the end of things — decay. And at the same time He saw other things live on. Amidst change there was constancy. He touched wind and rain. He felt love and hate, fear and courage, joy and sadness. The Great Spirit meditated to understand His vision. In His wisdom, the Great Spirit understood that His vision had to be fulfilled. He was to bring into being an existence that He had seen, heard and felt. Out of nothing He made the Sacred Fire, rock, water and the winds. Into each He breathed the breath of life. On each He gave with His breath a different essence and nature. Each

substance had its own power, which became its soul spirit. From these four substances the Great Spirit created the physical world of sun, earth, moon, and stars.

To the sun, the Great Spirit gave the power of light and heat. To the earth, He gave the power of growth and healing. To the waters, He gave the power of purity and renewal. And to the winds, He gave the power of music and the breath of life itself.

On Earth, the Great Spirit formed mountains and valleys, plains and forests, islands and lakes, bays and rivers. Everything was in its place. Everything was beautiful. Then the Great Spirit made the plant beings. There were four kinds: flowers, grasses, fruits and trees. To each He gave a spirit of life, growth, healing and beauty. Each He placed where it would be the most beneficial and would lend to the Earth its greatest beauty, harmony and order. After the plant beings, the Great Spirit created the animal beings, and conferred on each special powers and natures. There were four kinds: crawlers, winged ones, swimmers, and the four-legged beings.

Last of all, He made Man. Though last in the order of creation, least in the order of dependence, and weakest in bodily powers, Man had the greatest gift: the power to dream.

The Great Spirit then made the great Laws of Nature for the wellbeing and harmony of all things and all creatures. The Great Laws governed the world, and movement of the sun, earth, moon and the stars. The Great Laws of Nature governed the fire, rock, water and winds. The Great Laws governed the rhythm and continuity of birth, life, growth and decay. All things lived and worked by these laws. The Great Spirit had brought into existence His vision.

Our most important actions are determined by the most important objects around us. The four most important objects in all of existence are the Great Mystery, myself, my family, and the world itself.

Certain values are seen by Campbell as key to understanding human existence:

THE GREAT MYSTERY: The great, kind and generous one that is above everything. He is good and He looks after us. He is the giver and preserver of all life.
VALUE: generosity.

MYSELF: The Aboriginal person had a deep sense of pride in himself, because he was Aboriginal. He regarded himself as extremely important, because he was free, and because he could do hard things without showing fear or running from them. VALUE: bravery and individual freedom.

FAMILY: An Aboriginal person's attitude toward his family and fellow tribesmen was one that caused him to share with and to help them, and it made for a stronger unified race of people. VALUE: generosity of sharing.

THE WORLD ITSELF: All elements of creation. The earth, sky, plants and animal beings. The Aboriginal people regarded the world as one and related. It is sacred and because the Great Mystery dwells in it, the Aboriginal people hold it in great reverence. VALUE: respect.

There are four orders in creation: the physical world, the plant world, the animal world and the human world. All four parts are so intertwined, and they make up life and one whole existence. With less than the four orders, life and being are incomplete and unintelligible. No one portion is self-sufficient or complete, rather each component of creation derives its meaning from, and fulfils its function and purpose within the context of the whole creation. It is only by the relationships of the four orders that the world has sense and meaning. Without animals and plants, Man would have no meaning nor would he have much more meaning if he were not governed by some immutable law. There is a natural law. It is the law that everyone is ruled by, including all things in the creation. It is an absolute law. It is a law that has no mercy. It is a law that will always prevail. The basis of this great law is peace. And peace is a dynamic force. Peace takes a lot of effort. It is harder to keep peace than to have war. For the wellbeing of all, there must be harmony in the world to be obtained by the observance of these laws.

Man must seek guidance outside himself. Before he can abide by this law, human beings must understand the framework of the ordinances of creation. In this way, Man will honour the order as was intended by the Great Spirit. Both Sun and Earth were mutually necessary and interdependent in the generation of life. The sun illuminates, the earth sustains with beauty and nourishment. One cannot give or uphold life without the other.

Each morning as the sun rises, the flowers open, the birds begin to sing, the animals begin to stir, and the shadows fade away, the sun infuses life to all things. And each evening with the set of the sun, the roses enfold themselves, the robins become silent and the animals go to sleep. When the sun withdraws light, He also reduces life. In the spring when the sun grows warm, the whole world regenerates. In the fall when the sun is less warm, life departs. In giving life, the sun is father of all.

We, the Aboriginal people, have to be proud of our Aboriginal ancestry before we can be proud of ourselves. We can't be proud of our Aboriginal ancestry until we know what our Aboriginal values are. A people with a good set of values will live a long time.

Campbell believes strongly in the power of symbols, and specifically identifies the symbolic nature of Aboriginal spirituality and healing:

Symbols express and represent meaning. Meaning helps provide purpose and understanding in the lives of human beings. To live without symbols or signs is to experience life far short of its full meaning.

The Medicine Wheel is an ancient and powerful symbol of creation and the universe. It is a silent teacher of outer and inner realities of things possessed by human beings. It shows the many ways in which all things are connected and interconnected, related and interrelated.

The reason why various aspects of nature are used as symbols is because many of the human qualities reflected in the Medicine Wheel are hard to understand without living examples of nature. By choosing examples from the world or nature, people are able to look deeply into the nature of the gift that they seek to acquire, emulating that gift or quality and making it a part of themselves.

The Sweat Lodge

Perhaps the most important ceremony used in prison is the sweat lodge. It is used both for praying and healing. As many as twenty or twenty-five men might participate inside the lodge, typically constructed of a willow frame covered with canvas tarps. Four "rounds" ensue, during which the lodge is closed and made utterly dark. Water (sometimes laced with herbs) is sprinkled on heated rocks to create intense steam and heat. Individuals sing, drum, and pray. At the end of each round, the door is opened for a few minutes' relief. Then the next round starts. Campbell begins explanation of the sweat lodge ceremony by noting its central importance to the development and maintenance of a positive self-identity:

> Many Aboriginal people of today were reared without their cultural beliefs. The sweat lodge is used to re-identify ourselves with our traditional lifestyles and customs. The sweat lodge is used wholistically [sic] to assist in healing the imbalances of life which occur in the mind, body, spirit and emotions.

He then elaborates on the symbolism of the lodge:

> The sweat lodge is a domed-shaped structure built with either white or red willow sticks. Various numbers of sticks are used for different ceremonial purposes. The sweat lodge represents Mother Earth's womb and woman's womb. The sticks used to structure the dome represent the ribcage forming the frame of a woman's body.
>
> The four doors on the sweat lodge represent the four cardinal points where the Spirit Keepers of each direction enter the sacred lodge. There are four doors on the sweat lodge to represent the four cardinal points, the East, the South, the West, and the North.
>
> According to the legends of the Aboriginal peoples, the darkness within the lodge represents the womb of Mother Earth. Darkness removes distraction. Just as wisdom drives away ignorance.
>
> The rock represents the coming of life. The hissing steam is the creative force of the universe coming into action.
>
> The cover of the door is to the east, the source of light and wisdom upon the minds of men.
>
> The elements of earth, air, water, and fire are all represented in the sweat lodge.
>
> The fire which heated the rocks, is the fire that never dies — the light of the world — eternity, equality, unity and life.
>
> The vapours of the steam penetrates into your mind, your body and spirit to expel the illness you may have.
>
> The sweat lodge makes men brave. As the heat becomes more intense the urge to escape is almost uncontrollable. The noise of the steam, the heat, the lack of air, all in pitch darkness is very frightening. But you cry out to the Creator and the Rock Spirit to help you endure the pain and suffering.

The fresh cool air was never so welcomed, or appreciated as when the door flap is opened. How good it smells and tastes. You sit breathing it, absorbing it, enjoying it.

The sacred sweat lodge brings another element into healing: that the wellbeing of the body is directly related to the wellbeing of the inner being of a person. The inner being meaning your spirit.

Many values and behaviours are imparted to participants. These represent Aboriginal ideals, values to which all humans should aspire. These values, including generosity, caring, respect, and altruism can be contrasted with the insensitive, self-centred behaviour thought typical of many offenders.

The Sacred Fires represent life and spirit. Fire is warm, glowing with colour, surrounded by the night, yet speaking of day. Fire is promising, painful, dangerous, harmonious, visible at this moment, then moving into invisibility, alive, consuming, and finally disappearing into death. This is the fire that will help the generations to come, if they use it in a sacred manner. But if they do not use it well, the fire will have the power to do them great harm.

The Sacred Fires represent the Seven Council Fires of the clans: Loon, Crane, Fish, Bear, Martin, Bird, and Deer.

The Loon and Crane clans represent the chief clans. By custom, the Elders invited a man of their choice and offered the pipe of peace. Acceptance of the pipe signified acceptance of leadership. Its smoking is a solemn undertaking. In preparation, they studied history, tradition, grammar and speaking. Part of this training fostered eloquence, wisdom and generosity. In government, the wellbeing of the tribe superseded all other considerations. A leader was first in action, not a commander. As a speaker he did not utter his own sentiments, but those of his people. The leader was obliged to shield the feelings of his people.

The Fish clans represented advisors, giving direction and guidance, advising on custom and tradition, advising on policies and law, giving direction to clans and the wellbeing of the tribe. They were also the Seers, persons who foresaw or foretold events. These are the old ones who foresaw into the future through dreams and visions. They have acquired worthiness through long periods of training.

The Fish clans were also spiritualists, the old ones who were able to communicate with spirits. They have acquired this worthiness through a long period of training and suffering.

The Otter and Turtle clans represented healing. Initially healers became herbalists, herbalists became medicine men, and medicine men became philosophers concerned not only with preserving life and mitigating pain. From the healers came ethics. They offered guidance and principles for living the good life, whose end was to secure general wellbeing.

Healing went beyond the sick. It applied to the wellbeing of the tribe. More than this, it bordered upon metaphysics, psychology, ethics, morality and ceremony. It touched upon the training and education of the tribe.

Committed to the belief that long life was the product of good, upright living, the medicine men and women had to discover what constituted integrity in life, and having found it, lived it out.

The Bear clans represented the police or warriors who enforced tribal laws, and who kept law, order and peace at all times. The Warriors were leaders and became war chiefs like generals of modern armies. Below them were subchiefs, lieutenants, scouts, and squad leaders. Families, and tribe were protected.

The Bird clans represent farmers. Indigenous people raised natural food crops such as wild rice, potatoes, corn, squash, turnips and nuts. The Bird clan members were also diplomats, skilful in conducting relations between nations, and ambassadors, high ranking Elders speaking on behalf of their people and tribe.

The Deer clans represent peacekeepers, reconciling conflicts, preserving the peace between hostile nations.

The Seven clans were visible and living proof of the Seven Sacred Teachings and the Seven Principles of Life, which are: truth; faith; honour; generosity; justice; humility; and fortitude.

To every earthly thing Grandfather Great Spirit you gave power, and because the fire is the most powerful of your creations, since it consumes all things (including sickness), we place it here at our centre (the rocks) and when we see it and think of it, we really remember you. May this sacred fire be at our centre always, and help us.

Fire represents rekindling your spirit and reconciling with the Creator and your family and community. The sacred fires represent the circle — the path without end.

The heated rocks that are brought into the sweat lodge are also symbolic and impart certain teachings. So too does the water, often laced with herbs, which is sprinkled on the rocks to create the steam.

> The sacred rock is the symbol of life and spirit. The rock is a vital element for survival. The rock symbolizes many of our natures as human beings. The rock symbolizes endurance, strength, and sacrifice. We must learn to endure pain and suffering to find healing and growth.
>
> In times of turmoil, we find ourselves on the verge of exploding and destroying our lives and the lives of others.
>
> Rocks represent kindness and generosity. Rocks communicate our prayers to the Great Spirit and to the spirit world. Rocks have no eyes, no ears, no mouths, no limbs, and do not move, but by receiving their sacred breath (the steam), our people will be longwinded as they walk the Path of Life.
>
> Rock, your breath is the very breath of life.
>
> Water is a symbol of life and spirit. Water is a vital element for life for all living things. Water is a symbol of medicine and totality. The water represents the Thunder Beings who come fearfully, but bring goodness. Water flows freely and powerfully. Nothing will stop its flow.
>
> When we use the water in the sweat lodge, we should think of the Great Spirit, who is always flowing and giving His power and life to everything. We should even be as water which is lower than all things, yet stronger than even the rocks.
>
> We as Aboriginal people have been gifted with powers to use wisely. Our spiritual essence is to walk and flow freely with all and to become one with life.

Campbell describes other important aspects of the sweat lodge structure and ceremony, again invoking symbolism:

> The sacred winds represent life and spirit. Wind is a vital element. It provides oxygen for all living things. The sacred winds represent many of our human natures. Wind is cold and cruel. Wind is warm and gentle. The powers of the wind represent music and the breath of life itself.
>
> The tree symbolizes life and spirit. The tree provides shelter, sustenance, comfort and beauty. The tree represents many of our human characters and natures. The poplar tree represents kindness, gentleness, communication and medicine. You, trees,

are the protectors of the winged ones. Upon you they build their lodges and raise their families, and beneath you there are many people whom you shelter. May these people and all their generations walk together as relatives. Even the willow tree has a lesson to teach us, for in the fall its leaves die, and return to the earth, but each spring, they come to life again. Men die, but live again in the real world of the Great Spirit where there is nothing but the spirit of all things.

Offerings mean payments for deficits, shortcomings, and good health. Tobacco was a gift of the Great Spirit. Other offerings include prints,[2] oneself (through fasting and sweating) and other things, such as guns, dogs, knives, and horses.

Tobacco was the gift of the Spirit. Tobacco was in the nature of an incense. Sweet to the taste and fragrant to smell. No other plant is endowed with such qualities. Tobacco is a natural child of Mother Earth and Father Sun, and is the natural victim to be offered in sacrifice in the sacred pipe.

The darkness of the sweat lodge represents the womb of Mother Earth and woman. The darkness represents our ignorance. The darkness represents the void and emptiness within our mind, body and spirit.

When the door flap on the sweat lodge is opened, it is the symbol of the Great Spirit's light illuminating our ignorance that we may see not only with our eyes, but with the eye of the heart. We see light which destroys darkness, just as wisdom drives away ignorance.

The tarps used to clothe the structure of the sweat lodge represent the unity of all beings of the universe, the seasonal robes that cover the earth, and the robes that cover the sky.

Songs represent the utterance of the soul. Songs are poems chanted. They could be praise songs and they could be prayer songs uplifted to the spirits. Most songs were of a personal nature composed by individuals on the occasion of a dream, or an unusual moving event evoking every theme that moved man's heart and soul. These songs are chanted for different ceremonial occasions.

During the sweat lodge ceremony, the door is opened four times, representing the four portions of time and the cycle of life. This reminds us of the four ages of infancy, childhood, adulthood and old age, and how through the goodness of the Great Spirit, we have received the light in each of these ages.

The Sacred Pipe

The sacred pipe is another important component of Aboriginal spirituality. Campbell describes the origin of the pipe and its symbolism:

> A long, long time ago when our prophet the grandfather of human beings, the grandfather of all creatures, when this great and gifted being saw that his grandchildren were in great distress, and saw that they were quarrelling and drifting apart, he had a deep and sincere compassion for them. So he was ordained by the Creator to help the Anishnabe out of their troubles. Calling all his grandchildren to smoke the sacred pipe, he talked with them and a great peace, a great feeling of understanding descended upon them. Indeed, their hearts were filled with a new kind of joy. A new kind of comfort.
>
> And so it was, from that dim and distant day, when that great gifted being, the grandfather of men, the grandfather of every living creature stood upon the summit of a great mountain to light the red stoned ceremonial pipe, from the fire of peace. That same ceremonial pipe has been held as a very sacred and holy instrument ever since that time. The many mandates it represented were obeyed, unquestionably at all times, at all places and by everyone.
>
> But at the very beginning, when the newcomers began trading with the Aboriginal people, they failed to realize what the Aboriginal pipe stood for. All of that which the church, country, flag, all combined, was representative to the Aboriginal people in the sacred pipe. And it seemed to the Aboriginal people, because the newcomers did not, or could not, or did not want to understand the pipe's full meaning, the newcomers cast it aside as a silly, trifling and worthless thing. Indeed, they have a lot to learn from the ancient red stoned ceremonial pipe.
>
> A long time ago a strange and fatal disease afflicted the Anishnabe and threatened to wipe them out. For this dreaded disease there was no medicine, no relief or escape. Fear and sadness prevailed amongst the people who had not become ill. One of the victims of this plague was a young boy. After a short illness he died, leaving his family. In the land of souls the boy pleaded life for his family. Having pity, the Great Spirit promised that an intermediary who would teach the Anishnabe what was essential for their existence and wellbeing would be sent. In the

meantime they had to wait for their teacher to come before their miserable conditions could improve. The Great Spirit sent our prophet to teach the Anishnabe.

Our prophet, Nanabush, was born of a human mother, sired by a spirit. Our prophet possessed supernatural powers. Not long after his birth, his mother died. During his early years, our prophet was like any other boy. He had much to learn. What learning and wisdom he acquired came from his grandmother. By the time he grew into manhood, our prophet came to realize that he possessed powers not possessed by others. It was at this point that his grandmother told him about his mother's death. Our prophet set out to find his father and avenge his mother. He made his way westward toward the land of the great mountains. At long last as he sat pondering how he might find his father, he heard someone call his name. "Beware of your father. He has great powers. He knows that you are here and means to destroy you. Go to the place of flint, collect them, sharpen them, give them another force. They in turn will give you another power. They have in them the element of fire. It is the only substance your father fears. It will injure him but cannot destroy him."

While he was sharpening and polishing his flint, his father arrived. He greeted his father with respect but at the same time with fear and suspicion. He told his father of the purpose of his journey. "Father, I have come to avenge my mother's death. I have come to punish you for killing my mother, whereby I have been denied a mothers love."

"My son, you may harm me, but you cannot destroy me. Neither my injury, nor my death will restore your mother, or allow you to know a mother's love."

The battle began with no advantage on either side. When it seemed that the fight was going against him, Nanabush took out a flint and slashed his father's head, cutting him deeply. As soon as the blood began to flow, his father conceded. "Let us make peace. Return to the land of the Anishnabe. Teach them until they are strong. In this way, you and your purpose will be fulfilled."

Then his father fashioned the sacred pipe of peace. "As a remembrance of our contest and peace, take this pipe. Carry it with you always and you will know of a mother's love."

The moment that you decide, and say you are going to have or participate in a ceremony, your ceremony begins. There are preparations leading up to the actual ceremony. These are sacred vows and commitments you are making to your Creator. These sacred vows and commitments have to be honoured and fulfilled by the individual. These vows and commitments cannot be violated.

Man will smoke, and so the pipe becomes sacred. He speaks truth into the pipe and so the smoke becomes sacred. The stem carries truth and so the stem becomes sacred. But bowl and stem, without man, are nothing. Man is the truly sacred being. The pipe is an image of the truly sacred thing. The pipe is sacred, but not without Man's breath upon the stem.

It was foretold a long time ago, if the Aboriginal peoples should ever throw down the pipe and take up something different, that the Aboriginal peoples would have a hard time. They not only throw down the pipe, they throw down the family, the relatives and the tribe. For nothing shall ever sit above the pipe. The pipe meaning truth; the pipe meaning the old way; the pipe, a way of life that works. The pipe, a symbol of truth. And so the world, seeing the pipe, rejoices. Because all things come together in and through the pipe.

The pipe, bowl and stem are the pathway to the heart. The pipe, pathway to happiness and carefree living. The pipe, truth and holding truth.

The pipe is a messenger for the people. If you respect it, it will do good for you, and it will deliver your prayers and even more, then you have it in your mind and your heart.

The pipe ceremony begins with cleansing and purification of all people assembled. Then the helper or servant purifies all sacred objects to be used in the ceremony. Then the ceremony is identified to the spiritual world, whether it is a thanksgiving, giving or healing ceremony.

The pipe ceremony begins with the union of the bowl and stem being joined together by a pipe carrier's helper. The bowl is made of rock. The stem is of wood, derived from a tree which has a certain gift or characteristic. After the bowl and stem are united together, filled, and purified with sweetgrass, the pipe ceremony comes to life. It creates unity and harmony between all beings of the universe. The presiding Elder or Medicine Man then invokes peace of the Great Spirit and of the world to enter and infuse the pipe. There is prayer and there is chant. Then the Elder or Medicine Man takes up the pipe, offers it skyward, earthward, and to the four guardian spirits in the four cardinal directions.

From the sun's rays, the pipe received a portion of the power of the sun, and the Earth; from men and women — a human peace. And so, the pipe went from person to person, until all had touched and been touched by the pipe. The pipe was by touch and intent consecrated by all people. It possessed the spirit and medicine of peace. In turn, the pipe imparted peace to all who touched it.

After Nanabush and his father fought, they smoked the Pipe of Peace, as a symbol of reconciliation, goodwill, and harmony between them. His father explained the ritual of the pipe. The Anishnabe are to remember, as they smoke, their special relationship and dependence upon the sun, earth, moon and stars. Like the animal beings, their lives depend upon the physical world.

In each of the acts that made up the pipe ceremony, the smoking was considered to be a symbolic testimony of the beliefs and understanding about life, death and living. Only the pipe ceremony possessed a universal, and a more profound meaning than the other rituals. The pipe represented all relationships:

  – Man to his Maker
  – Man to the Cosmos
  – Man to the Plant World
  – Man to the Animal World
  – Man to Man
  – Man to his State

Tobacco is the sacrificial victim. In the immolation of the leaf was the tangible demonstration and evidence of creation, destruction, life and death. Each act in the smoking of the pipe reflected some belief about life, living, and being.

Campbell uses the sacred pipe in most ceremonies, and he has developed many teachings around it. One particular teaching pertains to the value of proper sexuality and is used particularly when working with sexual offenders. In this teaching, Campbell emphasizes that the pipe exists in two pieces that must be put together properly to communicate with the Creator. The stem is viewed as masculine and the bowl as feminine. When the stem is inserted into the proper place in the bowl (i.e., the stem hole, and not the bowl), the pipe comes together properly in unity. Furthermore, this unity of stem and bowl can only be achieved after the proper ceremony, which includes smudging with sweetgrass. The teaching imparts a view of proper sexuality, between male and female, and characterized by consent.

> The Pipe of Peace is an ancient symbol representing Father Sky and Mother Earth, man and woman. The stem of the pipe represents Father Sky and man. The pipe bowl represents Mother Earth and woman. The pipe bowl and the stem joined together means Father Sky and Mother Earth coming together as one. The pipe bowl and stem joined together means man and woman are joined together in a sacred act.
>
> But neither Earth nor woman conferred life alone. A woman by special act with man conceived and gave birth; the Earth by mystic union with the sun, through heat and rain generated beings and upheld life.
>
> The sacred pipe represents wholeness, completeness, creation and togetherness. The sacred pipe symbolizes harmony between human beings and creation.
>
> The pipe represents sending your voice to the Great Spirit. The pipe bowl is created from rock and comes in various colours: yellow, red, black, white. It is the earth.
>
> The stem of the pipe is wood and this represents all that grows upon the Earth. With this pipe you will be bound to all your relatives. From above the Great Spirit has given you this sacred pipe, through it you may seek and have knowledge. Through this sacred pipe nothing but good will come from it. Only the hands of the good shall take care of it, and the bad shall not even see it. All the people of the universe, all the things of the universe are joined to you who smoke the pipe.
>
> When you pray with the sacred pipe, you pray for and with everything. The more you use it, the more power it has. The sacred pipe means protection. The sacred pipe is used whenever we're in trouble, or whenever we're in council.
>
> We are to bring the ceremonial pipe into our midst and the spiritual essence of the pipe will immediately begin to cleanse our eyes, our hearts, and throats of all troubles and shortcomings. The sacred pipe was smoked by the Native scout to bind his words to the sacred truth. It was smoked in solitude and in reverence to the rising and setting sun. It was smoked that it might bring peace and solace to a troubled heart and mind.
>
> The sacred pipe was smoked by the Medicine people to comfort the dying and to aid the sick. It was smoked by the Elders for the people who mourned for the passing of a loved

one. In the early days of the Aboriginal people, no altar was ever complete without the sacred pipe. It was used at every function, at all spiritual gatherings and ceremonies, and was associated with all rituals and ceremonies. In the pipe ceremony, the four orders of life and beings are represented: earth, plant, animal, man. Earth, whose elemental substance is rock, made up the pipe. Tobacco, a plant, was the sacrificial victim. Animal was symbolized by the feathers or fur which was appended to the pipe. Man was the celebrant.

Rock is strong and enduring. Plant beings, animal beings, human beings all come to an end but the Earth lives on.

Just as the Anishnabe saw the sun as a symbol of fatherhood, so they saw in the earth, motherhood. A woman, by a special act with man, conceives and gives birth to new life. Therefore, she must sustain the new life. A mother gives birth to a child. She nourishes him or her, holds him or her in her arms. She gives him or her a place upon her blanket near her bosom. A woman may give birth to many children. To all she gives food, care, a place near her. A woman gives equally to all her children, from first to last, from strong to weak. All are entitled to her love and a place near her bosom in her home. Her gift does not diminish but increases and renews itself. Her robe is wide, her bowl bountiful and constantly replenished. On the robe of Mother Earth, there is a place for hunting and fishing, sleeping and living. From the bowl comes food and drink for everyone. For all young and old, strong and weak. The healthy and sick are all intended to share in Mother Earth's bounty and magnitude.

Mother Earth continues to be bountiful, sustaining all beings of the Earth.

In blowing a whiff of smoke to the earth, the people are honouring not only motherhood, but also they are honouring life-giving, the wonderful miracle that is shared by man and woman, permitted by the Great Spirit.

By the act, in offering a whiff of smoke to the sun, although the smoke was breathed toward the sun, the offering was, in fact, tendered to the Great Spirit through the spirit of the sun. In the same way, they were acknowledging that the Great Unknown could be known through His creations. What was created was not so much an act of power but an act of generosity, and an act of fulfilment of a vision. And each act of generosity had to be acknowledged in some tangible way. Therefore, the pipe ceremony was performed.

Tobacco and Sweetgrass

Tobacco is essential to most, if not all, Aboriginal ceremonies. According to Campbell, tobacco represents the unity of humans and the Creator. It is used as an offering to the Elders, and when something is sought. It may also be offered to others as a sign of respect, again when something is sought. Tobacco may be offered in bulk, such as in the form it takes in commercial tobacco pouches, or in smaller units, such as a cigarette. The latter is most common within prisons due to cost and the limited incomes of inmates.

Tobacco is one way that humans can touch the Creator. The smoke from burning tobacco naturally rises and can touch the spirits of the sun and wind. The smoke carries one's prayers to the Creator. Tobacco smoke may also be used to purify the body, mind and soul, as well as other sacred and ceremonial objects.

While the use of tobacco is common to many Aboriginal spiritual traditions, the use of other burning materials is more diverse. Sweetgrass is perhaps the most common of these, especially in southern areas where it grows, while sage may be more popular in northern areas.

Like tobacco, sweetgrass also represents "unity" between the mind, body and spirit. It is typically woven together into three braids, each representing one aspect of this unity. It has been suggested that single strands by themselves are weak and useless but when woven together they become stronger than rope. Each part of the sweetgrass represents a different stage of life. When the sweetgrass is joined at the ends, it makes a circle, the circle of life. Sweetgrass is used in a manner similar to tobacco: it is burned as a vehicle to communicate to the Creator, and it is used to smudge or purify the mind, body and spirit of the human as well as sacred and ceremonial objects.

The similarity between the theoretical literature on symbolic healing and the manner in which Aboriginal spirituality is presented by Elder Campbell Papequash is striking. He has even referred to his approach using the term "symbolic healing." More so than some prison Elders, he recognizes the need to educate the offenders about the meaning of the symbols as a first step on the spiritual path. He does this formally, through workshops and presentations, and informally, during actual ceremonies or private counselling. Many other Elders are considerably less formal than Campbell, relying more on the subtle teachings of the ceremonies as a form of education. As we shall see later in this book, the extent to which an offender first learns the meaning of the symbols, then accepts the basic principles behind them as a code of living, determines the therapeutic effectiveness of the encounter.

Many prison inmates are said to suffer from a variety of behavioural disorders, or "personality disorders" in psychiatric terminology, in addition to problems of alcohol and substance abuse. Many demonstrate "antisocial" behaviour, a lack of respect for the feelings and property of others, and antagonism toward authority. They often display self-centred behaviour. Aboriginal spirituality presents a variety of prescribed, positive values and behaviours that are very much the opposites of these "criminal" behaviours. Insofar as individuals come to understand these values and behaviours, the symbols and their meanings, they *may* begin to change their own behaviours and attitudes. To embrace the meaning of these symbols becomes itself a symbol of a new, emerging Aboriginality for many inmates. Viewed within the context of over a century of repressive, assimilationist government policies, Aboriginal spirituality has become central to this re-emergence of Aboriginal cultural identity. Earlier we saw how the loss of identity, or identity confusion, is viewed by many Aboriginal inmates and Elders alike to be at the root of their problems. But behavioural change is not easy. Indeed, the Elders stress that learning about spirituality, following the Way of the Pipe, is a life-long process, and there are many temptations along the way.

NOTES

1   In many ways, the development of biomedicine within the scientific tradition has been characterized by the struggle to jettison symbols from medical practice because of their alleged irrationality.

2   By "prints" Campbell is referring to lengths of cloth.

How mysteriously the Creator
works in people's lives!
— ELDER CAMPBELL PAPEQUASH

5 Following the Pipe: Elders and Spiritual Leaders

The backbone of Aboriginal spirituality in prison is the work of Elders and other spiritual leaders who offer spiritual services and healing behind the walls. It is not easy work. Difficulties dealing with clients who are troubled and imprisoned are compounded by the need to meet the security concerns of institutions and by the ignorance of certain correctional staff regarding the different nature of the spiritual and therapeutic services Elders offer.

Prison Elders, Healers, and Spiritual Leaders

A great deal of anthropological research on shamanism and traditional healing has documented how the "call" to the role is often predicated by a personal, traumatic event or illness (Eliade 1964; Halifax 1979; Achterberg 1985; Bennet 1987). According to Mircea Eliade (1964:33), in his classic volume *Shamanism: Archaic Techniques of Ecstasy*, "all ecstatic experiences that determine the future shaman's vocation involve the traditional schema of an initiation ceremony: suffering, death, resurrection." While the suffering is real, the death is symbolic, leading to the resurrection or transformation of the individual into one with the potential to heal. As

Eliade (1964:33) adds, "[n]aturally, this ecstatic type of experience is always and everywhere followed by theoretical and practical instruction at the hands of the old masters; but that does not make it any the less determinative, for it is the ecstatic experience that radically changes the religious status of the 'chosen' person." However, the key, notes Holgar Kalweit, is that the healer typically must heal himself or herself first, before healing patients (Kalweit 1992:1).

Shamans are special spiritualists and healers whose knowledge and abilities rise above the more common, practical medical knowledge as embodied in herbalists and other healers. While all healers, and in many societies most individuals, may have "guardian spirits," the shaman has a much closer relationship with these, one that allows him or her to communicate more directly with the spiritual realm. He or she has the ability to enter an "altered state of consciousness" in which communication with the spiritual becomes possible. The shaman may "fly" to other realms, or summon the spirits to this one. Scientists often refer to the shaman's ability to engage in "ecstatic" communion (Achterberg 1985; Hultkrantz 1992).

Not all Elders and spiritual people who work in prisons are "shamans." The term "shaman" was never used by inmates in reference to any individual. Inmates usually referred to "Elders," and in a few instances, to "medicine men/women." All of these act as healers, although many will not acknowledge it. It is highly inappropriate to call oneself a healer or Elder; this is an ascription best left to others. But Elders frequently establish relationships with individuals that become therapeutic, even if the Elder denies the ability to heal. Many of these spiritual people have personal histories that parallel those of shamans in the classical sense, and it is these experiences that make them particularly valuable within the prison context.

While not true of all Elders and spiritual leaders, many of those working in prisons are more than a little familiar with the environment behind the walls. These are not Elders in the traditional sense; they have not lived all their lives in a spiritual manner. Instead, we find personal histories of alcoholism and substance abuse, violence, and criminality. Many developed very bad reputations in their own communities and were often expelled or simply drifted away, spending time on skid rows in far away places like Vancouver or Toronto. They often lost their language and sense of identity as Aboriginal persons. In effect, they hit rock bottom.

> I became an alcoholic. I became a drug addict. I became a spousal abuser. I became very violent to the point where it didn't matter. I was just an out-and-out intimidating person.[1]

I used to be a terrible little guy. I used to get strappings every day [in residential school] and I grew mean that way and I grew to be ashamed of my people. And I was an angry young man when I got out of there. I was ashamed of my people. I didn't know where I fit in. The only place I fit in was when I was drunk. And I didn't give a damn who I was then, it didn't make no difference.

I was an alcoholic, con artist, b & e [break and enter] expert. I was good 'cause I never got caught. I was doing all sorts of things like that. I drank twenty-four beers a day. I'd wake up in the morning and my son or my wife would bring me a beer right in bed. I'd go have a bath and then I'd have another beer while having a bath. And I never took my marriage very seriously. I'd have two or three girlfriends all at the same time. I used to beat my wife all the time… slap her around.

Eventually, each of these individuals began to see their personal problems as related to the larger society, the legacy of colonialism and oppression, and to take steps to recover. Recovery was not easy, however, and backsliding was common. Identity issues became particularly important, as this Elder suggests:

During that time, when I left school and I came back to the reserve and I continued a little bit of Native culture. But then I left again but then I went to work in the White society for quite a number of years. And there I became an alcoholic, because to compete in White society, you had to be twice as good as your fellow man. But I was a very aggressive person, and I did that. Even on weekends when we drank, you know, if they drank one glass, I had to drink two glasses. If they drank one bottle, I had to drink two bottles to prove that I was better than them at all times. Not knowing that I was making a fool out of myself. And then I progressed more into alcoholism. Then I got married and had children, but my alcoholism progressed. I would go to these sweats every once in a while, maybe once a year and I got nothing out of it because I forgot all about the teachings of my father, my grandparents, my mother. And I went into the mainstream of society. The more I stayed away from my Native ways, the more I suffered and I became a person who blamed alcohol. But I came into Alcoholics Anonymous in 1963 and then I sobered up and then it was there that after eleven years of sobriety, I fell off the wagon. There was an emptiness that I just couldn't discover. Even though I was sober, there was still a vacuum in my life, and I could never pinpoint what it was. But there were benefits in terms of life for falling off the wagon. Materially, I lost everything. It was after about five years of drinking, that I reached out again. In my drunken state, I reached out and sought help, and that help was freely given to me by other Elders. I didn't go back to A.A. I went back to the traditional way, understanding the way our forefathers lived and learning about the value system of life. Learning the life of creation, how it supports mankind. And then I began my journey towards spiritual healing, mental healing, physical healing. It was through the patience of other Elders that I began to understand who I was, my identity as a Native person.

Another Elder related a similar story:

You know for the longest time I've had an identity crisis. I knew that I was brown skinned and I knew that I was Indian. But I did not really know what Indian was all about. Many times I was ashamed of my heritage because we were so poor. There were a lot of things that I suppose I wanted in life and I could not have. I didn't have any decent clothes to wear when I was growing up as a youngster. And even after I became an alcoholic, I didn't have the sufficient funds to buy myself decent clothes because all my money went to booze. I suppose the way we were brainwashed in school, in the boarding school, the residential school, I believe that had a lot to do with our identity. Because we were called 'good for nothing.' I didn't even know in those days what a 'savage' was. They called us 'savage' many times and they called us 'pagans' and I didn't know what a pagan was and they called us 'heathens'; I didn't know what a heathen was. They called us 'barbarians'; I didn't know what a barbarian was. And even the language that we spoke, they said it was the devil's language. And you know all these things did a lot of harm and damage to the Native people. I know I felt lesser, I felt very inferior and I knew that when I went to the school.

I come from a very happy childhood, growing up traditionally with my grandfather and my grandmother and I remember my grandfather was very kind and a gentle man. And I believed that this is where I have learned equality from. And now when

I understand the teachings of the pipe, I find this democracy and that is the democracy that my grandfather had left us. He left us a beautiful legacy. But then after my grandfather had died, boy, that was the greatest tragedy that had happened in our whole lives. That was the end of our traditional way of life for the whole family. And then the family started drinking. They started drinking. They became alcoholics, very dysfunctional.

It wasn't very long after that too, that I was apprehended by the missionaries, taken to this boarding school and it was very difficult for me to make those adjustments in boarding school because I did not know how to speak English and I had to adopt the foreign lifestyle, a foreign lifestyle that was really detrimental to the Native people. You know they cut off my braids. I had to learn to speak English. That was the end of my own Native tongue. It was gone. And after that I had to adopt a foreign religion and a complete foreign lifestyle of doing things and I had to make many adjustments in my life.

And that is where I lost my identity. And I accumulated a lot of anger, a lot of bitterness, a lot of frustration, a lot of resentment in that residential school. I used to think to myself there has got to be more to life than this, drinking, getting beat up and going to jail. I had those intentions but I could never accomplish anything good in life because I did not know that I had a very severe drinking problem. And boy I tell you, I suffered for years. I believe that I was on the streets for twenty-eight years. I walked the paths of blindness for twenty years. A lot of suffering and a lot of pain. And I could never see my reality. I did not know what reality was all about. I believe that I took everything for granted. I didn't know how precious life was.

It was necessary for some Elders to reach rock bottom before they were ready to change; spiritual as well as human intervention was ultimately necessary in a few cases to turn their lives around. These themes are clear in the story of this Elder:

And then one day I come home and says [to my wife], "You're moving, you're getting out. I'm not staying with you any more. I'm not changing and you're kind of stupid to stay with me. I want you to go back to your parents and maybe you'll find someone who will love you and care for you."

"No, I'm not leaving," she says.

I says, "You are" and I threw her out of the house and she went back to her parents. And I phoned her and she said, "I want to come back because I love you" and I said, "No, that's it."

One day when I came home from work I had a phone call from my mom that my wife was killed in a car accident and then all of a sudden it was my fault. If I hadn't sent her home, she'd never got in that car accident. She was killed by a drunk driver. And then, that was it. I wanted to commit suicide, it was my fault. I lost my son, I lost everything. I had money. I had thousands of dollars in my pocket and I had a house full of new things, but it wasn't a home without them. All of those things don't mean nothing. I had really lost somebody who I had truly, truly loved, who loved me for who I was. And she came to me two or three times after she had passed away. I know I was crying, I was mad at her and I yelled at her, "Why the hell did you die on me. It's all your fault." I was sleeping then. The pillow all of a sudden where she slept, starting moving where her head would be and the pillow started moving and the blankets moving and it was just like somebody hugged me. Boy that scared me, I'll tell you. That really scared me. And I says, "I don't want to live anymore."

I was getting ready to commit suicide and I went down in the basement and I had everything ready. I had everything ready to commit suicide and I was going to do it. I had my last beer and then all of a sudden, a knock came to the door. I went upstairs and answered the door and it was this Indian guy. This was before I knew about Indian ways. He come in and he says, "You got a choice. You either live or die. I'll help you now" and he sat down and talked to me for hours and hours and hours. And he told me about my wife and said, "In six months you're going to get a chance to say you're sorry to your wife."

I said, "Man, you're crazy. She's dead. How can I say I'm sorry?"

"Yes, she's going to be there and she'll kiss you and hug you and everything and you'll know it," he said.

"Man, you're stupid," I said.

He said, "Well you got a choice. Your wife sent you a prayer. You start on a journey. You keep up the way you are, you're going to die, and you're planning it anyways. If you live, you can take all that you've learned and those you learn about." What he said made me laugh. He says, "The greatest teachers are the con artists and the bull shitters. Those are the best counsellors and you fit the bill good."

I said, "Yeah, I am."

He said, "You got to quit drinking."

So after he was gone, I had a twenty-six ounce bottle of vodka left and I poured eight ounces of it into a glass and I drank down the glass and I poured the rest of the bottle down and I've never drank since. He just showed up. I never did see him again. Then I started going to [an Elder's] farm and I started following his ways and I really took it seriously. It was good.

And then that first year, I heard about a Sun Dance. I've never been to a Sun Dance. I didn't even know what they were, but I heard about them, so I went. And [the Elder] and some of the guys were saying, "Well you'll never make four days. You haven't got what it takes." But they knew I was stubborn and I'm not one of those that gives up and they were teasing me and saying, "You'll never make it. I'll have to take your place."

So I went to the Sun Dance that year. I got ready and [the Elder] helped me to get prepared. And he says, "You're not going to make it. Why should you go in?"

All those things... they were playing on my stubbornness. So I started and it was hard, it was hard. I think that year it was 108 [degrees] out. That one day I think it came up to 115 and on third day without food and water I said, "This is it. There's only so much a man can take." I think that year, thirty guys started and only five finished. And I saw people dropping out... see dropping out ain't so bad, it ain't so bad. I laid there and all of a sudden something flashed into my life. My wife! Her face flashed!

And I said, "You know, I hurt you. I wasn't a good man when I was your husband. But I'm trying to grow up now." I was hugging the ground. "But I'm trying now. I'm going to grow up," I said, "I'm sorry for hurting you, beating you, but I'm going to grow up and I'm going to help people."

Then all of a sudden a cold wind came around me, just me, but I was burning up and I felt her soft lips on my cheek and she said, "I love you. Go now."

And I did the Sun Dance because I didn't suffer anymore. And that's how I started.

Another Elder also related a personal story of transformation and spiritual intervention:

The reason why I go back into this is because I want to share the mysteries with you. In the latter part of my drinking career,

I think I progressed into chronic alcoholism. When you progress that far, you are beyond human aid. No one can ever help you. But things began to happen in the last eight years of my drinking. Somehow, you know, I always got into trouble and I ended up with a lot of kind people around me. One time when I was drinking I was put on probation. My probation officer asked me a bunch of things. And he says, you know, "I don't know what you are doing wasting your life on skid row." He says "you have a lot of potential." And he says, "you know you are a great leader, you should turn to your spirituality to become this great leader."

And I thought to myself, "Ah get me off this bullshit and get me out of here." I had to listen to him because he was my probation officer. No way I could get out. Anyways I think of that man and he was right, you know, he was right. I had the potential of becoming a spiritual leader. That is what he probably meant. And he told me that I would gain a lot of knowledge. And he was right. I did not know that I would gain this much spiritual knowledge in the last seventeen years of my sobriety.

And one time I was in a psychiatric centre and there again I met a woman who really discovered my potential. She was a psychiatric nurse and boy she showed me a lot of kindness and she took a liking to me and she would take me to a lot of activities. But before I left that psychiatric centre, she gave me her name and her address and her telephone number and she told me, "call me, I will try to help you." I was coming out of that psych centre vowing that I was never going to drink again. But it wasn't an hour and I was drinking again! But I look back upon that woman in my sobriety. There is no nurse, there is no psychologist, there is no psychiatrist, all the staff in this mental institution, they are not going to give you their address. I look back at that. Why did she give me her address? Why did she give me her phone number and why did she ask me to call her? You know, I always think today that she was put in my path by the Creator. The Creator was working on me already.

Then my father died in 1975. And my father was laying on his dying bed, my father lay on his bed dying and I don't know what happened but I sobered up when I came to my father. And I says, "don't worry about mom, I will take care of her." And what I said to my dad, you know, it must have given him a lot of peace because he sounded peaceful after I told him that I would take care of my mother and not to worry and that we were going to send him to a hospital in the city.

Anyways, my father died shortly after that. And here I was a full-grown chronic alcoholic, you know, couldn't even take care of my own life. And I promised my dying father that I would take care of my mother. You know, I look back at that, I made my father's death easier knowing that I was going to take care of my mother. It made him have a little more peaceful death. I look back at that and why did it happen? I was really quite fortunate that I was sober right through my dad's funeral and everything. Then I went back to the city and I drank for another couple of years. I ended up again in that mental institution. I ended up in many hospitals in the last two years of my drinking.

And then finally one day I had a spiritual awakening on the street. I had a spiritual awakening on the street and I did not know what was happening to me. I was awakened back to reality and it was such an overwhelming experience, you know, I will never forget that experience. It was so moving and it was so touching. When I talk about moving and touching, you know, I was moved to joy and I was moved to happiness. And for the first time in my whole life, my eyes opened. And for the first time in my whole life, I saw the dilemma that I was in. For the first time in my life I saw all my pain and all my misery and all my suffering. I never saw that in all my years that I had been drinking on the street. My eyes opened and I saw this reality. That was the first taste that I had for life and it was wonderful. It was just so amazing for me to experience what I was experiencing.

And at the same time I looked around and I saw all these other people suffer. I saw them with all their pain and all their misery and for the first time in all my life I looked at these people with a lot of pity. That was the first time that I experienced ever having pity on somebody, and now I wanted to help these people. But I knew right there and then how could I help these people when I couldn't even help myself? And it was such a humiliating experience! You know I realized for the first time in my life that I had a very serious problem and I knew right there and then that I was never going to drink again. And I knew that I was going to reach out for help. And that was humiliating because there is no guy on skid row, there is no guy on the streets who wants to reach out for help, because you have all this false pride, a false image of yourself.

That was the kindest decision that I ever made for me. And when I made that decision, that is when my recovery began. Right there. And then when I reached out for help, and you know when I came back to the reserve, to the old Elders. And I had such a hard time because I had a lot of anger, I had a lot of bitterness, I had a lot of resentment, I had a lot of envy to deal with. The Creator came into my life and the tears were running down my eyes.

I had said I blamed all these people for all my failures, and all my mistakes in life now. I thought that I hated my mother and my dad and I thought I hated the missionaries and I thought I hated the R.C.M.P. for always putting me in jail. But right then I realized that I didn't hate my mother and my dad. I didn't hate the missionaries. I didn't hate the R.C.M.P., I didn't hate my wife. Right then and there I knew that I was totally responsible for my own behaviour, my own actions. I was totally responsible for my own thoughts. I was totally responsible for my own feelings. I was totally responsible for my own misery. What an awakening!

Despite the spiritual experiences of some Elders, it would be a mistake to conclude that all of them have experienced this form of spiritual awakening. Some Elders simply came to a less dramatic, though no less significant, decision to change their lives. This often occurred after the realization that they were needed to serve a purpose much greater than their own interests.

Well I guess one time I was locked up in prison and I see these guys, these lifers making homosexuals, taking advantage of all these young people. At night time I would hear this crying, you know, this crying for their mother. Young people, you know. So I thought, well I have been in car wrecks, I have been shot at, I have been stabbed, and I am still alive. I said there must be a purpose. And I said I have searched all this time. Different churches that I've joined throughout United States and Canada and I never was satisfied with it. I said maybe I have to go back to what my grandparents believed and maybe I have to pray that way. So, when I thought about that, I thought well I have had a lot of experience on the streets. Drugs and dope and all that shit. Also in prison life. I've seen dead bodies in the prison, on the streets and the places where I've lived. So I said it's time, there must be a purpose in life. Maybe if I straighten out I can help somebody. I can help these kids that are crying at night. And I thought of it and I thought of it and I said, well maybe I should dedicate the rest of my life to helping people instead of hurting them.

There are still other Elders and spiritual leaders who have had only minimal interaction with the criminal justice system, or who have not had alcohol problems. Some Elders were introduced to spirituality at a very young age and stayed with it throughout their lives. These individuals also offer valuable services.

Negotiating "Elder" Status

As discussed earlier in this book, the healer is central to the process of symbolic healing, and in this sense Aboriginal Elders are central to Aboriginal spirituality. However, the status of "healer" or "Elder" is ambiguous and never clearly defined. Indeed, it must be negotiated in each therapeutic or spiritual encounter.

The question of who is an "Elder" is a thorny one. The general standard is acceptance by the "community" as an "Elder." This is a status that denotes a great deal of wisdom and experience, and the living of an ideal "Aboriginal" lifestyle. In practice, however, recognition is often quite ambiguous. A consensus rarely exists, and the demand for consensus may represent an unachievable standard. One segment of a community may view an individual as an Elder, but other segments may not. In one relevant study, Garro found a lack of consensus among residents of an Anishnabe (Ojibwa) community in Manitoba. "In the community, " observes Garro (1990:428), "there is often little consensus concerning who has been granted power; some individuals may refer to a specific healer as a medicine person, while others refer to the same healer as a herbalist, and someone else may voice suspicion that the individual isn't really gifted." "Acceptance of a healer's ability," she concludes, "is an individual decision" (430).

Age can also be an issue. The term "Elder" calls to mind an individual who is quite old, the wisdom of the ages etched on the face. However there are few very old Aboriginal people, and today "Elders" are often quite young. There are many in their fifties, for instance, who in previous eras would be considered too young to be Elders. Furthermore, there are very spiritual individuals who have earned the right to hold ceremonies at a relatively young age, in their twenties and thirties. They are not usually called "Elders" although this may be occasionally heard. These younger people are referred to in this book as "spiritual leaders."

Elders and spiritual leaders may be either male or female. However, cultural proscriptions reduce the role of female Elders, especially in men's prisons. For instance, during menstruation, females must not handle or be close to sacred objects or areas. Some female Elders interviewed in this study did not normally offer sweat lodge services or sacred pipe ceremonies. In these instances, male Elders were brought in. Some inmates have difficulties accepting female Elders. They may choose to avoid such individuals or to participate selectively in their ceremonies.

In effect, the status of "Elder" is an ascribed one. It is an honorary designation offered and used by others. Most Elders will have difficulty describing themselves as Elders, as this is culturally inappropriate. However, within prisons, this status recognition is essential to allow movement within the prison and to perform the job. Individuals are normally required to declare themselves as "Elders" and may even occupy an office with "Elder" on the nameplate. Many are uncomfortable with this, but accept that within prison *everyone* must have a label and a status.

Not surprisingly, there is tension within prison with respect to who is a "real" Elder, just as there is in the community. While not wishing to overgeneralize, it seems that Elders who work in prison are often singled out in the community for some of the harshest criticism from their own people. Aboriginal people, like other citizens, often harbour images of prison inmates that are unflattering and see no reason to believe they can be rehabilitated. Prison Elders, in contrast, believing that rehabilitation is possible, are continually frustrated by community views such as these which demean their work. They are often exasperated at the reluctance of specific Aboriginal people, as well as bands and communities, to lend support to the work being done by Aboriginal inmates.

Empathy is a key trait that makes certain Elders especially valuable. Some, having lived markedly unspiritual lives in the past, and having recovered, are therefore able to understand what the inmates are going through, and to provide excellent role models. However, their somewhat tarnished personal histories often render these individuals as pariahs in their own communities.

Regardless of personal criminal or addiction experience, all Elders and spiritual leaders who work in prison share fundamental characteristics with the offenders: they are all Aboriginal, and they have all experienced the oppression and racism that are rife within Canadian society. This sets them apart from all the other prison staff with whom the inmates must work and interact.

Working Within Prison

The work of the Elders and spiritual leaders in prison is very different from those prison staff most intimately involved in rehabilitation: the case management officers, the psychologists and psychiatrists, and the therapists and chaplains. In fact, while the basic thrust of prison rehabilitative programming is assimilationist (i.e., conforming to values and behaviours appropriate for the "White" middle class), the work of these Aboriginal therapists is directed toward spiritual and cultural reintegration and the need for Aboriginal inmates to develop better identities as Aboriginal persons. This is an effort to undo the damage done to both Aboriginal society and the Aboriginal psyche by colonization and assimilation.

Correctional perspectives view inmate criminality in terms of "criminogenic factors," that is, those factors seen to be the most immediate causes of criminal behaviour and which can be altered by the inmate. Alcohol or other substance abuse is seen in these terms. In contrast, while all Elders recognize the important role that such abuse has played in inmates' criminal behaviour, they look beyond the individual in seeking to understand criminality. They look to the history of colonization, the residential schools, and policies of assimilation, as the key to understanding. A specific individual's problems are therefore placed within the context of historical factors; these problems are invariably defined as a loss of culture and spirituality leading to a crisis in identity. Treatment, then, entails cultural and spiritual education with the goal of rebuilding self-esteem and pride as an Aboriginal person. One Elder stated:

> We see all this sexual abuse and abuses going on, broken homes. That's because we are products of the residential school era, and so oppressed that we turned on our own people. So we are trying to fix that somehow in our own way, in our traditions, our own teachings from way back.

This Elder compared the philosophy of the penitentiary with that of Aboriginal spirituality in explaining how identity is an essential ingredient in the therapeutic process:

I want to point out that institutions right from the beginning have been based on punishment, and slowly it's evolved to rehabilitation. They're starting to say that rehabilitation no longer works and they're even starting to look at healing issues. You know we're hearing now about these treatment centres, healing lodges, whatever you want to call them. Well it's still based on punishment. That's the underlying power of a penitentiary. The prison is punishment. You're punishing a person for doing something. Okay, I'm here because of the healing, because I understand healing, because that's what I'm doing with my own life is healing. Part of that healing, the very beginning of that healing is to know who I am. The only way that I can know who I am is to know where I come from, so I got to learn that culture, whatever it is that I have, that culture that I was born into. I have to learn that and learn the history of that culture, learn the traditions, the values, the teachings, the ceremonies, the language. The more I learn that, the more I learn about myself. The more I learn about myself, the more that I know where I can go. The more that I learn about myself, the better that I feel about myself, the more that I understand myself. As I understand myself, each time that I put another piece of knowledge into myself, that I call understanding of me, the more garbage it gets out, so the better I feel about myself. It motivates me to go where I should be going to become a good human being.

The following Elder expressed particular concern for those Aboriginal men who were raised within an urban environment and thus know little of their Aboriginal culture:

Because they need to go back to all them teachings to understand themselves and to feel good about themselves. Because a lot of our young people are lost out there, urban Indians who don't know anything about spirituality. The ones that are brought up in foster homes, those are the ones that have identity problems, you know. I think that a lot of these urban Indians, too, they have been brought to residential schools, ashamed of their culture, ashamed of who you are so you get very angry and you lash out. Breaking laws and stuff like that. The first contact [with spirituality] that most of them come into would be inside a prison or inside a jail like this. And for some that is the first time they have ever experienced a sweat and all of a sudden, the lights go on! They have been missing something all this time. Once they start learning these and they start going to sweats and stuff like that then they begin to settle down a little bit. They start realizing that we have something more than what the White guy has.

Another Elder, in describing his own personal journey, expressed the importance of a positive identity most eloquently:

> Today I am very, very proud of who I am because I know who I am. But again there is a lot of pain, there is a lot of suffering in getting to know oneself. And that's why I say identity is so important. My spiritual name gives me my identity. My heritage gives me my identity. You know I find my identity within the fire, within the sacred fires, the rock, the water, the air. I find my identity within the sun, the earth, the moon and the stars, all the plant beings and all the animal beings, and all the human beings. Because these are the elements that give me my identity because they are a part of me and I am a part of them. And this is the way. Through my spiritual name I am able to connect myself to all these spiritual elements in creation that give me my identity. And when I learn about these spiritual elements, I find all the wonderful and beautiful gifts that the Creator has presented to man.

His healing approach clearly centres on identity:

> I think the most important thing is to teach them about their identity. That's really important for their well-being. They have to know who they are. They have to know their history. They have to know their values. I have learned that a race of people with a good set of values is going to live a long time when they learn of caring and sharing. And when they have learned to respect themselves, then they will be able to respect others. When they have learned to forgive themselves, then they will forgive others.

Clearly the Elders do not behave like other prison staff, and this is not explainable simply by the fact that they are usually contract employees with little or no career loyalty to the correctional system. One key characteristic shared by all Elders is the fact that they are seen as trustworthy by inmates, in the sense that information gleaned about an inmate through counselling and ceremony is not normally shared with the other correctional staff. There are exceptions to this, for instance where an inmate discloses the intent to harm himself or others, but these exceptions are invariably made clear early in the therapeutic encounter. The establishment of trust and confidentiality is essential; it sets the Elders apart from other prison officials who routinely make records of their encounters with inmates and which are shared with other staff. Indeed, another distinguishing characteristic of the Elders is their abhorrence of written records and evaluations of inmates. These are seen as incompatible with Aboriginal culture and antithetical to the goals they are trying to achieve.

These issues are raised by the Elders:

> They don't have to make no appointment to see us. They can walk in anytime and see us. If we see one client, the two of us, all morning, we don't have a problem, because we want him to understand. Whereas when they go [to Case Management], sometimes they're told to get out of there before they start talking. They have a lot of problems. They're not being heard. We hear them. When a guy comes in here angry, we want to listen to that anger and let him get rid of it. We don't recommend that he should go to Anger Management and we let him deal with it himself, but we help him. And ten times out of ten, he walks out of here happy. It's effective. We don't see them for two or three minutes, or five minutes, and when we're busy, if somebody should walk in and we tell them, "Well right now we're having a session with this guy," they respect that. They respect that and they come back later.

> The case management worker, they write everything. I don't write everything, I use my brain. You never see me writing. I just keep track of the boys' names in the book there and I know what was done. When I started here, I told [the correctional staff] "I'm not going to be writing any reports. I don't work that way. I want you to understand that. If you can get another Elder that you want that wants to do the reports, you can."

Although it is a rare occurrence, occasionally a spiritual advisor is commissioned as a corrections officer. This leaves their fundamental role within the institution unchanged, as this individual suggests:

> I am an actual corrections officer. But I wear different hats out there. I am not seen as a corrections officer but I let them know

about it before I talk to them. You see, in my position as spiritual advisor out there, I also have the privilege of confidentiality whereas the other officers don't. Which means that I'm not obligated to report anything that is told to me when I am working with my clients. But the reason that I let them know that I am an officer is that I am compelled because of my officer status to report anything to do with security. Because I have had men come to me and say I am going to run away tonight. I have had them do that. So I make that perfectly clear so that they understand that. But they still don't see me as an officer. They see me as a counsellor or as the Elder.

The Elders have a philosophy regarding treatment that differs from other correctional staff. In effect, they adhere to the belief that no one can, or should, be forced to seek out their services or be forced to learn about Aboriginal spirituality. Individuals must make this decision for themselves. This sets their program apart from other programs, such as Alcoholics Anonymous, in which inmates are told to participate if they wish to achieve parole.[2]

The nurse said, "You're going to A.A." If you go up for parole, the parole people say, "Well you have an alcohol problem. You haven't attended A.A." If they don't attend A.A., none of them get paroled pretty quick. So they're told to go to A.A. They'll say, "Well you want parole, you got to go to Cog[nitive] Skills, you got to go to Living Skills, you got to attend A.A. Here's what you got to do." I don't do that. When we're at the sweat lodge, they show up and no one gets turned away. We run a lot of sweats. We'll do about three or four a week so everybody can get a chance. Whoever shows up... like the healing circle, whoever shows up, they show up. If they quit, they quit. That's it and nobody says anything.

There is nothing that I can do to heal anybody. The only thing that I can do is give him direction and guidance. Now whether he accepts that direction and that guidance is entirely up to him. If he refuses that, then there is nothing that I can do, nothing. I can take him to the sweat lodge. If he still refuses to open up, he's wasting his time and he's wasting my time. He's got to open up himself in order for that self-healing to come. I believe that we all possess a healing process that is in the mind... We take our time. We don't rush anybody into a healing process over night. We don't have healing powers to have that instant magic that they're healed now. We don't have that. It's a slow process. We deal with the whole individual.

And as far as people that are not interested in our Native program, we don't force them to come. We ask them. When they refuse us, we don't push them because of the danger of forcing them to come to something that they're not ready to take or they don't want to. It will hurt them more. And it happens in institutions where people are forced to take Anger Management because they had talked back to staff. Because of lack of training that a lot of people have, they think that this is a very angry person. So they send him to Anger Management whether he likes or not. And when you force a person to do something that he's not ready to do, he's not going to benefit.

The Elders are generally not concerned with an inmate's record or criminal offences. Unlike correctional staff, they do not make an inmate review his criminal past as a first step toward rehabilitation. The Elders start with the present and look forward.

When they go and see him [case management officer], their file is in front, and knowing that's his file, right away his attitude changes. So when he's having an interview, that file is open. "In 1972 [you did this], how are you dealing with that?" "Well, that's 22 years ago." I'm sure they have outgrown that, but the continuing of opening that wound... we try to not do that. We try to heal the wound by working with an individual.

I don't have no access to the files. That is the first thing I had asked. I do not want access to the files. I don't want to work that way. Because I know who they are already. I have a gift of knowing, just by looking at them and their voices. So I know because I was given that gift as a baby when I was born. Each and everyone of us has a gift, but we have to use it. We have to find what that gift is. There's a lot of Elders that know that. We don't have to go into the files to know a person. You can tell just by their behaviour, their speech, their actions, even looking at their eyes, you can tell. And sometimes you can feel it just by shaking their hands.

No, [I don't need to see their records]. They're human like me. I cannot judge them, ever, because I only have one judge and that's God, even though we have man judging them. It's not for me to judge them... When you're having a one-to-one with them, they feel sorry for what they did. But I'll always tell them, "I don't care how you got here or why you got here or how long you're here, what I'm interested in is what you're going to do about it, beginning now, to start maybe changing your attitude to a more positive one.

Not only are the criminal records unimportant to the Elders and spiritual leaders, there is a striking lack of concern for delineating the problems of particular inmates, in deference to the building of self-esteem. Stated one Elder:

You'll find some of them have been told they were no good. "You're no darn good" right from the day they were arrested. Right up to the time the parole board tells them we're going to try you out, even then, they're saying "Well you're a little bit good now, let's see how you do out there." We come in with a philosophy that there's a little bit of good in everybody, no matter how you got here, why you got here or no matter how long you're here. Let's focus on the good things about yourself. And then after that, maybe we'll start talking about the negative about themselves. When you get to that point, you'll create that healing circle around so that you can share some of the positive things about yourself, and if you want, you can share some of the negative things about yourself. If you're not ready to share the negative things about yourself, there's a sweat lodge over there that you can communicate with the Creator the best way you know how, the grandfathers, the spirits, the angels, whatever you want to call them. You can communicate by yourself the negative things that you're not ready to deal with somebody else.

Another feature that distinguishes the Elders from other prison staff is their willingness to meet with offenders after release, to provide spiritual and even financial assistance. Generally, correctional staff are not known for providing community support, and some fear that they may be accosted by released inmates. The Elders, in contrast, recognize that one is not an Elder only when one walks through the prison gate in the morning:

> I always tell them, "You've got certain conditions you must live
> under, here's my phone number. If ever you're having a hell of a
> rough time someplace, before you do anything, phone me."
> People have called me at 1:30, 2:00 in the morning.

This dedication to the pipe, however, has a personal cost.

Elders' Stress

The pressures of dealing with troubled human beings, especially within
a prison context, are enormous, and the inability to "leave it at the
office" leads to considerable stress for the Elders. Three of them shared
their thoughts on this topic:

> I find that if you are going to be involved with people in distress,
> living in despair, entertaining thoughts of suicide, you have to
> be available to these people. It is not a nine-to-five job. If it is a
> nine-to-five job for you, then you have no business there. We
> call ourselves 'caregivers', but are you just a caregiver from nine-
> to-five? An awful lot of these emotional problems fall upon me
> and I have to be very careful what I do with them. Like where
> do I go with my problems? What am I supposed to do? Here I
> have got this whole big bag of garbage, what am I supposed to
> do with it? Most ministers have what they call a support
> committee, you know, and they unload there. Whereas the
> Elders, I don't know of any having a support committee. But
> the only way that I get rid of that is through sweat lodges. So, I
> manage somehow.

> I still have tendencies to take my work home with me, something
> that's bothering me here. I usually want to share it with
> somebody. Like, you've got so much stuff being dumped on
> you here everyday, that you have to have an outlet of some kind
> to ventilate some of this stuff that you have. Although I speak a
> lot of times with a [another] spiritual advisor. He's helped me a
> heck of a lot of times, where I can go to him and say, "This is
> what's bugging my butt right now about this, because I heard
> this and I heard that and how am I going to strike it out" type
> of thing. He usually comes up with something that... sort of
> opens your eyes... tells me things like you can't straighten out
> all these guys in here. No matter how hard you try, you can't

straighten out all their problems. When you do that, you fall short yourself and you start feeling inadequate. And when you start feeling inadequate, you start asking for approval from some place. Maybe you take it home with you. You wait for your partner to pat you on the back and say you're doing a good job. That type of thing.

Maybe there's a reason why sometimes I feel a lot of burnout, because when I come in here, I'm not like the [other] counsellors. They can say, "I'm a counsellor," and it stays right here. "Now I'm here to counsel." After five o'clock, they can put their plate away and say, "I'm Bob Smith [a pseudonym]. I think I'll go for a beer." Sometimes I go from here and then when I get home and my [partner] says, "What's wrong with you?" it sort of wakes me up. Some of the things I hear in here, I have to sort out. Sometimes I take the long way home to unwind because I don't want to take some of these [problems] home to my kids. Sometimes after I put them to bed, then I sort things out and say, "Okay, here's what I have to do for so and so."

The Elders deal with stress in predictable ways: they consult with other Elders, often their mentors, or undertake sweat lodge or other ceremonies to reinvigorate their spirituality.

Problems Working within Institutions

There is also a great deal of stress related to problems with administration and security. In spite of directives from the CSC Commissioner's office, and the legislative and policy basis for Aboriginal spirituality described in Chapter One, the Elders, spiritual leaders, and inmates are still occasionally harassed. Every Elder has experienced this. It can be overt, such as when medicine bundles or pipe bundles are searched at the gates. This invariably desecrates these sacred objects, requiring the Elders to undergo extensive reconsecration. It can involve limitations on movement or access to inmates. It can involve the placing of unreasonable time limits on ceremonies. And it can involve both overt and subtle racism.

One particular incident is telling. A security drill was undertaken just as a sweat lodge ceremony was getting underway. The inmates were taken back to their units, and the drill was carried out. While the management argued that this was an unfortunate, but not deliberate, incident, in fact, security was aware of the sweat lodge ceremony, which was held every week at the same time and which they observed from a distance. The Elder felt, quite rightly, that such a drill would not likely be called during Sunday church service.

One Elder described the problems he experienced attempting to bring his sacred pipe into one institution:

> There you have to carry your pipe through the main building and people handle your stuff. They look for stuff even though I would never take nothing in there that secretly, neither would I take anything out, other than what I brought in. But most Elders will tell you that they don't like other people rummaging through their medicine bag, through the pipe. That is one of the biggest difficulties that I had there because it made me feel that these people have a very strong distrust for me in the way that they operated. I hated the day that I had to walk through there with my pipe. When that happens, I have to leave my pipe outside because it [should not] be desecrated by mishandling, misuse, many things that happen to pipes. I have to put it outside and let the sun, let nature and the wind, the trees, the birds, Mother Earth re-bless the whole thing and then I pick it up.

Another Elder related a similar story:

> Last year like I had a lot of problems here. And then I was stopped too and they searched but after they gave me that paper, like a memo, whatever they call it, and then after that I don't have no trouble. Because they have to trust me, because I know I can't bring in anything like that there, anything like scissors or a knife. I can't do that. But they were kind of suspicious of me. It's just like they don't trust me. In my bag, there's my clothing, sweat outfit, towels. They want to look in there too. But [they're] not [to look] in my case there where I keep my [sacred items].
>
> He [the guard] says "what have you got in here?"
>
> "Well I got all my Indian stuff here, my pipe," I says.
>
> "Well you want to open it?" He says, "you got a pass here?"
>
> I says "I got a pass here." Then when they look at it, and it just says a "medicine bundle."
>
> "It doesn't mean your pipe or your other stuff here," he says.
>
> "It's not here, it's not on the paper."

But then again the way they understand, these people, [they don't realize] that "medicine" means everything. But what they want to do is they want to see each part written down, the sweetgrass, the tobacco, and whatever, the prints, the whistle, and whatever. Even the blanket. So that's what they wrote then, so those guys could understand now. They don't want to bother. And that woman she upset my stuff too in the garbage. The case tipped over. That woman, she doesn't have the right to touch my stuff that I have in there because she's a woman. But she grabbed them and put them back in my case there.

As the previous Elder suggests, another problem relates to the presence of female staff in institutions. Many Elders believe that women are spiritually powerful, but Aboriginal cultures dictate that menstruating women, who are at their most powerful, must not come into proximity with sacred items.

It's very difficult in here. Like, I don't bring my pipe in here. There's a visiting room nearby. With all respect to women, there's women walking up there. Women are very powerful. They are a lot stronger than us, spiritually and mentally. Physically we are strong, but the strength that they possess, man doesn't possess that. And out of respect, I won't bring my pipe in here. I bring sweetgrass in here, but not my pipe. I won't.

As this Elder continues, it becomes clear that this issue is one that transcends work in prison; it is essential in all aspects of his spiritual life that the pipe be protected:

I don't take my pipe to hotel rooms because the pipe that I carry is very special... I can't take it anywhere where there's women, because the pipe has to be free, just like it was before it was put together. The tree is free and the rock is free. It never should be imprisoned. I wouldn't bring it here. Maybe I would bring it if I was on the top floor. That's the only place I would take it, but I wouldn't take it to a basement or middle floor or the 12th floor with a 13th, 14th and 15th floor. I wouldn't take it there, because to me, my pipe is very valuable and it's very sacred. I don't even take it inside my house. I have a special building over there at home where I keep all my medicines. Only I go there. And my oldest grandson, he can go in there. That's where I keep my pipe, all my medicines, my flags, tobacco. That's where I keep it. It doesn't go inside the house.

In the 1990s, the issue of contact with women, as outlined by this Elder, is very controversial. At one prison, for instance, one female guard was outraged when, at the beginning of a healing ceremony, she was asked if she was menstruating. She launched a grievance with the institution and contacted the local media, declaring discrimination on the basis of her sex. It is difficult for non-Aboriginal women to appreciate the significance of menstruation from an Aboriginal perspective, especially after having fought for so many years for employment equity and the right to perform their duties free from any gender discrimination.

Another form of harassment pertains to the restrictions placed on ceremonies and counselling work with the inmates. It has taken many years for the correctional system to realize that Aboriginal spirituality operates according to its own time frame. Unlike Christianity, it cannot be "practised" for an hour on Sunday morning. Pipe ceremonies and sweats can take many hours, and inmates occasionally undertake four-day fasts in their cells. Elders told of being informed that they had fifteen minutes to undertake a pipe ceremony. At one prison, sweetgrass ceremonies were held at eight-thirty in the morning, and were concluded by nine so that inmates could attend other programs. Conflict with other institutional programs is pervasive across the correctional system.

> This is what happened. I come in here, I build a sweat and I had my sweat on Thursday nights. At the same time there were three Chaplains in here, they were having catechism steady over here, Bible studies, or whatever you want to call it, on that night. All these guys were leaving the Bible study and coming to the sweat and there were only two or three in the chapel. So three chaplains with two inmates, I mean, that isn't going to make a very good report. So what are they going to do? They have to get rid of me or I am going to wreck their program, you see. So they hired another Elder. They gave me the excuse that they [inmates] had to go to education.

> I seen this guy come up to me and say, "What the hell do you think you're doing? You started Cree classes and I only had eight people in my class and they all went to your Cree classes. What the hell do you think you're doing?" I just about told him to take anger management himself.

Like when I am having these guys here, and I'm trying to talk to
them and there is a phone call here saying that they have to be
over there. Even when I'm talking, there is one staff [who] told
this guy, "hey, you are supposed to be over there in that program.
It is very important for you to be over there, and you have to be
over there," he told him. And I asked that staff, "what about
me?" I says, "'cause I'm working with the Elders and at the
same time I am an Elder by rights, and by rights I should have a
little respect too," I said. "And while I'm talking to this guy, he
belongs to me," I said. "If I don't let him go, you guys you can't
do nothing," I told her, 'cause that's what they told me over
here. "See there's little things going on here," I says, "it seems
like you people don't want to cooperate with the Native people
and at the same time too, you don't want to trust me. That's
what you are trying to say," I said. "These guys here, what
about me and my culture," I says, "they are not important?"

The stress of dealing with the ongoing problems associated with
security, and the inability of some correctional staff to understand
and accept Aboriginal spirituality, has proven incredibly frustrating
for all the Elders interviewed for this study. At least two Elders interviewed subsequently went on hiatus.

I'm sort of burned out or whatever you want to call it. I don't
care for prisons anymore. Why I am going to the idiotic place
and putting up with all that bullshit, you know, and all that
administration stuff and dealing with this. They are just like a
little house on the prairies, they have got their own way of life
and I don't think they want to change any. So what am I spending
my time for, you know?

It is not just the stresses that relate to the institutions that generate
problems. As noted earlier, many Elders work in the community as
well, and they provide assistance to released offenders. Furthermore,
those inside the walls often work longer hours than is required by
their contracts.

One spiritual leader was called upon to assist in a four day fast.
While not specifically a part of his contract, it was assumed that he
would facilitate the event. This effectively involved spending the better
parts of four consecutive twenty-four-hour periods at the teepee where
the fast was being undertaken. Then, when he took time off subsequent to the fast, in lieu of overtime pay (which was not available in

his contract), he was chastised by the contractor (a non-correctional agency) because regular Aboriginal programming was not available to inmates while he was away.

The Elders and spiritual leaders who work in prisons, along with the Native liaison personnel, are terribly overworked. While the correctional system seems willing to use them as token examples of their commitment to Aboriginal programming, it is reluctant to acknowledge that the spiritual services are unlike those offered by the chaplains, and that the healing services are unlike those offered by the treatment teams. Being an "Elder" is not a status specific to the correctional environment; Elders are on call twenty-four hours a day, seven days a week. Once an Elder accepts a sacred pipe, he is required follow the pipe, to help people whenever called.

Contracts and Correctional Contradictions

Many Elders and spiritual leaders who work in prisons have become spiritual at a later stage in their life. They function fairly well within the correctional environment because of their English language skills and knowledge of Euro-Canadian culture. Some Elders, however, are more traditional, having been born and raised within a spiritual, Aboriginal cultural environment. It is here that we find one of the most profound contradictions. The correctional system needs Elders who, on the one hand, can deliver culturally appropriate spiritual services, and who, on the other hand, can interact well with correctional staff and fit into the institutional culture. This means attending meetings, giving cross-cultural awareness workshops, interacting informally with staff, writing memos and reports, and evaluating inmates. In effect, Elders are expected to behave like the (invariably Euro-Canadian) chaplains and other correctional staff who are involved with offender rehabilitation. However, as noted earlier, most of the Elders are reluctant to take notes of meetings or write reports. They will, however, engage staff orally and play along with most of the rules of the institutional game. Sometimes, their ability to function within institutions provides them employment even though their spiritual skills may not be well developed. A bizarre example occurred at one institution where a non-Aboriginal woman was hired to provide spiritual services, including sweat lodge ceremonies, to inmates. The inmates protested loudly, including in the local media, and ultimately she was removed.

The manner of contracting for services is part of the problem. Contracts are tendered, and individuals or organizations bid on the work. This is a complex process in which the awards are invariably made to those with the best skills in writing contract proposals and bids, as opposed to those with the spiritual skills. For instance, one contract proposal called for an Elder to work thirty hours per week, outlining twenty-eight "deliverables" or separate contract demands. These not only included working with inmates, but also the provision of services, such as cross-cultural workshops, to the staff. Not only would the Elder would be responsible for providing counselling and ceremonies, but also for keeping detailed records of activities (for example, the "number and type of individual inmate interviews... group sessions... [and] spiritual ceremonies"). This is a great deal of work, and it is all crammed into a thirty-hour week. The eight-page call for tenders, including a system for awarding "points" in each category of deliverable, was complex and clearly aimed at organizations which had experience with contracts. The notion that spirituality and healing can be redefined in terms of contractual "deliverables" is objectionable and culturally insensitive.

At one institution an Aboriginal person who lacked extensive experience with Aboriginal culture was awarded a contract to provide Native liaison services. Supported by a large outside institution, this individual was able to write a good contract proposal, and therefore win the contract. It was this individual's *Euro-Canadian* skills and advanced education, not his knowledge of the correctional system, Aboriginal inmates, or spirituality, which won the contract.

Therefore, it is not surprising that many contracts to provide spiritual services are held by institutions, and not by individual Elders. These institutions, while often well meaning and managed by Aboriginal peoples, are nevertheless in the business of winning contracts and supplying services. It is virtually impossible for most Elders to win contracts as independents. Even when they work for a contractor, problems can arise. Service providers are supposed to conform to the details of the contract. But there have been many times where actual prison conditions necessitate an alteration in the delivery of services. An Elder may be required to suddenly leave the institution to obtain rocks for a sweat, or he may feel the need to spend an entire day with one troubled client. Such deviations from the contract can result in friction and bad reports.

In one case, a spiritual leader became embroiled with his boss, an Aboriginal man who worked for an outside institution, because the spiritual leader was unable to keep to a strict daily schedule (e.g.

nine to ten-thirty, crafts; ten-thirty to noon, videos). The reason? There were many offenders who required counselling, and this individual put them ahead of craft workshops and other scheduled activities. He was severely chastised for not fulfilling aspects of the contract. The contractor had virtually no experience with prisons, and little idea of what really went on, yet insisted that the contract be fulfilled to the letter.

In another institution, friction developed when the contractor decided to bring an Aboriginal healer into the institution, an action which was both offensive and culturally inappropriate in the eyes of an Aboriginal contract employee. Furthermore, when the employee was informed in a meeting that he would be required to assist this healer, he balked, feeling that he was unqualified to do this and that he needed to consult with his own Elders about the appropriateness of his involvement. He was also concerned that the inmates themselves had not been properly consulted about this new initiative. In his mind, the healer's program was being rushed, and there was no time to reflect on the suitability of the process. In the end, he felt forced to resign, an act that sparked a crisis meeting among the Aboriginal inmates. They demanded, and received, assurances that they would be consulted in the hiring of the new employee and in other initiatives emanating from the Aboriginal program.

The contradiction within the correctional system concerning the provision of spiritual services can be stated clearly: the Elders with the greatest spiritual knowledge and gifts are least likely to obtain contracts (or even bid on them) or fulfil the expectations of the correctional system. Aboriginal spirituality is becoming not just institutionalized, but corporatized. The correctional system wants Elders who work and behave, not like Aboriginal spiritual people, but like other Euro-Canadian staff. The inmates, in contrast, want Elders who are spiritual, who follow the ways of the pipe, and who do not appear to be a part of the correctional team.

This contradiction is evident in part of a CSC review of the work of one Elder, a man renowned in the west for his spiritual knowledge but who is also very traditional. Raised with spirituality from birth, he has spent most of his life on the reserve and speaks a variety of Aboriginal languages. His oral English, however, is functional but not fluent, and his reading skills are minimal. The report states:

> The quality of work is... sometimes poor when performed by ... [the Elder]... The concern remains the quality of the deliverables and the difficulties experienced by [the Elder]

adapting to the [institution]. The deliverables most affected were "liaising with Social Work in case management strategies" and "conduct workshops." [The Elder] does not share [another Elder's] abilities in the English language, in counselling and in interpersonal skills within a correctional environment. Consequently, the Elder program has suffered in the areas of leadership and problem-solving.

In fact, this report referred only to the Elder's reluctance to engage the correctional staff. His counselling and interpersonal skills were exceptional with respect to the Aboriginal inmates, but of course they had no input into the evaluation.

The Elders and spiritual leaders who decide to work within correctional institutions face many obstacles and are repeatedly frustrated by the correctional system's insistence to turn Aboriginal spirituality into something that it is not, namely European religion. One of the key areas of friction can be found in the fact that Aboriginal people see their spirituality as a form of healing, something that requires time, patience, and commitment. It is not directly comparable to European religious practice. Forced to operate within the confines of two of the most repressive European institutions, the prison system and the Christian church, they nevertheless have achieved many successes. However, "success" as defined by the Elders is somewhat different than that defined by the correctional system. Certainly the inmates react differently to Aboriginal spirituality than to other prison rehabilitative programs. It is to this issue that we now turn.

NOTES

1   Since there were relatively few Elders and spiritual leaders interviewed for this study, in order to protect their identities no cultural information can be provided.

2   Unfortunately, in some instances, Aboriginal inmates are now being told by prison staff to consult with the Elders, but this is contrary to the traditional philosophy espoused by the Elders.

I used to love drugs. I used to love drinking. Now I love going to the sweats. I replaced that addiction. I have become addicted to spirituality.

— ABORIGINAL INMATE

6 Finding the Way: Inmate Experiences

For many Aboriginal offenders, their first experience with Aboriginal spirituality has come in prison. While individuals raised primarily in Aboriginal communities may have had some prior exposure to components of spirituality, often this education was piecemeal and incomplete, leaving the individual feeling spiritually inadequate. Furthermore, some Aboriginal offenders come from communities where practices such as the use of sweetgrass and sweat lodges have long been absent, or from communities where such practices were foreign to their traditional cultures. Those offenders raised in the Euro-Canadian cultural tradition have had virtually no exposure to Aboriginal spirituality until their incarceration. Many of these individuals are desperate to learn anything they can about Aboriginal culture, and spirituality is often considered the essential, signifying ingredient. In this chapter I look at how inmates are coming to understand the symbolism of Aboriginal spirituality and act upon its teachings.

Understanding the Healing Philosophy

Symbolic healing operates at many levels. As we have seen, it involves learning the symbols that are used and manipulated as part of the therapeutic encounter. What remains to be seen, however, is the extent to which individuals hear the teachings and act on them to change their lives. Much evidence has been gathered demonstrating that many Aboriginal men have learned a great deal and have come to understand, and accept, the symbols as defining a new cognitive approach to life, one that includes a drug-free, crime-free future. The narratives that follow are particularly valuable when viewed alongside those offered by the Elders and spiritual leaders in the previous chapter.

The men are taught that spirituality is both a collective and an individual experience. They are taught to be independent in worship, in contrast to the hierarchical approach of Christianity. Inmates are taught that one can worship anywhere, at anytime, and that the spiritual path exists no matter where one is. The plan for leading one's life is to be in effect all day, every day.

> I sit in there [cell] sometimes and have a smoke, smudge myself. See it doesn't matter where you are, you're sitting in the toilet and can still be thankful. You don't have go to a cathedral or really fancy church, you know. You can go in the bush and give your thanks. That's the way I see it. I go in there when I want to be alone. That's what I do, sit and think. I don't have to go to no church or sacred circle or anything. [Traditional – Ojibwa]

> Because it is my understanding through the teachings that the grandfathers are all over the place. They know what is in your heart. They know what is in your mind even before you say it. So anyone playing with these ways is only bullshitting themself and only hurting themself. But if you take them and use them in a proper and a right way, and a good and positive way for the people, then these ways will always look after you. They will help you and it is a beautiful way of life. It may be a strict way of life but it is a beautiful way of life. If you look after these ways, they will look after you. That is just the way it is. [Bicultural – Plains Cree]

These comments indicate the pervasiveness of the spiritual path, which is all around and never ends. Aboriginal spirituality is not something that can be turned on and off, or that can be practised only for a few hours each week, in a specialized location. While the ceremonies may be central to its practice, clearly the path exists everywhere.

> Long ago the altars were built like this anywhere. This is in the
> Bible, right? Sometimes it was in the desert, the rocks... an altar
> everywhere. And so Indian ways is to believe in the altars
> anywhere you go. Where you start praying and talking to God,
> that's an altar. [Bicultural – Northern Cree]

Respect is one of the key values that is taught. Respect for others,
and especially for oneself, is essential if the offenders are to develop
proper attitudes towards criminality and their role in society.

> Like, for me, if there's a White guy who hangs around with me
> and he knows what he's talking about... I'll talk to him. Like,
> to me, I don't really care if he's a sexual offender or he tells on
> people anymore... I'm trying to get out of that now, because I
> want to follow my spiritual ways. Part of the teachings is to
> respect everybody, and that's been really hard because of the
> way I grew up. I'm still trying. [Traditional – Saulteaux]

One aspect of this respect is dealing with one's criminal behaviour.
Although the Elders emphasize the need to look to the future, other
correctional programming focuses on understanding the individual's
criminal behaviour. Many inmates go through a stage of denial in
which they refuse to accept that they have committed a criminal act,
or else lay the blame on others. Taking responsibility for their actions
is the first step in correctional treatment. Aboriginal spirituality assists
individuals in coming to terms with their past record and criminal
offences.

Sobriety and a drug-free existence are core values that are learned
through spirituality. Most of the men have alcohol or substance abuse
problems. In some instances their major offences were committed
while under the influence of a substance, acts that were very much
out-of-character for the clean and sober individual. Some men actually develop drug problems while in prison. The need to develop the
inner strength to avoid alcohol and drugs, both within the institutions
and after release, is absolutely essential for effective healing and avoid-
ance of recidivism or parole revocation.

The spiritual path is also a path of nonviolence, another essential
ingredient for healing men with anger management difficulties who
have often resorted to violent behaviour to solve problems. The men
are taught respect for others, for their bodies, and for their posses-
sions. The sanctity of the individual's body is an essential value; hence
both physical and sexual abuse is proscribed.

Sure I have my bad days, and go there [to Elders]. When I come back, I'm feeling better. Like there's so many times I want to get into trouble, pick a fight or something. But there's always something in the back of my mind with the Elders. Common sense comes in right there. I was taught that's not right, so I go in my room and smudge. Then I apologize to the guy and offer him a cigarette, and tell him I'm sorry for being rude. I never did that before when I was on the street. If the guy said something bad, shit, you got to go for it. That's the way I was raised. It's a hard habit to break. It's the Elder that's teaching me this. [Bicultural – Plains Cree]

The way of the pipe is not an easy way to follow. It would be much easier for the men to simply continue with their old ways, abusing alcohol and drugs, hurting people, committing crimes. The Elders are always very clear about this fact: following the Aboriginal way will be difficult, and there will be many temptations. The men understand the task they have set for themselves. This inmate touched on many of these themes:

So I started changing my life, started going back to the sweats, pipe ceremonies, overnight retreats. I started singing again, I started dancing. I started doing all these things again and for a long time, for a long time for nine months I kept going. "I'm doing good, I'm doing good." But I forgot my purpose in learning and things started to get rough again. I started wanting to go back to drinking, doing drugs, fighting, gambling and all that. I wanted to. Then I remembered what that old man [Elder] told me, "When things get tough, pray." It is so easy, but it is so hard, it is a hard thing to do. So I started praying. Life is still not easy but I'm alive. I'm living for today. I can't worry about what is going to happen next year, next month or tomorrow because I live for what's today. A lot of my questions in my life, there's answers in it today and it's up to me to look for them. Elders can only do so much. Ceremonies can only do so much. But you can do a lot for yourself... They accepted me for who I was and not what people made me out to be. They showed me good qualities that I have in myself. The understanding, the listening ability, everything. They showed me these things, now it is up to me what I want to do with these things. [Euro-Canadian – Dakota]

The men who become the most dedicated and serious with respect to Aboriginal spirituality become highly respected role models for the other prisoners. They buck the prison culture, the "con code," and live their lives for themselves and for their spirituality. This requires a great deal of courage; evidence in this research indicated that these men are sometimes subjected to harassment and ridicule by inmates who fail to understand the significance of the spiritual path. They are often greeted with suspicion by correctional staff who have difficulty accepting the sincerity that accompanies profound behavioural changes. These devout individuals are nevertheless envied by other inmates.

> They go to the sweats, they go to sacred circle, they go to brotherhood meetings, and all that. And they live that life. They are out of drugs, they are out of the muscling, they are out of the fighting, they are out of the drinking. [Euro-Canadian – Dakota]

Sweetgrass

It is now fairly common for Aboriginal inmates to be allowed to have braids of sweetgrass and sometimes matches in their cells (many believe it is inappropriate to use a lighter). Therefore it is available to them for prayer whenever they feel the need, and not just during ceremonial activities. The use of sweetgrass is pervasive. One man described the symbolism of sweetgrass as he understood it:

> The sweetgrass road, it's a very good road to follow. But you have to be sincere, open and truthful and really honest with the Creator if you want to follow the sweetgrass road. There's three braids of sweetgrass and there's twenty-six to thirty strands on it. One braid is your family, one braid is you, one braid is the Creator. But different people look at it in different ways. You pick it, you braid it, and you pray with it. [Euro-Canadian – Saulteaux]

Another inmate described how the sweetgrass is used to temper relations between inmates and promote harmony even when the Elders are not around:

One inmate called me into his cell, and he burned the sweetgrass and we smudged ourselves before we started saying anything, like to be honest with each other. And he started telling me what I was doing wrong, and that's how we dissolved our problems, by smudging ourselves. And I told him, "I've got a lot of respect for you, and I don't want to screw our friendship up in any way." And that's how I knew that whenever I wanted to talk to someone, I always burn the sweetgrass. I smudge myself and I get that person to smudge himself, and then I quickly say, "What's between us is true." And that's how I solve my problems, instead of going up to a person and saying, "Well, I've got a problem with you." Because you don't know how he's going to react, whether he is going to get pissed off at you and want to beef you out. [Bicultural – Plains Cree]

Sweetgrass also provides comfort to troubled inmates. It calms them down when they are distressed and allows them to focus their thoughts constructively. This individual found burning sweetgrass important to his mental health, helping him deal with suicidal thoughts:

I've always done that when I got feeling really desperate or suicidal, when I was in jail. I would come down and I would straighten out and burn my sweetgrass for a while. I learned to do that, you know. I do that without even thinking, to pray for guidance. [Euro-Canadian – heritage unknown]

The Sacred Circle

The Sacred Circle could be viewed, in one sense, as a ceremonial form of group therapy. The circle is an important symbol in Aboriginal spirituality since it represents the cycle of life that has no beginning and no end. Keeping the circle closed or unbroken is essential. After smudging and an opening prayer, the presiding Elder will often begin with a story or a particular teaching that is relevant to the men. The use of parables, or spiritual narratives involving figures such as Nanabush, is common. This provides an opportunity to deal with any issues that may have recently arisen and that require an Elder's guidance. Problems between inmates, and problems with correctional staff, may be raised, but specific individuals usually remain unidentified. The Elders speak to specific incidents, but in a way that highlights more general principles. For instance, the problems one man may be having with the presence of a non-Aboriginal inmate in the sweat lodge may be discussed in terms of the irrelevancy of skin colour in the eyes of the Creator.

The tone of the Sacred Circle is calm and sedate. In contrast to many group therapy exercises in prison, the Sacred Circle does not usually involve feedback or the challenging of specific individuals. Each person is given the opportunity to speak; they may pass if they wish, and they can speak on any topic that suits them, for as long as they want. Some will simply say how happy and honoured they are to be in the circle, but others will discuss problems they may be having. Most Elders use a speaking device, such as a "talking stick," "talking stone," or eagle feather, which moves around the circle. Only the person in possession of the device has the right to talk; all others are to listen.

The Sacred Circle is central to the process of spiritual education. As such, it is particularly important in helping inmates who are just starting their spiritual journey and are trying to sort out their identity.

> I think in the year that I've been here, I went three Thursday nights for the Sacred Circle. For the first time, I was proud of who I was and there was no shame in it, to talk about the cultural part of it, whatever I learned, you know, from the Sacred Circle or even the sweats. I was so full of energy. I wanted to tell people what I learned. It was just the little boy in me coming out. This is what I learned. So I was a little boy, full of energy, wanting to tell somebody. Last Thursday, I came to the Sacred Circle and I've learned more in that one than I did in the whole year that I've been here, other than the fact of what I learned in the sweat lodges. I wasn't aware of the role of the male or the female in my identity or culture. I wasn't aware about suicide. I wasn't aware of dreams. About what the Elder spoke on Thursday, it kind of blew my mind, but it also scared me. It scared me to the point that rather than shut it out, I want to experiment. I want to learn more about it. There's something here now. The seeds been planted, but I've been watering it. But it seems now like I want it to grow faster, rather than let nature take its course. I feel like I want to artificially use ultraviolet light and make it grow faster, but I can't. And I guess I'm learning patience, tolerance. I know there's so much to learn and I have quite a bit of time to do it. [Euro-Canadian – Ojibwa]

Another individual described the therapeutic benefit of sharing experiences with other inmates in the circle:

> It also gives me a sense of healing and self-healing when I listen to other people in a sacred circle. When I listen to other people, other brothers and sisters, they say, "Oh yeah, this happened to me." Sometimes it hits home, like that happened to me too. You're not alone, you know. Then when you talk about your experience or your thoughts or advice or whatever, to anybody, then everybody respects you. Because it's there for everyone. A guy is not there just because he says, "Oh, I'm feeling bad." And then when they got it off their shoulder, they take off. It's not like that. They sit there and they listen. They have patience. [Traditional – Saulteaux]

The ability to speak openly, without fear of retribution, is essential to the success of the Sacred Circle. Advice may be offered to others who clearly solicit it, but it is not normally offered in the circle unless it is requested. And the circle is never confrontational. This individual described how these aspects were important:

> I can speak my mind there too. Like I can share my outlook, what I learned, talk about things there. And sometimes when somebody talks first, I try to give my advice and everything about their problem. But I never say, "Well you have to do this" or something like that. I just talk about what I did when I had that problem too. [Traditional – Northern Cree]

The Sweat Lodge

For many offenders, prison affords them their first opportunity to undertake a "sweat." The data show that 64% of the inmates interviewed came from communities where sweats were absent, and 65% experienced their first sweat in prison. Overall, some 67% of the men had experienced at least one sweat in prison, and 34% had experienced ten or more sweats. The reasons for becoming involved tend to vary. The most commonly stated reasons were to pray and to experience the therapeutic benefits, both physically and mentally. Learning about Aboriginal spirituality was also an important reason, since much valuable teaching occurs in the lodge. There is also some peer pressure to participate as a sign of solidarity with the other

Aboriginal "brothers." But the therapeutic effects, as perceived by the offenders, are most important in the decision-making process that leads to the sweat. One offender described his introduction:

> Well, I seen a lot of people going to the sweats and it seemed like it was changing them, that they were becoming different because of it. I watched their attitudes, whether they were in prison, or whatever they are, and I didn't at first just jump right into it. But I watched, because I was always sceptical. I watched the change... They weren't as bitter, they weren't full of bitter and... hate. They seemed to have more compassion, more caring after practising it for awhile... It's been like a cleansing. It has given me a chance to cleanse my insides, my thoughts. It's a spiritual learning process. [Euro-Canadian – Metis]

Some offenders attend the sweats faithfully when they are offered. Others attend only for a specific purpose. Still others never attend at all. Some reasons for having a sweat included notions of sacrifice and suffering.

> I don't get into sweats unless I know somebody is really hurt, somebody is really sick and not getting any better. Then I get into that. If I know my mom and my dad is really sick and they aren't getting any better, I know I can use that prayer and that sweat. That is something I have to do for me to get them better. A sacrifice. Something for me to do to get them better. [Traditional – Slavey]

Making amends through prayer was also important. In the sweat lodge the men are taught to pray for others, especially those they have harmed, and not for themselves.

> Because that's where I leave all my defects of character behind. To pray for my loved ones and anyone I've hurt or harmed in anyway. [Euro-Canadian – Cree-Metis]

> [I sweat] to help clear my mind. To pray for my family and myself. I pray for everybody, all the brothers, my grandparents, my little brother in the spirit world. [Traditional – Chipewyan]

> The last sweat I went to was after my dad passed away, so I could let go of holding him here. But I mostly go to sweats for

my family, so the Creator watches over them and protects them. And to humble myself and show respect. [Euro-Canadian – Slavey]

Offenders identified spiritual renewal and an enhanced ability to cope with prison life as direct benefits of sweats:

It takes my anger away. Sometimes I feel real happy. [Traditional – Northern Ojibwa]

It brings up my spirit, especially when I come out of a sweat. When you come out of that sweat, there's nothing that can disturb you today. [Bicultural – Northern Ojibwa]

You have to go through suffering and pain, and you have to experience it, you have to sweat it, you have to learn how to pray, and in that way you come out refreshed like a new person. And I guess in a way you look at creation in a different light. All of creation... And in a sense it did provide that relief of pressure of everyday living, participating in sweats... because you have to sweat and you have to be exposed to the rocks which are hot, and you have to suffer a little pain, humility. But I guess that is a process that is needed and required for a person to start praying. And you don't just pray for yourself as an individual. You pray for all of creation, and you pray for your brothers and sisters. In that respect it was more or less known that you were suffering for the overall good health of everything else around you. [Bicultural – Chipewyan]

From where I am now [prison], it gets you away from being lonely, depressed, or even playing head games about the outside world. [Bicultural – Plains Cree]

One of the most vivid images generated during interviews about the sweat lodge was that of cleansing through sweating. Many men described an "evil" or "bad" essence that was removed from the body through the highly visible purgative mechanism of sweating. This essence was sometimes described more concretely as bad thoughts or poison, but most often it was impossible for individuals to articulate the specifics of what it was that was leaving their body. Nevertheless, the imagery of cleansing, whether of the mind, body or spirit, was pervasive.

> I think a sweat will give me a chance to pray for all the other people. It makes me humble myself. Like I have to get on my hands and knees to walk inside that sweat, so I am really humbling myself, and then when I go in there, I am asking to pray for other people that have a hard time understanding me, ones that I can't get along with. I pray for guidance and I pray for understanding... I think I get really cleansed. I sweat all the bad stuff out. [Bicultural – Cree/Metis]

Dealing with the pain brought on by the intense steam is part of the process of adapting to the sweats. The Elders suggest that if you are clean from drugs and alcohol and clear your mind, you can focus yourself on your prayers and the Creator will protect you.

> But now, I go there and I don't even burn. The first time I peeled, 'cause I didn't listen. And they [Elders] taught me, "go there and pray for your family, yourself, your Creator." So I did, I prayed hard the third round. I was burning like crazy. I told myself, "Why am I burning?" That's when I asked for help, and the pain went away just like that. I didn't burn. The fourth round was hotter, people said, but I didn't notice it. [Bicultural – Plains Cree]

It is evident from the comments above that the sweats also serve an important institutional function, by reducing stress and illegal activity within the prison. One man, displaying an understanding of the symbolism of the sweat lodge, described this aspect in more philosophical terms:

> In a prison environment, everything is negative or tends to be negative. It is hard to project positivity and receive positivity back because there is no positivity to come back at you. Thereby sometimes you have a tendency to absorb negativity. I go to the sweat lodge to absolve myself of all this negativity, to cleanse my mind, my heart, my body and my spirit. You come out and you are reborn because once again you are cleansed and you start projecting more positivity. [Bicultural – Plains Cree]

Aboriginal spirituality, like any form of therapy, does not usually spark a dramatic, instantaneous recovery among participants. Recalling that many of these individuals are very troubled, it should not be surprising that progress is sometimes slow, as this inmate suggests:

I feel good inside. I feel good about myself, I feel good for what
I'm doing. Ever since that I'm in a sweat, I start to look at other
people that I hurt. Like I don't want to hurt nobody no more,
unless they push me to a certain spot, because I have a temper
myself. But I'm working on that... When I was in [one prison],
I usually go to a sweat everyday. I never felt angry. I was in a
good mood all the time. When I came here [to another prison],
I kind of lost that. When I came here, I felt angry most of the
time. [Traditional – Chipewyan]

The struggle that some men experience in their efforts to follow the
way of the pipe will be discussed in greater detail in the next chapter.

Working with Elders

As we saw earlier in this book, the central focus of Aboriginal spirituality programming in correctional centres is the work of Elders.
Their work is concentrated mainly in three areas: offering sweats
and other ceremonies, individual counselling, and providing cultural
and spiritual knowledge.

The influence of Elders and spiritual leaders in the lives of Aboriginal inmates is pervasive. In the study of 249 Aboriginal inmates
in federal institutions, 55% indicated that they had sought out an
Elder for consultation while in prison. When asked to indicate a preference for the offering of religious services inside prison, 78% opted
for the Elder and only 14% selected a Christian minister or chaplain.

The decision to become involved with the Elders and the spiritual
programs is largely a personal one, but many influences are brought
to bear on the individual. Elders, as we saw, will not pursue or badger
anyone into attending a ceremony, but they will extend an invitation.
For some men, that is all that is required. For others, attendance is at
the urging of friends and other Aboriginal brothers, who extol the
virtues of spirituality. Inmates are often aware of the changes that
occur within certain individuals as they become more involved with
spirituality, and these observations may lead one to similarly become
involved.

Most Aboriginal offenders viewed the Elders with great respect and
reverence. Some suggested that any notion of playing "games" with
Elders, such as lying to them (as they might with regular prison staff),
was simply out of the question. Indeed, the contrast between the offenders' views of the Elders, on the one hand, and other correctional

rehabilitation staff, on the other, were quite striking. The Elders were considered to be significantly more empathetic, not only because they had lived the cultural experience as Aboriginal persons (including experiencing the trauma and racism discussed earlier in this book), but because they too had often lived troubled lives and had used spirituality to rehabilitate themselves. They were living proof that the spiritual path was a viable option.

> I feel that I can relate to this Elder. He has been through what I have been through. He was an alcoholic one time in his life. He was on skid row. He did things that I am doing now, and I ask him for advice, what changed him around. How did he do it? What path he took... Like I have one-on-one's with the staff, but it's not the same as talking to somebody that you can relate to. Somebody that's your own kind. [Traditional – Northern Cree]

> I can relate to these guys [Elders]. They've been through what I'm going through, and how they've changed their life is something that I want so bad in life for myself. And I admire these people turning their lives around and becoming somebody. [Traditional – Northern Cree]

Elders with prison experience were sometimes particularly valued.

> An Elder who has been in prison and has gone straight would know more and understand more than an Elder who has never been in jail or has never been an alcoholic... I can approach an Elder who hadn't been in prison or been a drunk... but pretty hard to talk to. [Traditional – Ojibwa]

A contrast was specifically made between the Elders and other treatment and correctional staff. The emphasis was often placed on the different types of learning or training each had received. A certain disdain for the training of the treatment and rehabilitation staff is evident from these passages:

> Well, these people [staff] are talking from a statistical point of view, from a book experience, like there is no practical at all... But an Elder, they are teaching you things that have been taught to them, that have been handed down. That makes it more valuable. [Bicultural – Plains Cree]

The treatment staff, all they know about us is what they learn in the book. I think the Elders is not what they learn in the book. I think he learns that in life... You end up going and sitting in the room with those nurses... you see that nurse sit in front of you and keep watching her watch all the time. Because a normal one [session] should be one hour. I don't know, it's hard to trust when you see a person act this way. You can't really trust that person, and yet they try to help us. The Elders... they do what they think is best for you. They don't mind sitting two to four hours with you in a room. Those nurses are different, because they have the guidelines to follow, and if they don't follow it, they end up in trouble. [Euro-Canadian – Cultural heritage anonymous]

Psychologists and psychiatrists in particular often received negative reviews from many Aboriginal inmates. Their power and authority were resented, and their ability to mystify, especially in their use of language, was not seen as helpful. In contrast, the Elders were valued because they appeared interested only in helping, not in keeping individuals incarcerated, and because they spoke plainly.

He [the Elder] doesn't try to manipulate your problem. He'll tell you straight out in a spiritual way so that you understand. Psychologists make a problem sound worse than it is. Their experience is from paper and books, not experience. [Bicultural – Northern Cree]

I had a death feast for my cousin and mother. That's what an Elder's done for me, pipe ceremonies, sweats, taught me a lot of things. Nothing a psychologist taught me. They just wrote reports about me, things I talk about as a kid... and they made everything sound bad. I don't understand what the purpose of a psychologist is, why they go to school that long just to learn the common sense of life. [Euro-Canadian – Saulteaux]

They [Elders] explain things to you, their way. Then you know what he's talking about. A psychiatrist, they really come and hit you with the high words and trying to get you confused and try to put words in your mouth. It's pretty confusing. [Traditional – Chipewyan]

An Elder's here because he cares. Shrinks are here because they get paid. [Bicultural – Metis]

One-on-one, private counselling was greatly valued by the inmates. They were able to talk about their culture and their personal histories, and to obtain advice and spiritual/cultural knowledge from the Elders.

> I talk about myself and the problems I have, and they give me advice, you know, how to have a better life out there. That's something that I've learned so much from these Elders... Like I go up there for a one-on-one when I am depressed, then I ask him why I feel like this? Why am I having so much guilt? What can I do to get rid of these feelings? And that's where they come in. And they make sense when they say something to me, because I can relate to these guys. [Traditional – Northern Cree]

> If I was feeling down and out, I would tell him why I was feeling down and out. I just come to them for counselling, sort of if I am having problems... When you are in jail, you kind of have an image that you want to maintain. So if you are hurting inside, unless you have a real close friend that you can talk to, you don't want to talk... So I used to go to the Elder and talk to him... I know what I told him wouldn't go no further. [Bicultural – Saulteaux]

Confidentiality is crucial in building the relationship between Elder and offender. The fact that the Elders do not normally record any information about individuals, or share that information, is particularly valued. Inmates are often very concerned that any disclosure they make will become part of their official file and possibly be used against them. As a result, they tend to hold back in their treatment programs. But with the Elders, there is no need to hold anything back.

> The Elder don't write down anything. These staff members write down everything you do... you go to the washroom, and they want to know about it. They give us this chart. You got to write down when we have a bowel movement and stuff like that. It's all crap to me... Like, for example, how long did I drink or use drugs. I just told them a little bit of each area, where I figured it would be good enough for them to take back to the office. Because I know that they take everything back there and write everything down. So I just tell them a little bit here and there, what they want to hear, just enough to get by these people. Talking to the Elder, I would tell him everything. But I don't trust these people [staff] because when they find out something,

then they push something else onto you, saying your problem areas are here and there's something else wrong with you. [Euro-Canadian – Cree-Metis]

Like they have all these psychologists and psychiatrists and programs and stuff like that. I only open in degrees. But with the Elders, it's like I can open right up. And even when I'm holding something back, I know they're looking right through me... It's important that they see the real me, instead of somebody, an image, that I'm trying to project. [Bicultural – Plains Cree]

Talking to the staff here, you are being judged. Talking to an Elder, you are not being judged, but you are being counselled. There's feeling, there's compassion ... It is that they [staff] judge what you do, everything you do, and it kind of makes a person scared to open up because what they say will be all written down. Whereas, when you talk to an Elder, it is all confidentiality and what's said is going to stay in that room. [Euro-Canadian – Metis]

Aboriginal and non-Aboriginal approaches to treatment often differ, as we have seen. Take, for example, the philosophy of many Elders that what is in the past is past, and that an individual should start today in his rehabilitation and look to the future. Those men who listen to the Elders are told not to dwell on their offences, not to dissect them or to try to understand why they did what they did. As we saw earlier in this book, Elders rarely inquire as to the nature of an individual's offence. This appears to stand in direct contradiction to the correctional philosophy of remorse, which demands that rehabilitation involve a thorough reassessment of the past, especially the criminal behaviour. In my research I discovered just how effective this approach is: though I never inquired about an individual's background, most men had been so conditioned to talk about it that they offered very detailed personal histories. One individual explained how the clash of treatment philosophies had seriously compromised his experience with the justice system:

I also took a life and I regret that. When you take a life, up north, they're very forgiving. Before I came up to the courts, my people and the people that I had injured had a meeting and they talked and they forgave one another for the healing. The

Elders, I told them exactly what had happened. They took a message back and then I was forgiven, so they expected me back, but the court system is very different. They take you to a penitentiary... I made them [Elders] look like liars because I didn't respect or accept their forgiveness for me to come back into the community, and I've never been able to get back. It made them look bad. The healing hasn't begun at all. After the Elders forgave me, I was told by them never to talk about this crime again. It's over and done with and there's nothing you can do about it. Look to the future. So I said okay. I came to court, was convicted. And then I came into correctional services and they wanted to talk about the crime. But in my mind, I was told by the Elders to not talk about it anymore, because you'd be insulting the spirits and delaying all kinds of things. Delaying your healing too if you talk about it. So I never talked about my crime to the psychologist, because I wanted to respect what the Elders had said. And I was told that I refused to face my crime and I'm in denial and everything else. Unremorseful. I was deeply hurt by those comments, but I wouldn't talk until just last year. I finally put something down on paper to explain what happened. I always thought at the time I wrote out on the piece of paper, the courts, if they wanted something out of me, they should have went and gone to an Elder to give them permission so I could talk about it. But they didn't do that. They go and accuse me of hiding behind my Elders. [Bicultural – Northern Cree]

This individual's perspective notwithstanding, the contradiction in this aspect of treatment philosophy may be less than it seems. While it is true that the Elders do not dwell on the past, remorse is very much a part of the spiritual tradition. For instance, the men are told that they should continue to pray for those they have harmed, and to seek the forgiveness of the Creator. But this form of remorse is expressed privately, often within the sweat lodge, or quietly through prayer. It is not done publicly and for the official record as with other prison programs. The offender is not expected to proclaim his remorse, although this may happen within the lodge or in the sacred circle. It remains primarily a private act, and therefore an act that is not recognized by the correctional system.

Many men found the Elders to be helpful in coping with the various stresses of prison life. This individual was ultimately able to make a commitment to undertake treatment at an RPC after consulting an Elder:

He has given me strength and he gives me encouragement to go day-by-day on my problems. And being in a maximum security jail, he said that I was a very young guy and he gave me strength with words like wisdom, to be strong, and it reminded me lots like my grandfather. How he taught my uncles. And what I picked up off him [Elder]. And I started using those memories, and you know everything was going okay. And I wanted to open up, so I started seeing a psychologist over there. I told her about this place [RPC], and we talked a few times, and one day I got called up to come down here and I took it. [Bicultural – Northern Cree]

Elders are also involved in crisis intervention within institutions. Episodes of acute anger or depression, and suicidal intentions, often require direct, immediate intervention.

Spirituality has given me strength, a will to go on living. I was going to kill myself last year. I wrote out everything, a suicide note, letters to my mom. When I was writing, an Elder came to my door, opened the curtain, and he was standing there with my feather. That feather saved my life. I've had that feather for eight years. [Bicultural – Plains Cree]

Through their teachings, the Elders are also able to diffuse some of the racial tensions that permeate the institutions. With such a large proportion of Aboriginal inmates, tensions between Aboriginal and non-Aboriginal inmates are common. And some Aboriginal men are occasionally racially victimized by other Aboriginal men. The Elders offer their services to all inmates, and this is made clear whenever tensions arise. As one Elder was fond of saying in the sweat lodge, when the door is closed and everyone is plunged into absolute darkness, there is no colour.

An Elder sets the mood of an institution. He sets the mood, he sets the pace of an institution because whether they follow the traditional ways of life, people respect an Elder. They will show him respect. There are very, very few that I have run across who disrespect an Elder. And I have known wardens to consult an Elder. I have known deputy wardens to consult an Elder. I have known your normal floor key-turning guard to ask advice of an Elder and show him respect by giving him tobacco. Because they see the good work of what an Elder does or a spiritual advisor does in a prison system. It is for the benefit of the entire prison, not just the Aboriginal population. There are less instances of violence and yet anyone can benefit. And there is no colour limit as to who can attend a sweat lodge, or a pipe ceremony or a sweetgrass ceremony or a sharing circle or sit at the drum. There are no colour limits. We are human, therefore, anyone is entitled to do that. There are no colour barriers and that is good because those teachings are for the benefit for all, not just for one race or one colour and not just for one type of person but for all people. It is a universal, holistic way of viewing, learning, and that is what makes it so vital to an institutional setting. [Bicultural – Plains Cree]

Elders, as noted previously, are particularly useful in helping those who are experiencing problems related to self-identity. The Elders teach the inmates to have pride in their Aboriginal heritage, even if they are of mixed ancestry, and reintroduce them to some elements of Aboriginal culture that can foster this pride. Generally, when they do this, they do not denigrate non-Aboriginal people or cultures, but instead accentuate the positive within the Aboriginal cultural framework. However, many Elders will place the issue of identity firmly within the historic context of oppression and assimilation. One Metis inmate explained in detail his identity problem and how the Elder helped him:

I see myself in the middle of both cultures because I believe the Bible to be the word of God. I always feel that I am an Indian inside a White man's body, and that's more or less how I feel… I've learned a lot about the Natives' history and my family's history by learning about the history of what has happened in the past and the way it is now. And it has really helped me to understand where I came from. And the things that I have learned about the Native spirituality and the cultures has helped me. I talked to the Elder and Native liaison guy in here once about having an identity crisis. Being a White Indian, I guess, is kind of hard. And I just come and talked to him about that. I just more or less told him my life story. He said that I have to go back into my history and see where I come from in order for me to see where I am going. Once I know my history and come to understand it, then I will be able to start healing from there. It has really helped me a lot to deal with my identity crisis, it has really helped me a lot to be more comfortable with who I am. [Bicultural – Metis]

An Ojibwa offender with little knowledge of his culture also found the Elders to be particularly helpful in establishing pride in his Aboriginality:

> But now I can hold my head up and be proud to pass on the knowledge that I've gained from the Elder to someone that wants to know... Like today, I'm proud of who I am. I know I'm a Native and that's something that will never change. It's something that the Creator gave me and it's meant to be. [Euro-Canadian – Ojibwa]

Many Aboriginal offenders, especially the more traditional ones, believe strongly in the power of dreams and visions, but dreams usually require interpretation. Other than acknowledging that they experience these phenomena, most men were reluctant to divulge specific details. Elders are usually sought out to help in understanding what meaning, if any, should be attached to dreams and visions.

> But sometime I don't like having those dreams, having bad dreams like that. Like, see, when I have a dream, I like to tell the Elder about it, because the Elder knows what to do... [after one dream] I told him about my dream and I told him I believe in my dreams. I respect them and then I'm scared, I told him. And he told me [what to do about them]. [Traditional – Ojibwa]

> My son passed away. Recently I talked to him [Elder]. And in these dreams I've been having, he's alive. And when I wake up reality would kick in and I'd feel bad. I was having them every night, so I went to talk to him. [Bicultural – Plains Cree]

> See, I'm not a pipe carrier... I just take care of the bundle for the whole group. Sometimes when I have that bundle, there's strange things, you know, happening. I feel like there's somebody else in my room sometimes. And I talked to the Elder. "When you have that thing in your room, you have to expect things like that, 'cause you've got a powerful bundle there and the pipe itself is powerful. You have to expect things like that," he says. "Things that you can't explain." And sometimes I feel there's somebody in my room, sometimes, and I'm scared. [Traditional – Ojibwa]

Some also expressed a belief in "bad medicine," the ability of individuals to cause harm, illness or misfortune to befall other individuals through spiritual means. In the survey, some 64% of the men indicated their belief in this aspect of spirituality. Not surprisingly, those who demonstrated a belief in bad medicine tended to be more traditional in their cultural orientation. Some men intimated that bad medicine was implicated in their problems, However, to discuss bad medicine openly is seen by many to be an invitation for something bad to happen, and therefore the research uncovered specifics for only a few men. Instances, and fears, of bad medicine can only be handled in a culturally appropriate manner, and the Elders and medicine people are the ones capable of dealing with these problems.

> I was real bad. I was seeing things... I get the feeling when I read a book, somebody is thinking really hard about me to destroy what I am doing. They do a good job of it. [Traditional – Saulteaux]

> I would like to find out if the guy I killed used love medicine on my wife. Because she goes and sleeps beside him at his grave... I feel bad that I did that thing, but maybe I'd feel better if I knew. An old man came to see me and said that someone had used medicine on me to kill that guy. [Traditional – Northern Cree]

Some traditional men, fearful of bad medicine, refused to become involved in ceremonies with the Elders, whom they believed had the potential to do harm as well as good.

> They talk about bad medicine a lot back home. When something happens, people know when you want to put it on somebody. He dies. That kind of scared me. So I don't want to really get involved. [Traditional – Ojibwa]

Other men presented more vague problems related to spirituality, such as this individual:

> I was having nightmares. They've been going on since I was a kid. I brought it up and the shrinks talked to me and everything. It's like somebody's in my room at night, like something evil. 'Til I started using sweetgrass. And it just seemed to stop. I started using the sweetgrass... you're supposed to do the four

corners of your room to take away evil spirits or keep them away and I started using it and it stopped. It's really amazing. I've never had those feelings that somebody was watching me in my room and some other stuff that was happening. It just seemed to go away. I have strong beliefs and it has got to have something to do with the sweetgrass or maybe my anxiety level went down, I'm not sure, but there's something in it. I mean, it's working. Well, I've been getting more sleep. I'm more relaxed because I had this feeling that somebody was tapping me and saying things in my ears when I was sleeping. It was really disturbing me, you know. It was pretty scary. [Euro-Canadian – Cree-Metis]

Having visions, hearing voices, experiencing disturbing dreams: all are phenomena that psychiatrists might categorize as pathological, and individuals who experience them as psychotic or schizophrenic. Clearly, these phenomena can be understood and treated within the context of Aboriginal spiritual and healing traditions.

There are many men who have come to understand the symbols inherent in Aboriginal spirituality and are healing themselves. It is an intense, profoundly personal process that is often hard to articulate to others. The spiritual path is demanding, and prison is a difficult place to learn and live the Aboriginal way. It should not be surprising, then, that not all Aboriginal men are equally touched by Aboriginal spirituality or understand and accept the symbols. We can learn a great deal about the efficacy of this form of symbolic healing by examining both the successes and the problems. It is to this latter issue that I now turn.

When I went to my first sweat, I straightened out for about three years. And then I started getting high and stuff like that again. That is when I quit going to sweats.

— ABORIGINAL INMATE

7
Obstacles and Detours

Not all Aboriginal offenders become involved in Aboriginal spirituality while in prison. Some avoid it altogether, while others become cautiously involved only in certain aspects. It is essential to our understanding of Aboriginal spirituality as a form of therapy that we examine the dynamics of non-involvement, partial involvement, and the critical perspectives offered by the men themselves.

Non-involvement and Critical Perspectives

Not everyone accepts Elders, sweat lodge ceremonies, and the other aspects of spirituality in prison. Not everyone engages the Elders in the manner necessary to establish the cultural base essential for symbolic healing to occur. Symbolic healing requires that the patient and healer agree to enter into the spiritual and therapeutic encounter, but there are a variety of reasons why this does not happen.

Occasional complaints about Elders can be heard. These complaints mirror those that are often heard on the outside. The central issue concerns the legitimacy of a particular Elder. Are they "real" Elders? Do they have the support of their community? A few men had serious difficulties accepting Elders who had criminal pasts, or who once had alcohol problems. Others were critical if an Elder lacked certain types of spiritual knowledge, or if they did not speak an Aboriginal language. The issue of remuneration was also raised by some men, who felt that the contractual approach tainted the Elders and what they represented. These concerns were not widespread, however, and often demonstrated a lack of understanding of Aboriginal spirituality and the constraints of the correctional setting.

A few offenders questioned the qualifications of the Elders they saw in prisons. This individual, for instance, was concerned about the eclectic approach of some Elders he had encountered:

> Some of the Elders are pretty good. Not all are level. Some of them are just a bit off. Like they've got things kind of scattered about, and they give me a piece of this, a piece of that... They give you one thing from one [culture] area, then they go to a totally different area and give you another thing. [Traditional – Slavey]

Another inmate was concerned that they had little input into the process of selecting Elders:

> We have no say, the Indian people have no say in who is going to come here and administer to our spiritual needs. They are having contract negotiations [to hire a new Elder] and we don't even know who is vying for the contract. We don't know anything. Sometimes I just feel like telling them, "Okay, fine, then you go to it yourself. You are going to bring in some hypocrites probably." [Bicultural – Plains Cree]

He continued by criticizing the whole concept of paying Elders:

> The Elders charge you now to do things, and they never did that before. That is one of the big things, putting value on things, putting price tags on things, putting dollar values on things.

Another inmate noted the inherent contradiction in correctional approaches to Aboriginal spirituality, discussed in the previous chapter, in which the least traditional people seem to have an edge in the hiring process:

> But there's other Elders that are really phony, super duper phony, so we just humour them. The phony Elders, they seem to have more say... They're listened to [by correctional staff] because they want to talk more, because they think the European way. And the ones that are really helping us, they never get any place. They're not hired by the agencies around here. [Bicultural – Northern Cree]

Individuals who had led lives of alcohol and crime could not be "real" Elders in the eyes of a few inmates. Some rejected the qualifications or validity of certain Elders. The following individual offered a wide-ranging critique of some Elders he had encountered:

> There's only about three Elders that I know that have come in that are recognized in the community. The rest of them live in [the city] and they don't have any following of people that support them. How they become Elders in my eyes, I'm still flabbergasted. And then sometimes you find some of these Elders are divorced. They're supposed to relinquish their Eldership if they've divorced or if their children are doing all kinds of things. Most of the Elders that come into the system also follow the clock. They come to work at nine o'clock and leave at four o'clock. European Elders. And they collect a pay cheque. They're selling their knowledge that came to them for free. I have a hard time accepting that. Some Elders [say] "Oh, you're too dangerous, I don't want to talk to you." An Elder is supposed to be able to stick with you no matter what you tell them. As long as that Elder has obtained his status in the way their community recognizes them, as long as they have a people. That's the main thing that I look at. As long as they have a people. And then you can ask them as to what areas they work with, they'll tell you. Some Elders would say, "Oh, we can talk about anything and everything." Oh, all around Elders, eh? Those ones I don't talk to either, because each one is skilled in one area, so I have a hard time with those ones. The ones with the community are the ones that I really appreciate. They have their honours all intact. Like I said, you meet a lot of Elders nowadays that are not legit. [Bicultural – Northern Cree]

These critiques highlight several misconceptions about Elders and the limitations of work within prisons. For instance, those men who express a concern over the fact that Elders are paid for their services do not realize that Elders and healers were always remunerated, in one form or another. Furthermore, "knowledge" was often paid for by novice Elders and healers, perhaps through service or apprenticeship to more established mentors. In the contemporary era, Elders who take on full-time responsibilities within a prison obviously need a source of income, and the inmates are in no position themselves to offer gifts in the traditional way as a form of payment. Individuals such as the one quoted above seem to feel that some Elders who work in prisons are somehow tainted because of their troubled past. However, the fact is that few Elders are willing to work in prisons. Some refuse because of perceptions that it is a frightening place, because it is not sacred enough, or even because they harbour negative stereotypical views of inmates as lost causes, much as the regular population does. Those Elders who were once inmates themselves or who had other brushes with the justice system are acutely aware of the type of healing opportunities that are needed in prison. These Elders are exceptional individuals.

Some men believed that their problems were too severe for an Elder to be of assistance or that mainstream correctional programming was more appropriate. Such individuals were expressing a belief in the limitations of Aboriginal spirituality as a form of therapy.

> But I think for the type of problems I had, I needed serious professional help. Like I'm sure an Elder would help a lot, but to really help me, I think I need serious, professional medical psychologists help. [Bicultural – Metis]

Other men were simply not ready to accept the Aboriginal way or else still believed that they could work out their problems on their own, without assistance of Elders or other counsellors.

> I was sort of shaking it rough. I didn't know where I'm at and why I did all these things I shouldn't be doing. That's why I went to talk to the Elder, and he asked me to go to the sweat, and I agreed but I didn't show up again until today. I didn't want to blow my whole day in the sweat. I understand my problems so I just gave up without letting anybody know. I don't want to go back to the sweats. I wouldn't go back to talk to the Elder. I can talk to them to be nice, but I'll never talk about a problem. I'm getting rid of the problem right now. I'm working on it. [Traditional – Plains Cree]

> You know, I just spent too much time drinking to get involved, and when I wasn't drinking I was too busy trying to straighten out my life. I didn't have time for neither church or Native traditions... I'm trying to cope with what is going on in my head. That is tough enough. I don't need to go to [Aboriginal] Brotherhood and get another set of moral codes, if you will. That moment will come in time once I get my head straightened out here. [Traditional – Ojibwa]

Sweat lodge ceremonies are taken very seriously by most offenders, yet some refuse to participate despite their belief in them. For these men, to sweat within the prison environment would be sacrilegious. Clearly these individuals do not completely share in the symbolic world that the prison Elders are trying to construct, one that allows for spiritual activities within the prison walls.

> Well, I could participate in this thing [sweats] but to me I don't find it's being in the positive thing. And in a place like this there's not too much positive thinking. There is always a negative here and there. If you've got everybody thinking in the positive, then it is good to go into it. But if you get a negative here and there and you go into a sweat lodge and somebody gets scared, it is a sign of negative, being negative. [Traditional – Slavey]

> It's not sacred ground. It's behind a fence. It's not freedom. Guards who walk on the grounds don't offer tobacco to show respect for the grounds or rocks or anything. [Euro-Canadian – Saulteaux]

Others felt the need to learn more about Aboriginal spirituality and sweat lodge ceremonies before they participated.

Some men simply did not believe in sweats, or else were fearful of them. For the uninitiated, the darkness, cramped quarters, and intense heat can be very frightening. These individuals tended to be bicultural or Euro-Canadian in their cultural orientations, and they rejected the world view and transactional symbols of Aboriginal spirituality. In some instances these individuals were active followers of fundamentalist Christian churches. The following individuals clearly failed to comprehend or accept the symbolism inherent in the sweat:

> I know that you get really hot in there, and that is why I get chicken. Don't know whether I can stand the heat. Like I say to

myself I can, right. I got a low self-esteem of myself, and that is what stops me from going. [Bicultural – Cree/Metis]

But I don't like doing his sweats, they are too intense. It seems stupid in a way… You get burned really badly, and I don't care how much you pray or anything, it's not going to stop you from getting burned… I think it is kind of, well to put it bluntly, retarded. To go and sit in a sweat house. I would rather go and sit some place comfortable in a sauna and sweat just as much rather than going in a small place with a bunch of Indians singing songs and praying, you know, "Oh great-grandfather." Just sounds kind of phony, and getting my ass burned off and my lungs burned. It just kind of seems silly, so I just quit. [Euro-Canadian – Cultural heritage anonymous]

Well, I could go to a sweat if I wanted to, but there are things that they say that I can't agree with. Like when they say that their prayers are carried to the Creator through the smoke, and I don't believe that. I heard that they believe that woman was created first, and I can't believe that because the Bible says differently. [Bicultural – Metis]

Some individuals who did not believe in sweats nevertheless expressed a belief in spirituality by noting the possible consequences awaiting the non-believer who participates.

If you don't believe in it, why play with it? It's a very serious thing to play with. If I go [to sweat] and don't believe it, then I could hurt myself. [Traditional – Northern Cree]

Spiritual Violations and Unethical Conduct

Aboriginal spirituality defines and prescribes a strict ethical code of behaviour, yet evidently some degree of unethical behaviour regarding spirituality occurs. This should not come as a surprise. These are, after all, prison inmates. Many of them are experiencing alcohol or substance abuse problems and have experienced the more tragic aspects of life. Furthermore, the Elders do not exclude individuals who, in their view, are not as serious as others. What is surprising, then, is that there are so few violations. Occasionally, an inmate is caught burning sweetgrass or sage to mask the smell of marijuana or hashish. A few individuals have been known to enter the sweat lodge while on drugs. Such violations invite their own form of sanction. One inmate related the following story:

> But those sweats that I attended over there, some of them were pretty powerful. Like you wouldn't even believe what goes through there. This is how powerful it is. At one time we had an inmate in there and he gave the Elder a bale of tobacco to pray for him inside the sweat so we all went in there and he told this certain person to lie down. Like this guy was taking drugs, smoking hash or shooting up. And all of a sudden it was dark in there and you couldn't see nothing. The next thing I know he [the Elder] started chanting these words, started talking in Cree and singing in Cree to the grandfathers to get this thing out of this person. And the way he said it, I could tell it was working because the guy was on the ground there inside the sweat and it's hot in there and dark. And he [the Elder] starts rattling, starts moving this rattler around, chanting these words and using the feather, and all of a sudden this guy, he started to sound like he was puking, and you could just feel it, you could feel everything in there. I guess the grandfathers were in there and just like the Elder said, you could feel it. You can feel them in there. The Elder told this guy to get up after that and he started chanting these words again and this guy started puking right inside the sweat. And I knew right there and then that it was true, man, it is a powerful thing. You can't fool around with it. And then I guess it stopped for a while. He felt better and then all of a sudden he [the Elder] started singing a song in there and that guy started puking again. The Elder was yelling, yelling and saying "get out of there, you devil, get out of there," and that guy was puking again. Everybody just sat quiet, they never bothered saying anything, nobody would even breathe. And then finally it was over and then he sat in there with us and we all started praying for him. It was just a powerful thing to see. [Bicultural – Plains Cree]

A few individuals focused their criticisms on what they saw as the hypocritical attitudes of some participants. This individual suggested that the form of Aboriginal "culture" presented to inmates was more about politics and race than about spirituality. He argued,

It's a power control, power trip. I think it is a power trip for a lot of inmates. I didn't like that. I've never followed it before, and I have just seen different attitudes in people who did follow it. I didn't like that attitude... It was like they walk around with these red headbands on, the tough guy attitude. [Bicultural – Saulteaux]

These individuals, perceiving hypocrisy, refused to participate in Aboriginal spiritual programming even while accepting the symbolism:

I don't use this religion thing to get out of here, because I don't believe in it. It would be disrespectful for me to use it to get out, so I don't even try. [Bicultural – Ojibwa]

I don't feel comfortable to do this in prison. The way I look at it, most people take these programs to help them get out of prison, and I don't feel comfortable going to a sweat with people who don't understand what it's there for. [Bicultural – Saulteaux]

A few men were so disturbed by what they considered to be hypocritical and unethical behaviour that they refused to participate in Aboriginal ceremonies. They complained about some men who appeared devout around the Elder and the sweat lodge, but who reverted to prison behaviour, such as swearing, fighting, and drug taking, once back on the ranges.

The majority of the people in prison that take these programs, they're not doing it for themselves. They are what we classify as "main street warriors"... When they are doing the program, great, they are totally into it. But when they come out of the program into the population area again, they get back into drugs, the homebrew, the [loan] sharking, beating up people. You see a guy getting into sweetgrass, the cedar, tobacco, the drum, the dancing, and he will go back into the system and he will go and have a toke, he will go beat some sex offender, he will go and beat anybody as long as he fits into the prison system. And then tomorrow he will go and do his sweats. You see two different people right there... I guess I can't blow it on them, but it is pretty well impossible to have two sets of attitudes in prison, and I don't want to be like that... The reality of the thing is nobody is what they are in prison. [Bicultural – Northern Cree]

Me personally, I believe that in Indian culture there is no room for drugs and alcohol. And it kind of bothers me that I see people get high and then they go to a sweat, and after they come from the sweat they get high again. I mean, that's hypocritical, phony, you know what I mean? [Bicultural – Saulteaux]

Even among the devout followers of the spiritual path, backsliding can occur. The pressures to use drugs and alcohol in prison are enormous. Yet, such use is fundamentally incompatible with a belief in the spiritual way. The result is that, occasionally, an individual makes a decision to remove himself from the path, avoiding the sweats and Elders, so that he may engage in drug and alcohol consumption without feeling guilty that he is committing a spiritual transgression. For these individuals, falling off the path is not necessarily failure, but more like a detour. It also serves as a profound indicator of just how important Aboriginal spirituality is becoming in their lives, even if they are not yet wholeheartedly committed.

If they say we're going to have a sweat or a pipe ceremony the next four days from now, I ain't going to touch the dope from this day until after the ceremony. [Traditional – Chipewyan]

Well, I was at a [social event] and I guess it would have been my fault. Nobody forced it down. A guy came over and said, "do you want some pills?" And I said, "okay." He gave me a few pills and I figured I would put them in my pocket and I would give them to somebody else. Maybe I wanted to take them, I don't know. Maybe subconsciously I wanted to eat them. And then he said, "take them," and I said "yeah." And I ate them and I got high that day. And I thought, fuck, have I been missing this all this time. So I was kind of fucked up for quite awhile. And after I straightened up, I talked to a psychologist, and I was pretty honest with that psychologist. And I told him that I got high, and that I was choked at myself for getting high and I wanted to see the Elder. I seen the Elder and all the Elder basically told me was that we are all human, we are all going to stumble and fall. Not to feel bad about falling off the Red Road. So that kind of comforted me a bit, and I could justify it in my head. And I said, well I'll get high for a year, and after that... I will get back to my Native culture and take it from there. [Bicultural – Saulteaux]

> For me, like I didn't go into sweat because I was smoking dope all the time. I wasn't being honest, you know... I respected it. Like I only stood outside. If I went into the sweat and I would come back out and I would be clean, but a couple of days later I would have done what I was doing before, smoking up and all that. That's still disrespectful. [Bicultural – Northern Cree]

Occasionally inmates are prescribed various medications while in prison. This compromises the belief of the Elders that all men must be free of drugs before they can participate in spiritual ceremonies. Most Elders are willing to allow medicated men to participate, however, if removing them from their medication is not acceptable to staff or if such action might result in inappropriate behaviour that could threaten the safety of those involved in the ceremonies. In this case it is not seen as unethical to engage in spiritual activities while on prescription or mood-altering medication (especially if the inmate is forced or influenced by staff to take it). Nevertheless, some men take it upon themselves to stop using their medication so that they can participate in the culturally prescribed manner.

> Cleaning. It [sweats] cleans me, gives me peace. It helps me to understand. Like they pump me full of pills here and all that, and they get really mad when I don't go in there [sweat lodge] on medication. I fast. It just cleans my whole body. It spiritually lifts me. [Bicultural – Metis]

The existence of sex offenders in prison represents an ideological problem for Aboriginal spirituality, founded as it is on the principles of tolerance, respect, and the equality of all human beings. The negative attitudes of many inmates towards sex offenders, and sex offenders' own apprehensions, demonstrate clearly that Aboriginal spirituality is simply not a panacea for escaping all the prejudices of society as a whole. It too must come to grips with its own contradictions. Many Elders work hard at reconciling the principles of Aboriginal spirituality with the repugnance some men have for sex offenders, with varying degrees of success. They try to promote a view that all the inmates are equally human in the eyes of the Creator, and an individual's crime is not important. I have heard some Elders suggest that sex offenders are even more troubled than other inmates, therefore needing special care and attention from the Elders and support from the other Aboriginal participants. This attitude is in direct conflict with prison culture, in which sex offenders are ranked at the bottom of a hierarchy of offences. Sex offenders often hide their offences to avoid persecution; beatings are common. This individual expressed his view that Aboriginal men, more so than others, should never engage in sexually deviant behaviour:

> When I see an Indian guy, like a rapo [rapist], it bugs me. A White guy doesn't bother me at all. But when I see an Indian guy, it bugs me. Because they are Indian people, and that's not part of our culture to go and hurt women. And then they try to get into their culture [through spirituality]. That bugs me. Why didn't they think of that before they started going out raping women? [Bicultural – Saulteaux]

There are two problems. The first is that some men refuse to participate in ceremonies if sex offenders are also participating. One such individual stated emphatically:

> If they can't control their urges, they are weak. Then I figure they will weaken my spirit, you know? [Bicultural – Saulteaux]

The second problem is that some sex offenders so fear for their safety that they choose not to participate:

> In my case, I'm a sex offender. I can't let my guard down even for a minute. Even a traditionalist would go out of his way to punch your head out if there is a sex offender, because the prison code says he has to. And everyone abides by the prison system first, then themselves last. That's just the way it is. [Traditional – Ojibwa]

Security is always a primary concern in correctional institutions. There is no aspect of prison life that is not scrutinized by some inmates looking for opportunities to escape. Although rare, there have been a few serious breaches of security related to Aboriginal spiritual activities. One Elder told me a story of an incident that occurred when he was in the sweat lodge with some inmates; at the end of the round when they called for the doorman to open the lodge, nothing happened. The men began to yell because of the intense pain, and eventually one got the door open from the inside. By this time, the doorman had already scaled the first perimeter fence and was part way up the second! That was as far as he got. He fell and broke his leg, an outcome that continues to be seen as a form of spiritual retribution for his act. In another incident, a couple of inmates actually tied up an Elder in the sweat lodge and made a brief escape. Gross violations such as these attract spiritual punishment; many inmates shake their heads in disbelief when these stories are shared, dumbfounded by the stupidity of the offending inmates who would now certainly face spiritual repercussions.

The Elders themselves seem to accept inmate transgressions as inevitable; they realize that their clients are often extremely troubled and that the temptations and pressures within prison to use drugs or alcohol, or to escape, are strong. Nevertheless, in interviews the Elders expressed dismay whenever a particular offender was involved in an illegal or unspiritual act, especially if that individual had been working closely with the Elder and had been seen to be making progress. Inmate transgressions are not punished by the Elders, as this would be against their spiritual philosophy. Rather, the Elders pick up where they left off with the inmates, accept them back into the circle, and re-establish the therapeutic relationship.

Aboriginal Spirituality and Christianity

Christianity is by far the greatest factor in the men's decision not to become involved with Aboriginal spirituality. The mainstream Christian churches, such as the Anglican, United and Roman Catholic churches, have had a strong grip on Aboriginal communities for over a century. Some Aboriginal offenders, often traditional men who were raised in these communities, believe that Aboriginal spirituality is fundamentally opposed to Christianity. Even stronger views are held by those who have become "born again" Christians, usually while in prison. These are often individuals with less Aboriginal cultural upbringing. This inmate's views were typical of Christian attitudes among inmates:

> When I was raised with Christian beliefs, I was taught Native beliefs were heathen, so I never tried to understand it. [Bicultural – Metis]

And these attitudes continue to be expressed within prison. One inmate referred to the tension and conflict that exist between Aboriginal spirituality and Christianity:

At [one prison] there was some Christians that were saying that this is pagan stuff. They are Bible readers and they come there and read the Bible and things like that, and say, "how come you are going to that sweat? You should come here because this is better for you. This other stuff is pagan." [Bicultural – Metis]

Another man described his own anxieties which resulted from the existence of the two belief systems:

I am torn between the two now because I always prayed to God, but there is this other god, Mother Earth. Every day I look for some kind of boost to help me make it through the day, and I think of the God I was raised with... being Indian. And yet I have this problem being able to comprehend another spiritual being... 'cause I feel good praying to God, but this isn't supposed to be my God. It is supposed to be someone else's God... Now there is this other thing, and I don't know quite where I am supposed to be. But when I go to powwows and I hear the drumbeat, I feel something about that. Not just the beat, I feel something. I feel something pull me in this direction. I feel stronger. I feel better and cleaner, like more serene when I am at a powwow. When I go to church, I feel sort of shameful – it is just different. Like I said, I was taught the Anglican way. Yet I feel better when I go to pow wows and stuff. [Bicultural – Plains Cree]

Such conflict inevitably leads to a decision to make a choice between Christianity and Aboriginal spirituality:

Like I don't get involved in any Native programs... Because of some of the things which I don't believe in... Sweetgrass, I don't believe in that. I don't believe in what they call "praying to the grandfathers." I don't believe in that, and I have my own faith in what I believe in... Christianity, that is what I believe in. And I go to church but I don't participate in any Native culture. [Euro-Canadian – Cultural heritage unknown]

I can do this Native spirituality to a certain extent, but if the Native spirituality ever said "give up Jesus and start believing in the four directions and the great grandfather," I would say, "stick your great grandfather. I am going to stick with my Jesus." [Euro-Canadian – Cultural heritage anonymous]

Cultural Compatibility

A premise of this study is that one must be aware of the different cultural orientations of offenders and Elders. The spiritual traditions of Aboriginal peoples, both at the time of contact and today, are different. Most institutions have just one Elder, and at best two, who must work with Aboriginal inmates from a variety of cultural heritages. Inmates are not free to select the Elders they wish to work with; they are presented with whichever Elder is employed at that institution. It is inevitable that the therapeutic and spiritual relationship will cut across cultural boundaries. If the Elder comes from one cultural tradition, will his ways be alien to Aboriginal offenders from other cultural traditions and therefore be rejected? Whose form of spirituality is being communicated? Can symbolic healing ensue in such situations?

In general, most Aboriginal offenders were unperturbed by the cultural traditions underlying the spiritual programs they received. Very few men rejected an Elder because of cultural incompatibility. While some 60% stated that it was important to have an Elder from their own culture, over 90% agreed that an Elder from another culture could still be of help to them. Most of the Elders working in the institutions researched were from Plains cultural groups; however, the form of spirituality they followed and taught may well have been that of another culture, or more eclectic. For instance, a number of Elders who were interviewed had undergone some training in Lakota spirituality. It is easy to see how generic Plains beliefs have come to dominate in prison programs.

Surprisingly, those offenders with the firmest roots in an Aboriginal culture were largely unconcerned with the nature of the spirituality being offered; indeed, they too suggested that a sort of pan-Indianism exists, viewing all Aboriginal spiritual traditions as fundamentally the same, with only minor differences in procedures. However, it was also clear that the offenders have come to believe in a common spirituality as a result of their interaction with prison Elders. These Elders have been forced to enhance the common themes and symbols, and downplay the significance of differences, as a means of establishing the common world view necessary for healing to occur. For instance, outside of prison, the direction in which the sweat lodge faces, the colour of the prayer prints offered to the Creator, or even the number of rounds in the sweat ceremony, might be culture- or Elder-specific and very important. The possibility of spiritual sanction for doing something "wrong" might exist. But inside prison, the importance of these symbols is de-emphasized in deference to broader principles. The interaction between healer and patient, or Elder and inmate, becomes a search for the lowest common denominators linking their cultures and experiences so that the therapeutic encounter has some hope of success. Both the healer and the patient take on the responsibility of redefining the essential elements of their own cultures to arrive at a common base. According to one traditional inmate:

> I know we don't understand each other [in Aboriginal languages] but we sort of see that we have something in common. He's an Elder. He shows me how to pray. He teaches me about Native spirituality... We talked about that [cultural differences between Sioux and Cree] and it's [spirituality] about the same thing. A little different. Siouxs are Siouxs and Crees are Crees, and they do things a little different... but it's not something that I should be aware of because I like what I am doing with this Elder here. [Traditional – Northern Cree]

Another traditional man echoed these views:

> Elders, I guess I respect them because the Native people, they almost do the same thing. A little different, but almost the same everything... It doesn't matter, I guess, who the Elder is. [Traditional – Northern Ojibwa]

Some bicultural offenders also suggested that the cultural differences were unimportant:

> But to me our religion is all the same anyway. It doesn't really matter, you know, what tribe you're from. We still all believe in the same thing, that we're from different tribes but we're all the same. [Bicultural – Northern Ojibwa]

> No, that doesn't bother me because to me the original people of the northern continent was... the Aboriginal people, and spiritual beliefs or lifestyle was interrelated or similar in one way or another. So I have to learn from them, and I also have to learn from my own people. [Our] Elders that have known this type of spirituality have long passed, so the Elders from the brothers south of us, they tell us they could teach us, so we have to learn from them. [Bicultural – Chipewyan]

An inmate who had been adopted as an infant by a Euro-Canadian family, echoing the above views, suggested that as a "blank slate" in terms of Aboriginal culture, it was easy for him to accept various cultural traditions:

> If you are Mic Mac you got different ways to do it. If you are Blackfoot, you got another way to do it. But I think they come down to one principle. But maybe for me it was more easy because I don't know how my people do it. [Euro-Canadian – Cultural heritage anonymous]

Indeed, offenders like the one above, with no knowledge of their Aboriginal heritage, were least likely to be concerned about the cultural background of the Elders. Having little or no pre-prison knowledge of Aboriginal spirituality, they make no comparisons. These individuals are searching for their Aboriginal cultural roots and identity, and they are willing to allow the Elders to define a world view for them. They absorb everything they are taught, and question little.

> Like, sometime in my life I'm going to go back to that reserve, and I'll start learning the ways of the Blackfoot people. You know the Crees, the Chipewyans, the Blackfoot, I look at them all as one race anyhow, and one religion... I think all our beliefs are the same, it's just that we do things a little differently. [Euro-Canadian – Blackfoot]

> I had a very good partner... he's a Blackfoot. But even today, I don't look at cultures within our culture. I look at it as all one, you know. Being Native is Native. I don't care if you are Blackfoot, Sioux or whatever race. It is all Native. [Euro-Canadian – Cree-Saulteaux]

Even if the Elders spoke an unfamiliar Aboriginal tongue while praying, it was not generally a problem.[1]

> He used to pray in his language. He used to pray in Cree. I couldn't understand him but he used to tell me later on... I told him I couldn't understand Cree. I used to ask him how he was praying and he told me. [Bicultural – Chipewyan]

Yet there were some cases in which the fact that the Elder came from a different cultural background was of concern. This was particularly true for the traditional man quoted below, who clearly articulated the discord between cultures that prohibits symbolic healing:

> I want to talk to an Elder, but... I need an Elder that has been where I'm from, and knows something, so he wouldn't misunderstand what I am saying. I need an Elder from where I am from... I need an Elder that's from there, that understands the drinking, the behaviour, the negative, like why I am thinking negative... Cause we're [the Elder and him] from different grounds. He could say something and it could be from his, and not relate to mine. There's a negative in between. [Traditional – Chipewyan]

Another man, Euro-Canadian in orientation, expressed difficulties with one Elder's approach, contrasting it with what he had learned from another Elder:

> I didn't support what he [Elder] was doing. They were following practices that I didn't agree with. Others felt the same way, but out of respect didn't say anything. [Euro-Canadian – Metis]

This individual expressed the attitude of those who had fundamental disagreements with the way a particular Elder undertook ceremonies: out of respect for the Elder they said nothing, but tended to avoid participation.

One interesting and potentially problematic byproduct of the cultural education process that forms the foundation for symbolic healing is that a few Aboriginal offenders, including very traditional ones, have come to view their own cultures as somehow deficient because they lacked familiarity with certain key elements of the spirituality they were being taught in prison. As noted earlier, some offenders came from communities where sweats were no longer practised, where sweetgrass or sage were no longer burned, and where the concept of the pipe ceremony simply did not exist. They may nevertheless have lived a fairly traditional lifestyle, having been raised on the reserve or in the bush, spoken an Aboriginal language, and been involved in activities such as hunting and trapping. As such, they would no doubt have obtained a form of spiritual and cultural knowledge related to land and reserve activities. But this process of education was informal, in contrast to the more formal instruction they experienced in prison. As an example of this, consider the words of one offender, a traditional man from a northern Ojibwa reserve:

> When I was brought up... I didn't even know what Native culture was... I didn't understand it... Nobody even told me about it, you know. Maybe if I was brought up in a cultural way, if I understand what life is all about... maybe I would have understood the meaning of Indian religion. Because kids that are brought up in their culture, Native culture, they follow it. [Traditional – Northern Ojibwa]

This individual began to view himself as a-cultural once in prison, and the contradiction between the cultural life he had lived and his perceptions of it is striking. The following offender, a traditional Cree man from northern Alberta, had spent most of his life in the bush or on his reserve. Yet his belief that his upbringing was culturally inadequate is clear:

> I never really learned about nothing deep down Native, just that we were staying in the bush and surviving, and staying in the reserve and how it is. But I never really learned about nothing like the Elders and stuff like that... I never even heard of sweat lodges before I came to [prison]. Never seen one. I never seen pipe ceremonies. There was no pow wows where I came from. So I have seen all this stuff since I came to prison. [Traditional – Northern Cree]

Another offender, a traditional Slavey from the Northwest Territories with very little experience in a Euro-Canadian setting, described his a-cultural existence in even more dramatic terms:

> In that prison I got involved with my Native spirituality, got involved with sacred circles, Native sweat lodges and pipe ceremonies... There was something that was missing, knowing that I was a Native person and ... there was no culture in me. No cultural background grown up with... Where I come from in the Territories I never heard them do stuff like that. [Traditional – Slavey]

Much of the cultural "stuff" he described may *never* have existed among his Dene people!

Some of these individuals actually appeared to be developing identity problems because of their exposure to the Aboriginal spirituality programs in prison. Furthermore, these problems seem to have been an essential component of their own personal healing process as they embraced the spirituality and symbols of the Elders with whom they came into contact. Ness (1980:167-168) has argued that participation in religious healing rituals can have both positive and negative emotional effects and that "for some individuals, participation in non-medical healing activities may be emotionally and behaviourally disorganizing." The data presented here suggest that this occurs for a small number of offenders. The outcome was not always negative, however, and there were cases where individuals transcended cultural boundaries to become, in effect, competent and even respected members of other spiritual traditions.

Aboriginal spirituality within the prison walls is not without its problems and controversies. For a variety of cultural and religious reasons, and reasons unique to individuals, Aboriginal spirituality does not strike a chord with every Aboriginal offender. This is not surprising, of course, and it has never been suggested that it should be otherwise. The Aboriginal way is a difficult way to follow, in prison more so than anywhere else. The ambiguities and contradictions found within society are often exaggerated within prison and play a profound role in shaping individual behaviour and decision-making. Added to this is the pervasiveness of the so-called "con code," a blueprint for living one's life within prison which promotes values and behaviours that are often at odds with those of Aboriginal spirituality. Given these facts, it is perhaps more surprising that so many Aboriginal men manage to follow the spiritual path as they work to heal themselves. What follows in the next chapter are the stories of four such individuals.

NOTE

1   English is usually the language of instruction in group settings. An Aboriginal language may be used when Elders are involved in individual counselling.

I feel that if I do get out, that if I follow the right road, I can survive out there. I can make it out there. If I follow the right life, I can make it no matter what.

— ABORIGINAL INMATE

8
Case Studies in Spirituality and Healing

The case study method is a common, effective presentation tool in anthropology, psychiatry, and medicine. It provides detailed qualitative data which reintroduce the human dimension into social inquiry by providing a more focused examination of the issues as they are experienced by individuals. As we have seen so far in this book, the manner in which Elders and offenders interact and learn about spirituality, and hence define the therapeutic encounter, is complex. In this chapter, I wish to provide four case studies that highlight these complexities while reinforcing the main themes of this study: oppression, trauma and issues of identity; personal and spiritual transformation; the importance of culturally appropriate assessment and treatment; the need to accept experiential reality as a dimension of human experience; and the manner in which Aboriginal spirituality complements other prison treatment programs.

Case One

This first case presents an excellent example of an individual whose behavioural change was most remarkable.

"Jack"[1] was an individual of mixed ancestry. His father was Aboriginal, his mother Euro-

Canadian, and he grew up mainly in the city. I first met him at a Native Brotherhood meeting. My first impression of Jack was that he was an intensely angry and suspicious man, spewing venom with every comment. He shouted angrily, denouncing everyone including the police, the judges, the prison staff, and finally me. He was particularly upset that I proposed to examine the case management files for those offenders I interviewed. In his view, the files contained nothing but lies concerning his background. He complained that once something was written in the files it was seen as "truth" and was never removed. A man's reputation, based on the documents in his file, followed him everywhere and conditioned prison officials' responses to him.

Jack's case management files generally supported my initial impression of him as an angry, bitter individual. When he was interviewed by me, he was in his early thirties and was doing a long sentence for a violent offence. He had committed that offence just one day after release from a previous sentence. His criminal convictions began at age 16, and he had at least seven convictions between the ages of 16 and 21. His most serious offences on the street involved armed robbery, hostage takings, and gun battles with police. He had been in some form of institutional care since the age of twelve.

His prison record documented many incidents of violence, escape, and other prison infractions. He had spent more than two years "in the hole" (segregation) and in the "special handling unit" (SHU), a secure unit designed to handle the most dangerous offenders and available only in some prisons. According to one report in his file, "up to approximately one year ago, his behaviour in prison was disruptive, rebellious, and often a threat to institutional security." As a result, he had served time in most prisons capable of handling dangerous offenders. He let it be well known that he hated anyone in authority, especially prison guards, and believed that both the guards and other inmates were constantly out to get him. One report stated that "he showed no signs of major mental illness, although he is very sensitive to real or imagined slights." Another documented that "[t]he patient had deteriorated into a paranoid agitated state and had developed some delusions concerning a couple of other inmates... There was also considerable mood disturbance and he had in fact made a significant suicidal gesture by cutting quite deeply into his arm."

An earlier attempt at obtaining treatment at one RPC had ended in failure after only three weeks; he requested to be transferred back to his parent institution "because the open discussion of personal problems and the atmosphere of the unit were making him very anxious." While waiting for the transfer, Jack asked to be secluded in the most secure unit in the institution: "He has stated that he cannot handle being around other patients and staff in an open environment."

In a psychiatric interview, "[h]e stated that he hated people and the system had made him avoid them, especially women and now he was forced by the same system to be in this atmosphere wherein he had to deal with a lot of women. His hatred for people is very apparent... He has poor control of his temper, his frustration tolerance is low and often has the urge to take it out on other inmates." Jack was diagnosed as having a "personality disorder," including a substance abuse problem, "difficulty coping with stress resulting in aggressive behaviour, and difficulty interacting with authority." Indeed, many prison staff were fearful of him.

Although Jack had originally rejected my request for an interview (and did so quite vehemently), eight months later he was more than willing to sit and, in his own words, "do the best I can." This quite remarkable turnaround will be discussed shortly, but first I would like to elaborate more on his past from information obtained in that interview.

Jack's father had grown up on a reserve, but Jack himself had spent relatively little time there as a child. His formative years were spent in the city, and he never learned his Aboriginal language. He had very little cultural knowledge of his people.

Evidently his childhood was quite disturbing, filled with alcohol and violence:

> My dad was an alcoholic and my mom used to take lots of beatings, lots of screams, stuff like that. And I saw my father rape one of my sisters. And then I said, "fuck that shit," and I ran away from home.

His description of his prison experiences was considerably more graphic than what was recorded in his files:

> I find the time I spent in jail wasn't easy, either. I watched a few hostage takings, took part in a riot... had both guards tied. I spent six years in the SHU out of fourteen years... The rest I spent in normal population, but I was bad ass up there. They kicked me out of [one province]... they booted me out after a few years there... they transferred me back [to another prison]... got in a riot there. They made me spend two and a half years in the SHU over that. I come out of the SHU and [my home province]

didn't want me. So they sent me to [another province]. [There]
I did the same thing. I escaped... did lots of pipings [beatings],
stabbings... So I spent lots of time in seg[regation] and they just
booted me out... When I arrived at [one prison], they [guards]
tried to torture me, tried to hang me, smashed three of my ribs.
I got nineteen stitches in the back of my head. They really did
put a number on me. And all those friends that I had when I
first came in when I was sixteen, most of them today are dead.
The pigs killed them. So I don't know, I got a hatred, a hatred.
I just can't handle them around me.

Despite his pale complexion and his relatively weak links to his
Aboriginal heritage, he was subjected to racism and some taunting
as a child. His response was to fight, and he was ridiculed by his
father if he appeared to have lost any of these encounters. On two
different occasions, after witnessing his father rape his sister, he attempted to kill his father, but he was charged with assault only once.

The most pleasant memories of his childhood were the brief times
he spent on the reserve, where he was sometimes sent to live after
getting into trouble in the city. He stayed primarily with his aunt and
uncle, from whom he received a very cursory introduction into his
people's culture and spirituality. On the reserve he found a refuge
from the racism of the city.

By the time he entered prison as a young adult, and despite this
early exposure to an Aboriginal culture, he knew very little about
Aboriginal spirituality. Ultimately, he would experience a personal
and spiritual awakening. He explained his reasons for becoming involved in the prison's Aboriginal awareness and spirituality programs:

I saw some of my friends, they were there before me — they were
in the SHU and when I hit [the prison] I don't know, I saw a
change in those guys. They were fucking nuts like me before... I
couldn't understand how come they were changing like that. And
they used to tell me, "You try this, you listen, you see. You try
this and you see." So I put myself into it, and I believe it today.

It was in prison that Jack experienced his first sweat, and began to
learn more about Aboriginal culture. But his real awakening came
when he entered an RPC and began to work with the Elder there.

When I started to talk to that guy it was easy to relate to him.
He knew a few of my friends. That was our first conversation

there, about of a couple of people we knew. And then we talked about myself. And I was sitting in my cell one day and I said, "fuck, that's not my dad. That's what I would like to have fucking gone to my dad [for]." So to me he is a friend, he is a dad. He's everything, that guy. And he was the first person to come along and be willing to put everything on the line for me, so that means lots to me. He was the first person that came along, crossed my road and asked me if I wanted help, and was willing to give me a hand... And you know for me that means a lot, because I never had anybody come along and ask me those things before. I wish somebody did, but it never happened.

Then Jack added, thoughtfully and reflectively:

Now it's funny. I never feel that I want to beat anybody up. I never feel I want to escape. I never feel like taking hostages no more. I just want to be out with [the Elder] and learn about my people, and learn about me. Learn about me more.

This remarkable change in attitude was noticed by correctional staff. Reports in Jack's file stated:

Since being here, [he] has developed a relationship with the Native Elder. The Elder has offered him ongoing support in the community... On the unit, [his] participation in groups has been consistent. He has always been attentive, but his active participation is limited.

A great deal of [his] efforts at identification of self have been through the Native Brotherhood. He has worked closely with the Native Elder... In fact, they have bonded to the extent that [Jack's] plans for MS [mandatory supervision] release are to reside with the Native Elder.

RPC staff, in general, were quite surprised by the change in behaviour. By the time I interviewed Jack, he had been at the RPC almost a year, and the intense, angry man had given way to one who readily smiled and joked with the staff. It is not possible to say to what extent the work of the RPC staff, and prison therapists at other institutions, contributed to this remarkable change relative to the work of the Elder. A report in Jack's file stated that, in 1986, he had started therapy with a prison psychologist, signalling "the start of a change in his behaviour which continued throughout the eighteen months he was [there]." But there is no denying that the man who arrived at the RPC appeared to be as tense and angry as any person could be.

Jack places most of the responsibility for his transformation with the Elders he has worked with, and particularly one at RPC. However, other aspects of the RPC program have contributed as well. Jack states:

> A year ago, I wouldn't talk to anybody. I wouldn't talk about myself. I would fight all the time. At least once a day I would fight. I don't say that to try to look bad or nothing, but that's exactly the way I was. I was really hurt and I learned how to talk about that hurt. Talk about it. I spent lots of time with the Elder. Spent lots of time with those psychologists down in the psychologist's office here. Spent lots of time by myself, reading those handouts they gave to me.

According to Jack, the Elder was instrumental in helping him remain calm and deal with the stresses of prison life, stresses which contributed to his poor incarceration record:

> Usually lots of time [the Elder] used to come and I wasn't ready to go [to the sweats]. And I fought four times and I used to tell [the Elder], "forget the sweat," because I was so angry inside. [But] I would go in that sweat and I would pray hard and I would ask him for understanding and that did help me. No matter what anybody says, that did help me.

One particular incident seems to have been the turning point for Jack. Despite having been physically abused by his father, Jack was particularly troubled when news of his father's death reached him, followed by news that he would not be allowed to attend the funeral service. Indeed, he was so upset that the security staff became nervous that he might become violent. Once again, the Elder was there to assist.

> I asked [the Elder] for a special sweat, there. He made a special sweat. And it was for me and my father. And I was sitting down and I asked him for more understanding. I went through what basically I went through when I was a kid. I talked basically about all my life... the pain and the hurt. And he showed me how to pray, how to get a better understanding of myself. And since I did that, I do feel better, because when you grow up like

that, you just keep those things inside you. That's why you
become so bitter.

In a separate interview with the Elder involved, Jack's story was corroborated. The Elder explained that Jack broke down and cried in
the sweat as he related his story, particularly his difficult relationship
with his father. Because of his image in prison as a tough "con," this
was something he simply could not be seen doing. In the security of
the sweat lodge, alone with the Elder, his true pain came out. The
Elder saw this as a turning point.

Jack's relationship with the Elder was quite different from that he
had established with the nurses and other staff at RPC. He suggested
that there was a great deal he would not bring up in his counselling
sessions with the nurses, and he mocked them for always looking at
their watches to gauge session time. As Jack said, "[it's] hard to trust
when you see a person act this way." He had obtained some benefits
from the group therapy sessions, in his estimation, but his lack of
trust of the staff clearly inhibited his participation. In contrast, his
work with the Elder was built upon a foundation of trust. His respect
for the Elder stemmed, in part, from his respect for the knowledge
the Elder had gained over the course of his life, and he contrasted
this with the knowledge of the nurses:

> How can somebody who's twenty-four years old, twenty-five
> years old, sit down in front of you and talk to you about life
> when you're a lot older? I don't know. To me it's hard to
> understand. If somebody is able to talk to me about life,
> somebody is going to be older than me, somebody that has seen
> more than me... I can learn from that person. Somebody younger
> than me didn't even go through half what I've gone through.
> How can I learn from that person?

Jack was subsequently transferred to another prison to await his
statutory release date.[2] The Elder had invited Jack to work with him
as his helper, an offer that Jack received enthusiastically. He had been
in prison since the age of sixteen, and he stated emphatically, "I don't
want to fuck up the next thirty years." However, he also recognized
how seriously institutionalized he had become, and that he still required treatment in order to adjust to life on the outside.

> Actually, I seriously believe I've hurt a lot of people and I have
> to try to make up for it. More sweats to go through. More

suffering I have to give for the people that I made suffer all my life. I wish to help some other people like [the Elder]... I want to be working with some kids, try to give them understanding, talk with them. Because I remember when I was a kid, that was one of my dreams. To see somebody come along, sit down, kind of talk with me and tell me what's wrong. I never had that happen when I was a kid, and I know when I was a kid I was needing that. So maybe that is the way I will pay back... But I am not going to go [home] until I am strong. Until I can walk on my two legs without worry. That is the time I am going to go there.

In the end, Jack's release plans were changed, and he was unable to reside with the Elder. However, two years after his release, the Elder could report that he was still out of prison, and that they had been in contact several times over that period. The Elder's invitation to come and stay at his place remained open, but it is difficult for newly released offenders to obtain permission to travel outside their parole jurisdictions.

Case Two

Case Two presents an interesting clash of cultural understandings of normality, abnormality, illness, and treatment. On the one side, we have the clinical reality of the biomedical system determining a variety of psychopathologies and relevant treatments; on the other side, we have the experiential reality of the offender and Elders identifying problems and treatments which are culturally-based.

"Bill" was from a Plains Indian cultural group. He had spent the first five years of his life on the reserve. At age five, when his father was killed, he was placed in a series of foster homes, first on the reserve and then off. In the latter cases, his foster families were non-Aboriginal. Over time, he lost his ability to speak his language and became increasingly distanced from his Aboriginal culture. He was introduced to Christianity as a young man but once in prison was exposed to Aboriginal spirituality. This caused him a great deal of confusion and inner conflict since he saw the two as fundamentally opposed.

Bill was serving a relatively short sentence, less than four years, when I interviewed him. His criminal record showed primarily property offences, especially break and enters, thefts, and a few assaults. In prison, psychologists and psychiatrists began to diagnose various psychopathologies and prescribe courses of treatment. Early in his criminal career he had been described by a psychologist as having "deficits in ego functioning" and as being "antisocial, egocentric, dominant and insensitive." A few years later, it was noted that he "had been acting strangely and pestering other inmates regarding his/their religious beliefs." He was also accused of being involved in a "racial uprising" in one institution, pitting "Indian against white." At this time, he was diagnosed as schizophrenic, "somewhat delusional, hyperactive and genuinely presenting concern from a management standpoint." Another assessment at the time referred to him as "borderline psychotic," an individual who refused to open up and discuss his feelings or experiences.

While in prison, he encountered an Aboriginal Elder from his area and began to consult with him. Subsequently, he made a decision to stop taking his medication, an action that concerned the prison staff. However, they were prepared to monitor his progress with the Elder and allow him the opportunity to "see what he can do, along with the Elders, to help himself and to stabilize his mental state." In one report, staff noted: "He has obtained an amulet from the Elder, and seems to be working within a Native spirituality framework to regain some stability and sense of direction. Speaking with him it does not appear that at present there is any inclination towards self-harm or suicide. He seems to have identified fairly strongly with the Native counselling and spirituality framework, and it seems to be providing sufficient structure, and support for his needs." However, it was recommended that he seek treatment at one of the Regional Psychiatric Centres (RPC).

In contrast to previous assessments, a more current psychological assessment uncovered no evidence of perceptual abnormalities or formal thought disorders, no impairments in cognitive skills, and no evidence of depression. But it did uncover a phenomenon that baffled the assessor. The existence of a conflict between the psychological approach to etiology and assessment and the emerging understanding of the offender, based in his rediscovery of Aboriginal spirituality, is evident from the report:

> At interview... [he] described an elaborate delusional system which, on his request, is not being further described in as much as he wanted to protect the protagonist involved in his beliefs. Despite there being some cultural elements in his delusions, for example "bad medicine," that could pose difficulties in diagnosis, on further exploration of his symptoms... it was felt that the

content of his delusional system was too bizarre to pass for a normal experience.

This passage is remarkable for a number of reasons. The offender was expressing a belief in "bad medicine," a belief that other individuals could cause harm, bad luck, or illness through spiritual means. This belief is common among many North American Aboriginal cultures. The author of the psychiatric report quoted above appears to accept the inmate's experiential reality concerning bad medicine: at the inmate's request he does not describe it in detail (on the belief that to discuss it further would harm the individual who "sent" the "bad medicine" — this alone is telling of the transformation that the inmate was undergoing). However, the psychiatrist rejects the premise of bad medicine as a "delusional system" which is "bizarre" and not "normal experience." This begs the question: normal for whose culture? Within certain Aboriginal societies, as I've noted, "bad medicine" is experientially very real. But clearly, the standards of assessment being applied in this case are those of biomedicine, which is blind to the reality of such phenomena. It seems that the point has been missed: cases of "bad medicine" can only be diagnosed and treated within the culturally appropriate framework.

I interviewed this offender at length and was able to obtain more insight into his view of his problems. He began by explaining his understanding of "bad medicine" and its effects on him:

> Physically I was starting to have very slow thoughts and a great deal of those slow thoughts involved devious thoughts all the time. Very wicked thoughts, breaking out, running away, or fighting, or not caring about anybody. Those thoughts were going through me and those are bad and very hard within the Christian way. And I prayed "please Lord can you not let these thoughts overcome me anymore." And anytime those thoughts start to strongly overcome me, I would pray. I would pray hard to the Lord... and physically what was happening to me while these thoughts were occurring in my head, I noticed I couldn't sit still for very long anymore. I would always be wanting to be on the move, constantly on the move for one reason or another. I couldn't stand still. And I can't understand that overtaking me. It was really tiring me out.

Conflict concerning his Christian beliefs was also involved.

What had happened to me there was one day I couldn't understand why this and that was happening to me so quickly all the time. And I was praying, I was praying just my regular prayers. But something was holding me back at the same time. People would say "Gee, we see you want to be a Christian but something is holding you back. What is it?" And I tell them I don't know. I am putting all my heart and my faith, and I am praying three or four times a day, and I am reading in the Bible, and I don't know what is holding me back and I didn't fully understand.

As a result of these problems, Bill met with the prison chaplain but gained no insight. So he sought out the Elder.

I had heard of bad medicine being used among our people at times. I didn't know much about bad medicine. I did know one thing about bad medicine, that it can cause whoever uses it on you, no matter where you are, to have the ability to control you in some way or another. It is a spiritual control of you sort of like a devil within a devil. It can be good or it can probably be bad this medicine that can be put on you. This is what I was aware of bad medicine being used on people. There is such a thing as good medicine too and like I was saying the good medicine comes from such people like our Elders. And they know that they are quite capable of using magic or whatever they have to use to overcome people or be with people and to give them strength in what they do to help them pray in better ways. And the Elders know what they are quite capable of doing. And that is the good medicine. This is why I trust an Elder a hundred percent more that I would trust anyone else. So yes I was aware of the effects that it had on people before I discovered that it was on me. I didn't know it was on me. I did know that it could be used for the good or the bad and most cases that I heard, it was always for the bad because people tend to use it on other people, to use it to control one. And when they get this control, they take everything, their property, their family, their money or your spiritual sense is gone and you are just like a walking zombie or dead man. And in some cases a few people have actually ended up dead or committed suicide.

Bill did, in fact, begin to think of suicide as an answer to his problems. He decided to consult the Elder. It was not an easy decision, because his Christianity was still influential:

So when I made my decision, I was held back for about two weeks. Something inside me wouldn't let me go and see the Elder. Finally one day I swore and I got mad and I don't care what happens, this day I'm going to see the Elder and going to see what is going wrong. And when I saw the Elder he detected some bad medicine on me, some disease on me. It was located around my neck area and this is what had caused me to be all discouraged and things happening in a strange way for me that shouldn't have been happening. So when I finished talking to the Elder, he told me that if I want to remove that medicine I need to attend a sweat lodge ceremony, which I did the following week. I went in there and he removed the bad medicine. Unfortunately a lot of damage had been done with me personally, my thinking had gone all haywire and had led me to a place such as this.

Bill quickly began to understand the broader issues linked to "bad medicine." He began to see not only how it worked, but more importantly, he began to see how he could heal himself and change his behaviour. The opportunity for revenge was available, but he was no longer interested in causing harm to another individual.

It is hard to say when this medicine may have been placed upon me. I suspected a few people. And the Elder that removed this, when I made an appointment to attend his sweat, I told him prior to that sweat I knew just as much as he knew. He could not only send this medicine back to whoever sent it to me but he could give me a rough description of who this person was, whether it was a male, or a female. He could give me a description of how he or she may have looked and a very good chance of locating that last place where I picked it up. But prior to this sweat I told him I didn't want to know about where it came from, who it came from, or when I got it. I told him that. I told him I don't want to know because I don't want to hurt, physically hurt whoever put it on me. And he told me that was a very wise and good decision on my behalf and said part of removing this medicine involves me praying for whoever used it on me. I have to pray for that individual no matter what the circumstances were, and that is what I do today. I pray for whoever used this medicine on me that a better healing and better way of life will happen to this individual.

There was still much to learn about "bad medicine," however. At first Bill did not fully understand how his "protection medicine" (the "amulet" described in the psychological report quoted above) was to be used and safeguarded. Another Elder gave him a hand.

> What had happened is he had given me protection and I had a misunderstanding of how I was to look after this protection. My understanding was that I had to wear it twenty-four hours a day practically. I can take it off prior to a shower, take it off before bed, you know as long as I had it near me it was good enough. So yeah I have kept it nearby and when I smudge, I often smudge all my pictures and my protection badge — smudge all of it. In the morning and in the evening, I smudge.

But a different Elder detected some problems with Bill's behaviour and sought out the cause.

> The Elder here asked me if he could have a look at my protection. When he saw me wearing it he asked me, "is that your protection?" And I said "yeah." And he said "I don't think it's working," and he asked me if he could have a look at it. And it was up to me to show him what was given to me. And I let him have a look at it and he said, "you have wrecked it, you have water in it, and have killed the spirit." And he gave me a new one.

Just as the psychiatric staff had, the Elder perceived some problems with Bill's behaviour, in particular his behaviour in ceremonies. The Elder described the behaviour as "inappropriate" to me. For instance, during a Native Brotherhood meeting, after everyone had smudged with sweetgrass and the guest speaker had started, Bill rose, lit the sweetgrass, and started to smudge everyone again. The speaker stopped and allowed Bill to proceed. It took about ten minutes, but no one said anything to Bill; his behaviour was simply accepted. The Elder later discussed this and other behavioural problems with Bill. Bill explained that he was worried that he sometimes did things "backwards" (like entering the sweat lodge backwards) or at the wrong time. The Elder, recognizing the specific cultural group of which Bill was a member, revealed that his people had a proud men's society, the "Clowns," who were brave warriors but whose trademark behaviour was to do things backward and at inappropriate times.[3] Whereas the psychologists had described his behaviour as bizarre and delusional, the Elder placed it within an Aboriginal cultural context, noting that this behaviour was Bill's unique gift from the Creator. Bill was greatly relieved, and even proud, that he was in fact carrying on one aspect of the noble heritage of his people. The manner in which the Elder explained and transformed what was perceived by psychologists to be pathological behaviour into a unique attribute for which Bill should be both thankful and proud underscores the very different approaches of the two healing traditions. Biomedicine identified an abnormality, a psychopathology, which was de-problematized by the Elder when placed within its within its proper cultural context.

As a result of his work with the Elders, Bill began to understand the meanings behind the symbols of Aboriginal spirituality. He began to understand how he could follow a new path in life.

> It has brought me closer not only to reality in this modern day, but it brought me the reality that we are here for a certain amount of time and we are to do our best while we are on earth among each other. We are to do good to each other to the best that we can. And don't even be violent if we can overcome that. Be peaceful, as peaceful as possible with mother nature, the earth. We have to practice, learn. It must be passed on to our children so that they will have a good life too. That's what it has done for me. It has brought me a greater deal of understanding. My [old] way of understanding the modern way of living was we had to kill each other or not care for each other. That was my way of thinking a few months ago. And that was my way of surviving out there. You had to have something of value to be living out there and I discovered you don't need anything of value but yourself. You need to be a good person, that's all.

Bill also clearly grasped one of the central tenets of Aboriginal spirituality: the need to eliminate selfishness and work for the healing of others, even those who had harmed you. In so doing, one commits to a personal transformation. Bill's vow to undertake a Sun Dance is profound.

> I have a child with a heart condition. So what I had done in my prayers and meditation is I made a vow and a promise to Mother Earth and to the sun, that I would perform a Sun Dance for this boy to help heal him. The Sun Dance involves piercing of the breasts and piercing somewhere up on your higher back, and

you attach to rawhide rope to what they call a centre pole. And you are dancing and praying and you are using an eagle whistle at the same time to perform the ritual. I have also come to understand that you can't do anything wicked once you've performed this Sun Dance. I can't even steal or think too badly of people. I have to be a very gentle man after that. And this is what I intend to be, a very gentle man.

It would be incorrect to suggest that Bill made progress only with the Elders. Aboriginal spirituality can often be seen to work in conjunction with other therapeutic programs. In fact, working with the Elders tends to make some offenders more receptive to prison programming. Bill found some value in his work with the psychologists and psychiatrists at the RPC.

I'm trying to understand that myself, why I'm here at the RPC. But I'm starting to understand it a little bit with the nurses that are here and the psychiatrists. They told me that I had some misconceptions about what life is all about. And from what I have discovered through spirituality, I did. This is my understanding now through the psychologists and the nurses of me being in here. Because I needed some mental attention as far as getting a better grasp of what life is supposed to be all about. And spirituality and the Elders are helping also and they are doing a very great job so far.

Case Three

Case Three is interesting because it describes an individual who experienced a "spiritual awakening" and whose personal transformation has involved extensive ceremonial fasting within prison.

"Jeff" was serving a life sentence for murder. His ancestry was mixed: his mother was Cree and his father was French. As a result, he thought of himself as both Metis and Cree. At an early age, his parents separated and he went to live with his mother. This was followed by a string of foster homes, some of which were Native and some non-Native. Although raised for the first few years on a reserve, his ability to speak Cree quickly faded and his upbringing became centred on the Euro-Canadian culture. His exposure to Aboriginal spirituality was minimal, and to some extent negative.

I never experienced anything culturally or spiritually until about the age of eight or nine when I saw sweetgrass in my Aunt's house. I saw it on the wall. I don't know whether it was more ornamental or if that's just where they kept it. When I pointed it out and asked them what it was about, they told me to leave it alone and not to play with it, and that was the end of it. Same with the sweat lodge. There was one next door to my aunt's, a sweat lodge large enough for about four guys to fit into. Just a small lodge. And I asked about that also and I was told not to go play around there and it wasn't explained to me. So that was my cultural and spiritual education.

Jeff's early years were tumultuous. He became involved with alcohol, drugs, and crime at a young age, and he experienced and witnessed a great deal of violence within his family. Jeff was forced to become a trauma survivor.

And until then I guess my family was into alcohol and they were just moving here and moving there constantly; I just never had time to settle down, really getting into school. So within that, at the age of ten I would guess, I started getting in trouble, drinking, sniffing, stealing, learning how to fight. And I took to it pretty good because that's how I survived. I was able to survive that way. Take care of my younger brother. My older brothers and sisters pretty well went their own ways and not much attention was paid to this younger kid to follow. They were just doing their thing. There was a lot of physical violence right from our upbringing. The first memories that I can think of are of violence. That's how far back I could go and that's the only thing I can think of is violence. About the age of fifteen I was pretty well on my own, stealing to survive. Violence was a way for me, a way of life, and that's what brought me in here. I just couldn't exist outside anymore without direction, without knowing who I was. Just the way I was taught to survive. The way I took up as survival was violence, and I didn't know how to help myself. And when I gave up, I took lives.

Jeff brought this "violence for survival" strategy into prison. Fearing the violence associated with penitentiaries, he decided to make an impression right away. If violence was a way of life on the street, it could also be a way of surviving within prison.

And when I was in the institution, I had made up my mind I was going to take a life, just a life of the first guy that came on to me the wrong way. I was going to stab him and that was going to be the way I was going to take care of myself. I had already gotten down to the lowest point is how I saw it, and one more [murder] wasn't going to make a difference. To just settle me in the system. Like he would be a lesson to others.

Luckily, Jeff's intended course toward a new, prison-based career of violence was averted when a friend convinced him to attend a sweat lodge ceremony. Something about it seemed to strike a responsive chord, and Jeff began to find some answers to an identity crisis he had been experiencing.

My first experience in a sweat? It was a Sioux sweat, run by a Sioux from South Dakota. And I enjoyed it, I enjoyed it. I knew that this was me, this was my identity from sharing with the Elder, from him sharing with us, and starting to know about the Native way of life. I could identify with that. This was the way I wanted to go because there wasn't any judgement put on me by the Elder, by my peers. In the lodge everyone is equal. I was still pretty confused for awhile. [But] I knew that this was my identity. This was who I was.

Like many of the Elders who work within the prison system, Jeff experienced a profound moment that changed his life. He referred to it as a "spiritual awakening":

I had my first spiritual awakening after about my tenth sweat, I would guess, where the spirits came and touched me and the Creator came into my life as a spiritual awakening in the lodge. And you know this kind of disturbed me because I knew that this is for real and the path that I was on wasn't what I wanted. That's probably why I was in there in the first place. I took lives because I disrespected my own life and all living life. I was a pretty sick person. There's only two ways to go. And I couldn't handle living violence anymore, prison life, the screwed up way, thinking you don't have no friends, everybody wants something. You always owe somebody something. I was tired of that. I was either going to go out and kill as many guys as I could, kill anybody that looked at me the wrong way, said the wrong thing to me, even talked to me. I was going to kill them. I was thinking of killing a bull [guard]. That was the point: I could go that far if I wanted to. I couldn't get any further than that. Or on the other hand, I looked at what I found within the system, which was spirituality. I had to make my choice. Spirituality, I knew there was a way of life [there]. I knew that was me, my identity. And I chose that over taking lives and going the other way because it is just death and there is nothing there. Some people, they know it's their identity but they don't take it seriously because maybe they didn't have that spiritual awakening. I think to begin with you have to have that spiritual awakening to really become sincere and know that it is for real.

Jeff's spiritual awakening led him to become increasingly involved with Aboriginal spirituality programs. There was some conflict between these and the other prison programs that he was expected to take. He was often told to make a choice between the two types of therapy, a thinly veiled suggestion being that the institutional programs would be the "right" choice. He persevered, taking his involvement in Aboriginal spirituality to what may be the pinnacle of what is allowable, and possible, within prison: he decided to fast. At the time I interviewed him, he had just completed his second four-day fast.

His first fast was done in his "house" (cell). Another inmate also undertook a fast at the same time in a neighbouring cell. The fast was explained to security, and a sign placed on the cell doors stated that the inhabitant was not to be disturbed. This was hardly an ideal situation, but circumstances dictated this approach. The second fast was quite different: Jeff was the only faster, and he was able to stay in the sweat lodge on the prison grounds for the four days.

Jeff felt the need to continue his spiritual education through fasting, but the first time he was not at all certain what would happen. As he explains:

> One of the things is my expectations were all, I guess, thrown out the door as soon as it started. We utilized the Elders' services for use of the pipe and I myself had no upbringing with Cree, the Cree way. I just went through it with them like by following their directions. I was very insecure about what was to come. I was having, like, self doubts, but that's good. These were good things that happened to me.

Jeff nevertheless admits that this first fast was "extremely hard." Why, then, did he decide to undertake a second? From his explanation, we can clearly see that he was coming to understand the nature of the symbols of Aboriginal spirituality and how these fashion a blueprint for life:

> I have obligations to myself and to my Creator as a Native person to carry on these fasts. It is like progressing the spirituality to attain something which is what I fasted for. If I want this help, rightfully I should give something of myself. And that is the ultimate sacrifice, myself. Something I want to do the rest of my life. I was prepared after the first one to do more.

Fasting is more than simply not eating. A great deal of preparatory work is required. Using his own limited funds, Jeff was required to purchase tobacco and prints and arrange for the meals of his helpers and the Elder that would supervise him. The helpers had important functions to perform to ensure that the fast would run smoothly.

> I chose them because from experience I know that they have been working the lodge area. They have been trying to help themselves, they have some knowledge of sweat lodges and what's to be respected. And I had one head helper and three others under him that would do the work that they were told. They were out there doing their duties preparing my place of fast. They helped with the sweat lodge, set up the sweats, filled up the pipe, helped the Elder out. Whatever needed being done, they were there to do it. And they did an excellent job.

As with any activity inside prison, security is a concern. Jeff recognized the legitimacy of the security issue and decided to work with prison staff. He realized that the staff had legitimate reasons, in some instances, to be wary. He also suggested that the Aboriginal inmates and Elders have a responsibility to ensure everything runs smoothly. There are serious spiritual consequences for sacrilegious behaviour.

> This is a big concern; it has always been a big battle between Native inmates and administration — the trust factor. There has been incidents in the past where the institution has been scarred by guys attempting to escape from here. But that [sweat lodge] isn't a place to play and sure not a place to escape. These are the things that concern us as Native people, also, because it

is not like just because a person's brown and attends a sweat they can just say, "okay, we are going to give you all the trust in the world." It is just not like that. I can see where they are coming from, security-wise, and we also have those concerns. And we also have to take a lot of consideration when it comes to putting anyone out in the fast and when it comes to having them out in the lodge, when it comes to giving them an eagle feather. These are things that have to be considered by the Elder, by his peers. These things are very respected by most Native people. Like, there is very few that play around with that and when it is played around with, they are usually taken or they're given some help to educate them.

Jeff, together with the Elder and the Native liaison, was able to work out a plan that met the concerns of security and that entailed minimal disruption to the fast.

They did five counts throughout the day and all they did was tap on the lodge and I would tap back and that was their count. They didn't have to see me. I guess they spent time in the teepee [next to the sweat lodge] and when they did, they were instructed that if I needed help I was to tap on the lodge. They would inform me when the Elder or my supervisor had just left and he would be right back. So that was pretty good. They were really interested in what was going on there and they took part in it. And when it did come time for them to take their position there to spell the Elder or Native liaison, they were readily there. They were very interested in what was going on and taking some information in about the lodge and the teepee and about the fast. They had asked a lot of questions about the fasting themselves.

From Jeff's perspective, this second fast was very successful, and he greatly appreciated the assistance he received. His involvement resulted in a change in attitude toward the other prison rehabilitation programs. As he noted, "I'm just going to take the good from the program, and being able to fast is a plus while I was here. So I'm going to walk away feeling good." However, he denied that his involvement with Aboriginal spirituality was simply a way of coping within prison. It was a new road to follow. He stated emphatically:

No, it is a way of life. When I get out of here, like this is just the tip of the iceberg, you know what I mean, in prison. It's just an awareness. It's a beginning, I mean it's just very little knowledge compared to what is out there. And there's a lot, like a lot of the ceremonies. There's ceremonies that people figure are dead now that aren't around. It's just they're not publicized, that's all. There's a lot of teachers out there with gifts, gifts that are unheard of and again, a lot of the people that are very gifted are unheard of, like they're not publicized. They don't work for anyone, they work for the people. Give them that tobacco, that's all they need for payment, or cloth. They don't work for the government or anything. I mean this is the beginning here, it's an awareness and you can find something and there is knowledge. You need this knowledge here, this beginning in order to go out there on the street, to participate because this is like, I don't know, some place where you could start to identify, to know what you really want and out there the opportunity is there. It presents itself, it's for anyone. Just up to a guy to take it from there.

Case Four

"Bob's" case is remarkable because it highlights several important themes. Not only does Bob undergo a significant spiritual transformation, he also seems to undergo a cultural one, blending elements of his new found spirituality with his original Indian cultural orientation. His transformation is so successful that it attracts negative attention from some staff within the prison who are suspicious of his sincerity. This is compounded by Bob's reluctance to become involved in prison rehabilitation programming, which he sees as inappropriate for Aboriginal people. Bob also displays the dedication to Aboriginal spirituality that suggests he is on his way to being recognized as an Elder; indeed, he seems to be at an earlier stage typical of many current prison Elders. Unlike Jeff, Bob was actually able to engage in spiritual activities outside the prison.

When I met Bob, he was serving a life sentence. He had grown up with his family in the north, and had spent a great deal of time on the traplines and hunting. He spoke his Indian language fluently. His religious upbringing, however, was Christian, like so many other northern Aboriginal people. While in prison, he began to study Aboriginal spirituality, particularly the Cree way (he was not culturally

Cree), and slowly his behaviour began to change. It became clear to him that, while culturally he was "Indian," spiritually there was a void.

> Well, I grew up trapping as a matter of fact. I grew up right out on the land. I know I grew up much more traditional than a lot of traditionalists of today. But I look at it as sure I grew up culturally, but I was not spiritually connected to my identity. Culturally connected, but not spiritually connected. Basically my understanding of the teachings that were given to guide our people in their spiritual journey, I grew up without that direction. I grew up with the direction of the Anglican Church to guide my spiritual walk. Yes, I grew up with the physical, cultural part of it, very traditional, but not the spiritual connections to my identity. Like, really trying to get in touch with my own identity about what being a Native person was about. Traditionally, culturally yes I knew how I grew up, I know my roots were living off the land and growing up like that. But the whole philosophy behind being Native, I didn't have that connection. And that's what I felt was really lacking in my life, was that identity, the whole identity of what my journey as a Native person entails. I wanted to be connected right to the core of what my people are about, being Native, with my identity through the teachings of my people, with a whole different philosophy to guide my spiritual life.

Bob had dedicated many years of his life in prison to the arduous task of learning Aboriginal spirituality in all its complexity. He had internalized the symbols and developed a new plan for his life.

> And since connecting to it, having to learn the disciplines of five fastings, and through sweat lodge ceremonies, it is a whole different way rather than just this concept that if I believe, I can be forgiven for all the garbage that I have caused. But through the Native way, it is like I've got to earn my way back in the good graces of the people I've harmed. And that's okay with me. That makes more sense to me, you know. A lot of the teachings are already within yourself, and it's like how much discipline you put into digging that out through fasting and through those ways that I've struggled for the knowledge that I have come to understand. Now I understand and that's what really gives me a sense that I earned it and I'm just not forgiven

today and I can forget about all the garbage that I have caused everybody. It gives me the sense that I've earned my way back somewhat through the understanding that I have now. That's satisfying.

Bob's commitment did not come about instantaneously as the result of a particular spiritual awakening. It developed more slowly, aided however by long stretches in segregation and the Special Handling Unit. He began to find what he was looking for when he met a Cree Elder in prison and began to learn the Cree way. This resulted in a synthesis of cultural and spiritual elements that formed his emerging, new identity.

> Well the central belief system that I have is of the Cree culture, is of the Cree people. My cultural upbringing is [anonymous] so those two are definitely combined. I definitely combined those two in comprising my own identity. But the other parts that I have picked up, like from what I have learned from the Sioux. They were the first ones that taught me that I went to a sweat with, the first ones that I went on a fast with and that was the beginning of my journey. And now having met this Cree Elder and having connected to him as in having been given a real good understanding of my walk in life, that really connected me to the Cree teachings of spirituality. So that really is important to me and that's something that makes sense to me.

As his spiritual journey progressed over the years, it became necessary for him to move beyond the confines of prison to further his spiritual education. There were clear limits to what he could achieve within the prison context. Therefore, with the help of an Elder, he applied for a pass to attend a three-day spiritual retreat. With the approval of the National Parole Board, his request was granted. He described the many years of perseverance that culminated in this important event:

> Well it was after having initiated programs for about two, three years there, and really being involved in sweat lodge ceremonies all that time. Being involved in a lot of fasting, just initiating different programs like a family counselling program where the guys would be able to bring in their wives, their children, and being counselled by the Elders and given direction and that. Just different programs and building up credibility over the years

about not just what I was about but what the whole Native Brotherhood was about, and creating an awareness within the administration to the point where they even took the initiative to ask for a sweat lodge. And the whole administration came out and went to a sweat, myself and an Elder. So it was after creating a lot of awareness with them, and them understanding to the point where they respected that what I was involved in was just barely scratching the surface of what Native spirituality was all about. And in order for me to be exposed to the real hard core traditional teachings, I would have to kind of go out into the mountains with the Elders in order to really progress in that area. It also had a lot to do with the Elder we had working there; he had a lot of credibility. And you know he really thought that I should be exposed to some of the teachings, some of the traditional teachings. Be exposed to some of the real critical ceremonies, I guess. And it was him kind of initiating the idea with me that I've got to go out there, I've got to be involved with some of these ceremonies and that. It was just me applying for the pass and talking with the warden. I was really supported by the Elder. He thought that the work I had done with him over the years, the work I had done with the Brotherhood, that I had come to a point where I was ready for this type of exposure to that type of ceremony. I had earned that and I think from the overall feeling of the administration at that point, you know, the credibility I had built up within the institution, that they had a good idea that I was pretty sincere about what I was about. The warden really went out to back me and went in front of the National Parole Board. He really expressed that I be given the opportunity to go out and be exposed to these ceremonies.

In the eyes of many, Bob's spiritual retreat was viewed as highly unorthodox, unwarranted, expensive, and dangerous. The guards' union was quoted in the local press as opposed, dredging up arguments that they hoped would pander to a public fear of criminals and corrections. They emphasized not only that Bob was in prison for murder, and therefore a threat to the guards who would accompany him (and by extension a threat to the community), but that the trip would be costly in terms of overtime for the guards and the rental of camping equipment. When the media caught wind of the excursion, after it had started, they played to the public's fears with screaming headlines such as "Killer's camping trip sparks anger," "Killer con camping furore grows" and "Camping killer con backed."

Typically, much smaller type was used to note that this was a "spirituality leave." Even Doug Lewis, federal Solicitor General, was called upon to defend the correctional decision. While a local town councillor offered her opinion that Bob was unlikely to return to prison from the trip ("It's so beautiful outside, why would he?"), Bob completed his ceremonies and returned quietly to prison, only then to learn of the controversy.

> It was actually a very low risk situation that he [the warden] was letting me go and there was very low risk that I was going to screw up. There was just too much loyalty attached to my Native spirituality, to my people. I would never screw that up. No, it's almost like taboo I guess to me [to think of escaping], when the thought can't even enter. That's what it was about. I went out there and I was in ceremony. Like we would start building lodges in the morning and the afternoon we were in ceremonies and we were in ceremonies until four o'clock in the morning. So we were in ceremonies around the clock. But even going out there and prior to going out there, taking off, I knew that was out of the question, so no use even letting it enter my mind. And I think that is what the warden understood. He understood there was very low risk involved.

Despite the opposition of the guards' union, Bob found three guards willing to escort him, one of whom was Aboriginal. They gave Bob the space he needed to undertake his ceremonies and maintained a low profile in the camp of more than one hundred celebrants. But they also attended some ceremonies, and one guard went into the sweat lodge. Bob clearly made an impression on them:

> I thought they were excellent. On the very last day of the ceremony there was just myself and the guards. They had come to me and asked me to do a pipe ceremony with them, just me and them. They had come and offered me some tobacco and initiated a pipe ceremony between myself and them. And they wanted to go right to the top of one hill so the three of us went and climbed the top of this hill and had a ceremony up there just prior to coming back.

There was ample opportunity to escape:

I was in ceremony all the time and they weren't there. Like they would be out around the main fire where all the cooking was going on and that type of stuff. I was involved in a lot of the preparation whereas they weren't around at all. And a lot of times, when the ceremonies went to four o'clock into the night, they were nowhere around. I would be in the ceremony all those times and sometimes from one o'clock to four o'clock in the morning and they would be in their teepee sleeping.

Yeah, it was pretty good. I think one of them stayed awake and stayed around the fire, but there was no real necessity of them keeping me in their sights at all times or anything. I mean I was taking an axe myself and I was going away out into the bush and just chopping wood myself at times. Like no one else around, just myself going out in the bush chopping wood and coming back to camp. They trusted me.

That was one thing that they told me when I first went there, because I remember when we got there I told them, "Listen. I don't want you guys worrying about me taking off or anything because I have come here for specific reasons."

And they said, "We are not worried about you, we are not worried about it at all. You go and do what you have to do."

That's all they told me and that was good. It was perfect.

The reports of the guards involved were very positive, although they had difficulty sleeping and complained of the smoke ("Officers who cannot tolerate smoke should not go on such an escort. Every ceremony and every event included smoke"). They described Bob's behaviour as "impeccable and above reproach."

Despite Bob's involvement with Aboriginal spirituality, and the progress he was making, throughout the latter years of his prison term he encountered a great deal of friction because of his view that most prison rehabilitation programs were not appropriate for Aboriginal offenders. He was a strong vocal critic of these programs. An early report described him critically: "[He] does not... fully participate or accept the Living Unit concept... Most of his efforts are feeble or display a false front. He regards rules and regulations and those staff members who enforce them as superfluous in regards to his objectives."

A few years later, it was noted that "in most CMT [Case Management Team] meetings time is spent discussing the frustration he encounters as he feels his spiritual needs are not being met due to restrictions he believes he is placed under by CSC policies." He was described as "self-directed" and unwilling to accept "compromise" in treatment; in other words, it was recognized that he was rehabilitating himself almost exclusively through Aboriginal spirituality. He continued to emphasize that psychological counselling was unnecessary in his case.

His files clearly document the progress he was making with the Elders. For instance, one entry stated, "[He] is sincerely devoted and involved in his own Native Spirituality and Culture. He does not take it lightly. [His] last alcohol/drug related institutional conviction was a year and a half ago. [He] does not have much faith in institutional run programs... [He] maintains Native Spirituality heals and helps people wholistically [sic]." It was even noted that he was beginning to work with younger inmates and that he seemed to have a calming influence with many who were agitated or distressed. Another report described him as possessing "a great deal of insight and understanding of himself, others, his environment and the world in general." It was again noted that he had "overcome many problems" and no longer had a substance abuse problem as a result of Aboriginal spirituality. Another entry stated, "The Case Management Team takes note of the extraordinary personal and spiritual changes for the better that have occurred in [his] conduct and deportment, indeed, in his whole outlook on life." A particularly telling report stated that "the course that [he] has set himself is not an easy one. It is a process that involves many steps, or levels of spiritual consciousness; this process continues through a lifetime and becomes progressively more difficult, yet rewarding. [He] has taken this completely to heart and has demonstrated, through his consistent participation in the ceremonies, to this point that he is serious. He himself speaks quietly, but with conviction, of the change that [spirituality] has allowed him to make in his life."

Despite these accolades and admissions that he was undergoing a profound personal transformation, his request to transfer to a lower security institution was denied on the grounds of "unaddressed needs" resulting from the "lack of in-depth psychological/psychiatric intervention and substance abuse programs." Bob realized that a lower security designation would allow him even more contact with the Elder he had been working with, and he agreed to a psychological assessment by Dr. Joe Couture, the Aboriginal psychologist whose paramount role in establishing Aboriginal spirituality in prisons was discussed in Chapter One.

Couture's approach is unorthodox, and it would not be wrong to suggest that some CSC psychologists find his work difficult to accept.

As someone who has learned spirituality from the Elders, as well as earned a psychology degree, he accepts the reality of the spiritual from both scientific and experiential perspectives. He therefore combines the two approaches in his assessments. Typically, he will undertake a ceremony, such as a sweat lodge, with an inmate, and afterwards he will utilize psychological tests. He is much in demand by Aboriginal inmates because he accepts the inherent therapeutic nature of Aboriginal spirituality.

In Bob's case, Couture wrote that "his progress is attributable to the exigencies of Native spirituality. His continuing inner changes, against a positive history of sustained growth, is of course conditional upon his present substantial diligence in Native spiritual ways. Ultimately he will be successfully paroled."

Apparently, Couture's assessment was still insufficient and additional treatment programming was called for. As a result, Bob agreed to a transfer to one of the Regional Psychiatric Centres for treatment.

> Well I had been asked to go there for some time for a psychological assessment. Because that's one of the prerequisites that is required for anyone applying for an initial review or applying for a parole hearing that they want a psychological, psychiatric assessment done on the person. So it was to meet those requirements that I came there. But the last couple of years prior to that I was very opposed to Native people coming down and being assessed by kind of what I see as the Europeans' standards, European values. I had also felt that Native Elders should be allowed to do assessments. I thought that, myself in particular, when I had gone out on a pass to the mountains if there was any opportunity for an assessment to be done on me, that is where it should have been done, by the Elders seeing me under those types of conditions. In that type of setting a lot of the truth kind of surfaces about a person. I feel that is where assessments done the way Joe Couture does them can produce a lot of truthful results. I seen a lot of people come to the Regional Psychiatric Centre over the years and go back to the institution and have their assessments done and be granted paroles on that assessment and a year or two later they are back in for reoffending. So I question this whole [fact that] it's mandatory almost to be assessed by a Regional Psychiatric Centre.

Not surprisingly, Bob was initially reluctant to engage in RPC programming or develop a treatment contract. However, over the months, he began to see that there was some merit in what he was learning, and that he could actually use some of these new ideas in conjunction with his Aboriginal spirituality.

> Well when it comes right down to it I still feel if a person is sincere, the Elders can establish that through spirituality, through his involvement in that way. And that a person doesn't have to come down to a Regional Psychiatric Centre to go through the type of programming that they put you through here. But by the same token I think that a person is exposed to different perspectives of looking at things by coming through these programs, and that can be helpful. So it was very difficult for me to accept when I first came here, and having fought it for a couple of years. I just said okay if I got to be here, then I will open my mind to looking at things from a different perspective and taking what I can from the thing. And I don't think it's because I came here that I can go back now and be deemed kind of a low risk factor for release in population. I think that was already in existence before I came here and I think the fact that I went on a pass to the mountains before I came here, and it was a successful pass, that you know that in itself should have been enough rather than putting me through this. But yeah, I think that the type of awareness that this place [RPC] helped create within me can [also] be carried out in the prisons as well.

Bob became such a success at RPC, such a role model in the way he combined Aboriginal spirituality with psychological programming, that he was actually asked to remain at the institution after his program had been completed! He agreed and continued to work with other inmates. In an interview, Bob reflected on his beliefs about Aboriginal incarceration and treatment:

> It really comes down to sincerity. If a person wants to change, he'll change. I just feel that if they put a lot more emphasis on Native programs in the way of spirituality, maybe allowing more people to go to the mountains, being exposed to that type of ceremony, maybe having programs in the institutions where the families can get together, more emphasis redirecting the funding towards Native thought. You know it could be this whole thing about Native recidivism could be turned around. We've got to do something that Native people can connect to, value, and identify with. I mean, over the years I've seen guys go out on

passes and the first opportunity that they get, they're escaping, because they have no loyalty to the system, the CSC or with the parole boards. They have no loyalty. [But] once you connect to them with loyalty, then changes can occur and they will respond with being responsible.

Bob is currently out on parole.

These cases demonstrate in considerable detail the various kinds of personal, behavioural and spiritual transformations that some individuals experience when they become involved with Aboriginal spirituality. The changes that such individuals undergo are truly profound. Yet, true to the nature of symbolic healing, each man's responses to healing are unique. It now remains to examine how, and why, this form of symbolic healing "works" in a more general sense.

NOTES

1   "Jack" and all other offender names are pseudonyms. Aspects of their cases have been altered to further protect their identities.

2   Statutory release is automatically available to inmates at the two-thirds point in their sentences. This is different from parole, for which the offender must apply. Statutory release can be denied through a special hearing process.

3   The anthropological literature on Plains Indians makes reference to the existence of men's societies known as "Crazy Dogs" or "Contraries," whose descriptions are compatible with this Elder's notion of a "Clown" society.

How do I justify what the Elder does?
I know what he does, but I can't explain it.
— PRISON WARDEN

9
"But Does it Work?"

How effective is Aboriginal spirituality as a form of therapy? This is not an easy question to answer, and in some ways even asking it is problematic. Aboriginal spirituality can be seen to be therapeutically effective within its own cultural context, and some Euro-Canadians are perceptive enough to detect important behavioural changes in men who become involved. The problem arises in part when it is judged by inappropriate standards of definition, proof and measurement which are derived from a very different cultural and historical context, namely that of the non-Aboriginal, western culture and its scientific tradition. In this concluding chapter, the complex issue of efficacy is initially framed within correctional understandings of success in treatment. However, as we shall see, in viewing Aboriginal spirituality as a form of therapy, the issues surrounding the question "Does it *work?*" are much broader.

Correctional Perspectives on Treatment and Efficacy

If we wish to assess the therapeutic effectiveness of Aboriginal spirituality within the context of prison treatment modalities, we require an understanding of the goals of prison treatment in general. Criminologists, it seems, have for generations been arguing the relative merits of punitive/dissuasive versus rehabilitative goals of incarceration, and there is hardly any agreement about which should be the ultimate aim of our prison system. Furthermore, there is also no consensus on what types of rehabilitation programming are most effective. While there is much discussion of what "works" and what does not, an accepted definition of "works" remains surprisingly elusive.

Criminologists Curt Griffiths and Simon Verdun-Jones (1989) argue that for many years the dominant view in corrections was that "nothing works," leading to a shift away from rehabilitation. Eventually this position softened, evolving into a more cautious support of some programming that may reduce recidivism. These authors point out the obvious contradiction of correctional programming when they write: "While correctional treatment programs were designed to develop self-confidence, the acceptance of responsibility, and independence of thought in inmates, the regimen of prison required total obedience to institutional regulations governing every aspect of the offender's life" (1989:415). They note that many inmates were reluctant to engage in institutional programming because these were foisted upon them by administrators who, according to the "con code," were seen as the enemy. Ekstedt and Griffiths (1988:241-242) argue that the "medical model" upon which correctional programming was based usually lacked a clear statement of the objectives of treatment. Attempting to assess the effectiveness of treatment programs was difficult because there were no acceptable standards of success.

Recidivism is one measure of success that the public, and many criminologists and forensic psychologists, implicitly assume should be the goal of treatment. Is a released offender able to lead a crime-free lifestyle? In a paper entitled, "Does Correctional Treatment Work?" D.A. Andrews *et al.* (1990) surprisingly fail to define what they mean by "work," but the paper suggests that they, too, accept recidivism as the ultimate measure. Furthermore, having reviewed an impressive array of literature, Andrews *et al.* conclude that "some service programs are working with at least some offenders under some circumstances." However, they do move beyond recidivism to identify what they term "intermediate targets." These include: "changing anti-social attitudes, feelings and peer associations; promoting familial affection in combination with enhanced parental monitoring and supervision; promoting identification with anticriminal role models; increasing self-control and self-management skills; replacing the skills of lying, stealing, and aggression with other, more prosocial skills; reducing chemical dependencies; and generally shifting the density of rewards and costs for criminal and non-criminal activities in familial, academic, vocational, and other behavioral settings" (Andrews *et al.* 1990:374-375). Yet, in the end, these authors return to recidivism as the one true measure of correctional treatment effectiveness.

Griffiths and Verdun-Jones (1989) suggest that recidivism as a measure of program success is flawed. For instance, those who return to criminal activity but are not detected are classified as successes. Furthermore, there are many factors other than prison programs which might explain post-release behaviour. Recidivism is, in one sense, an end-stage measurement that does not capture behavioural changes that occur en route; an individual might dramatically alter an aspect of his behaviour, such as kicking a drug habit, but still be picked up for a post-release offence. Within the literature there is no clear indication of the time parameters for which recidivism is tracked: is an offender who is crime-free two years after release considered a "success"? How about after five years? And, of course, recidivism can only be used to measure success *after* release from prison. It offers nothing to our understanding of the efficacy of treatment while the individual is still incarcerated. Using recidivism as *the* measure of program effectiveness is problematic because it tells us little about the mechanics of motivation or behavioural change and the process of healing.

Many forensic psychologists appropriately seem content to achieve "intermediate targets" in their work, and the use of psychometric instruments to diagnose problems and monitor behavioural and attitudinal change is common. The granting of parole is another measurement of success since the completion of rehabilitation programs is a criterion which is given serious consideration by the parole board. In some respects, an even more modest measure of success is the completion of the programs themselves, after which a certificate is often awarded and a notation added to an offender's file. But institutional measures of the effectiveness of Aboriginal spirituality are lacking, and one does not see inmates receiving certificates in "sweat lodge" and "sacred circle." Institutions do not even keep accurate records of the involvement of men with Elders and spiritual programs; they do not attempt to gauge behavioural changes related to these programs; and they do not attempt to measure recidivism with respect to dedication to Aboriginal spirituality.

This lack of concern is in part due to the fact that Aboriginal spirituality is not officially seen as a rehabilitation program; it is seen as a religious program, one that may have some therapeutic benefits in the sense that all religions do, but one which is not inherently therapeutic. But we must also admit that Aboriginal spirituality as a form of symbolic healing and therapy is not easily understandable by many people. The usual methods of assessing the therapeutic effectiveness of prison programs, monitoring recidivism and psychometric testing to measure behavioural and attitudinal changes, may both be inappropriate methods for assessing the therapeutic effectiveness of Aboriginal spirituality. Simply put, there is no accepted definition of "success" with respect to Aboriginal spirituality, and consequently no measures of its therapeutic effectiveness. There are no "hard" data. No numbers.

Aboriginal Spirituality as Symbolic Healing

Aboriginal spirituality thus exists within a correctional void in which there are considerable ambiguities around the definition of "success" in treatment and the appropriate means to measure it. Aboriginal spirituality has the potential to heal individuals, but perhaps not in a way that is easily observed or understood within the correctional setting. It would be useful at this point to return to the discussion of symbolic healing which was first introduced in Chapter Four, but which now can be refined within the context of Aboriginal spirituality programming in prison.

Thomas Csordas (1983:334) suggests that what he calls "religious" healing, a form of symbolic healing, "does not necessarily include removal of symptoms, but change in the meaning the patient attributes to the illness, or an alteration of the patient's lifestyle." This form of healing necessarily results in a transformation in which the patient "is persuaded to change basic cognitive, affective, and behavioral patterns" (356). "The net effect of therapy," writes Csordas, "is to redirect the patient's attention to various aspects of his life in such a way as to create a new meaning for that life, and a transformed sense of himself as a whole and well person" (360). Arthur Kleinman (1988:134) also believes that "healing, as a sacred or secular ritual, achieves its efficacy through the transformation of experience." James Dow (1986a:56) links religious healing and shamanism to psychotherapy, arguing that they "invoke similar psychological processes"; Daniel Moerman (1979) and Kleinman (1988) refer to all three as forms of symbolic healing. Dow (1986a:59) continues, stating: "We assume that there are psychological processes in which symbols affect the 'mind', which in turn affects the body." Describing the work of one Otomi Indian healer, Dow (1986b:135) has documented the healer's form of "transformative psychotherapy" as relying "not on physical remedies but on symbolic communication between the healer and the patient." To this we can add Kleinman's (1988:137) observation that "[e]ven if there [is] no specific effect on pathology, patient and healer will feel better and believe in the efficacy of treatment... The therapist convinces the patient he has changed for the better and perhaps to do so needs to convince himself as well." "But of course," adds Kleinman, "such powerful psychosomatic processes do alter pathology, even serious pathology."

As pointed out in Chapter Four, it is essential that the symbols that are communicated and manipulated by the healer be understood and accepted by the patient. This requires extensive education. The healer has the paramount role in this relationship since, in the first instance, he or she must convince the patient that his problems can be understood within the context of the cultural and symbolic system. This is a particularly acute problem in prison, where there are men from a variety of Aboriginal cultural traditions, including some with no understanding of Aboriginal cultures at all. The men must be educated in one Aboriginal way while in prison, or at least negotiate symbolic meaning with the Elder, so that the symbols can become meaningful to all.

Unlike psychotherapy, the healer's role in symbolic healing is more proactive and interactive; healers explain both how and why healing can occur, and in so doing they convince the patient that healing is possible. Dow (1986a) invokes the work of French structural anthropologist Claude Lévi-Strauss, who argued that the healer is, in effect, also a symbol onto whom the patient transfers his or her emotions in a process known as "transference" (Lévi-Strauss 1967). The healer becomes "a living transactional symbol" (Dow 1986a:65), an individual who previously had been healed and therefore provides living proof of the possibilities of transformation and healing success. Trust and empathy are crucial in the development of the relationship between patient and healer (Kleinman 1988:117), and it is precisely these characteristics that are extremely difficult if not impossible to foster within the prison environment.

Aboriginal Elders and spiritual leaders, including those with some prison experience or who are recovered substance abusers, are able to transcend the barriers to establishing trusting relationships that prison engenders. In prison, the "healers" are the Elders and spiritual leaders who are the embodiments of ideal cultural values. In this analysis, it matters not if they are culturally validated "healers"; in fact, many of those interviewed did not view themselves as healers at all. By establishing relationships with inmates that become therapeutic, they transform into therapists and so assist the patients to heal themselves. They exemplify knowledge, wisdom, altruism, and kindness. They often speak of the demands of following "the pipe," including the tenet that they must place the needs of others above their own. They walk a path that is free from alcohol or drugs, but a path that requires ongoing, constant reaffirmation through ceremony. They are symbols of all that is believed good about Aboriginal society, and some are also symbols of recovery from the bad, as survivors of trauma and physical, sexual, and substance abuse. Most important, they are symbols of transformation, proof that one can face oppression and still be healed. No other correctional staff can offer such powerful symbolism.

The Elders are also able to place the individual's problems within a broader context so that they are more understandable and more manageable. Dow (1986b:142) notes how the "mythic reality," that aspect of culture that relates to healing, must be "particularized" to each patient. In other words, although a symbolic healing system exists, each patient must be made to see how it relates to him specifically. This study has demonstrated how the Elders expand upon the notion of particularization. They situate the inmates' problems in historical context, by emphasizing the damage or trauma that has been perpetrated upon Aboriginal people by colonial society. In so doing, they relieve the individual of much of the blame (but not the responsibility) for his actions, since historical processes can be clearly seen as liable. The inmate is made to feel less "bad" and therefore more worthy as a human being, and he is brought to see how criminal behaviour, substance abuse, or distorted thinking can develop. But in particularizing the individuals' problems and linking them to broader historic forces, the Elders also insist that the inmates are responsible for change. The process of transformation begins with the individual.

Although there are pressures within institutions to participate in Aboriginal programs, men are not normally told by staff to participate nor are they informed that failure to participate will be noted (and therefore likely be detrimental to their ultimate success in parole). The Elders maintain the view that each individual must make the decision to seek out the spiritual path; once the decision is made, the Elders will offer as much assistance as possible. Individual responsibility for seeking healing is fostered as the logical first step in personal transformation.

Of course mainstream correctional programming also seeks to transform individuals. Much of it operates on a model that stresses the straightforward communication of information and works on the assumption that individuals, once apprised of the "facts" of their criminal behaviour, can be brought around to accept that change is needed. This form of treatment seeks to control and redirect their thought processes towards more socially acceptable, non-criminal goals. However, these goals are often interpreted by Aboriginal inmates as "White" goals which, by definition, are unattainable by Aboriginal men. Some men see the related therapeutic processes as serving only to further their assimilation and oppression.

Correctional programming places great emphasis on the criminal past, self-confession, atonement, and the depersonalization of the self. There is little patience for those inmates who view their problems as part of broader historical or cultural processes. Kleinman (1988:117) has contrasted psychotherapy with traditional or non-Western healing systems in a way that is relevant to this argument. He writes: "Non-Western healing systems... usually do not regard [individual] insight as a necessary ingredient of therapeutic change, nor are individuation or personal growth explicit treatment goals. These contrasts illuminate the radical differences between egocentric Western culture and sociocentric non-Western cultures, and disclose that culture exerts a powerful effect on care." Aboriginal spirituality can be seen as a therapeutic system that emphasizes the need to heal Aboriginal *people* as a collective through the healing of each individual (this is the essence of "sociocentric" approaches), in contrast to Western treatment that focuses on the individual alone. Aboriginal spirituality appeals to each inmate to heal himself and hence work towards the healing of his people. Indeed, the healing of both self and community becomes their *responsibility* as Aboriginal persons.

The Problem of Scientific Hegemony

One major problem for understanding Aboriginal spirituality as a form of therapy is the hegemony that the biopsychosocial model has in institutional programming. Built upon the positivist tradition of science, this model demands proof that programming "works." For symbolic healing systems in general, and for Aboriginal spirituality in specific, such proof is not always forthcoming. Scientific descriptions of the sweat lodge illustrate this problem.

The sweat lodge experience has been described by scientists as having placebo effects and as entailing an altered state of consciousness (Swartz 1988; Wilbush 1988). It has also been suggested that the sweat lodge can have physiotherapeutic benefits (Adair *et al.* 1988), possibly involving the release of endorphins, and can contribute to bodily cleansing (Kunitz 1989). The psychosocial benefits of the sweat lodge in the treatment of alcoholism has been discussed as well (Hall 1986). Indeed, sweats have become commonplace in Aboriginally controlled alcohol and drug abuse programs in Canada and the United States (e.g., Hall 1986; Grobsmith and Dam 1990; Waldram, Herring and Young 1995). These explanations for the effectiveness of sweat lodge ceremonies diverge from those of the Elders, however. The scientific view seeks to understand the physiological responses of the body (sensory deprivation, endorphins, altered states of consciousness), looking for "evidence" that something scientifically explainable is happening. In contrast, Aboriginal explanations focus on the importance of prayer and sacrifice, and the role of the Creator in protecting participants from the heat and in fostering healing in the broad sense. It is simply accepted that healing occurs without the need for a detailed explanation of how it happens.

These two understandings of the sweat lodge are not incompatible; one need not be seen as more or less "right" than the other. The problem lies not in the multiplicity of views but in the privileging of scientific perspectives of Aboriginal spirituality and healing.[1] It is inappropriate to evaluate the sweat lodge experience only in scientific terms. Science has difficulty accepting the existence of the spiritual; spiritual beliefs are seen as irrational and superstitious. Therefore, science often appears to apply standards of proof for matters of spiritual healing that are even more rigorous than would be applied to biomedically-oriented treatments.

Interestingly, one prison psychologist told me that, in the end, they are not really certain what kinds of prison programs work. They *assume* that if a man has a problem, and you educate him about it, then he *may* change for the better. But they often do not understand why this happens, or what effect one program has on the others. They seem to start from the assumption that if the treatment modality derives from the scientific intellectual tradition, there is a greater likelihood that it works (even without proof). In other words, these treatments are legitimized *a priori* because of their intellectual heritage.

Clearly, then, it is not simply a matter of "proof," but rather one of bias.

The artificial dichotomy of "objectivity" versus "subjectivity" entrenched in scientific discourse is relevant here. "Objectivity" is considered the backbone of scientific inquiry: all research must be seen to be free of bias of any kind. This of course implies the existence of absolute "truth" (which only science can observe), as opposed to other kinds of reality. Objectivity refers to the supposed ability of scientists to distance themselves from the object of study and then claim mastery over it. Expert status, we are told, is achieved through the unbiased quest and discovery of "truth" as science defines it. But, as anthropologist Pamela Downe has suggested, "objectivity is what the Euro-Canadian patriarchy calls its own subjectivity."[2] Bias is as implicit in the objective understanding as it is in the subjective. This hypocrisy goes largely unnoticed, of course, and there are few criticisms within science as damning as that of "subjectivity." Howard Becker's (1967:240) insights are significant here when he asks: "When do we accuse ourselves and others of bias?" The answer, not surprisingly, is: "when credence is given, in any serious way, to the perspectives of the subordinate group in some hierarchical relationship."

From the "subjective" views and experiential realities of the many offenders and Elders quoted in this book, it is clear that there have been some definite therapeutic benefits to Aboriginal spirituality programs. Indeed, "to ask whether spirit [or symbolic] healing works in terms of removing the pathology is to alter the focus of attention. Spirit healing works insofar as Spiritualists [and Aboriginal offenders] have pain and insofar as they do not present themselves for treatment" (Skultans 1976:191). Both Kaja Finkler (1985:5), and Roland Littlewood and Simon Dein (1995:342), have argued for the acceptance of so-called subjective means for evaluating therapeutic effectiveness. The latter authors suggest that successful healing can not be measured by "some objective criterion of health external to the understanding of healing — as biomedicine still argues — but rather [is evident] in the acceptance by patient and others that a transformation of bodily state or sensibility has been effected."

Nevertheless, scholars who attempt to examine forms of healing in different cultures are often criticized for using poor or sloppy scientific methods and for accepting anecdotal information as evidence rather than subjective hearsay. So, while Kleinman (1988:130-131) notes that "systematic evaluations" of the outcomes of traditional healing have revealed success rates on par with those found in general medical care, Finkler (1985), Carol Browner *et al.* (1988),

Joan Wiebel-Orlando (1989), and Robert Anderson (1991), all suggest that indigenous healing systems have not really been adequately assessed in terms of efficacy from a scientific point of view. Even Elizabeth Grobsmith (1989:145), who has written about spirituality among Native American inmates in Nebraska, has adopted the scientific, biopsychosocial approach to understanding its effectiveness. Her tone is one of scepticism; proof is attainable only according to methods she (and science?) deems acceptable. She writes, "It is very appealing to state unequivocally that involvement in native [sic] religious activity provides definite positive rehabilitation for Indians in a way that conventional treatment programs do not... Systematic analysis of Indian spiritual activities compared with conventional approaches must be done, however, if *we* are to substantiate these claims" [emphasis added]. The "we" she refers to is, of course, non-Aboriginal society and its scientific tradition, and in the more immediate sense correctional officials and forensic psychologists. Furthermore, her insistence on *unequivocal, definite, and positive* evidence of rehabilitation that *exceeds* that of "conventional approaches" is yet another example of the excessive burden of proof required by spiritual healing.

I would suggest that proof such as that demanded by Grobsmith is largely unattainable, and untenable, at this juncture. As I have demonstrated in this book, Aboriginal spirituality pervades all aspects of an inmate's life, and it affects his involvement with other prison programs. Methodologically, it may not be possible to separate the effects of more general prison programming from those derived from Aboriginal spirituality. This issue is minor, however, compared to a more critical one: why should Aboriginal spirituality be "substantiated" anyway? How could this form of healing ever expect to receive a fair hearing when the very methods used for the assessment are derived from, and continue to inform, a cultural system that historically has oppressed Aboriginal people and currently feels compelled to criminalize them and throw them into jail?

An Alternative View of "Success"

Aboriginal spirituality and healing are not about issues of recidivism. Indeed, "healing" itself is not the point of Aboriginal spirituality: it is more of a consequence. The notion of "success" as the scientific model defines it, implies the existence of a logical end-point to treatment at which time some measurement of effectiveness or "cure" can be applied. But defining the end-point for many traditional healing systems is problematic, since the *process* of healing tends to be emphasized more so than the cure.[3] Does Aboriginal spirituality as a form of healing have a time-frame? Is there a "cure" that terminates the relationship between the healer and patient and signals the end of the patient's transformation? The Elders suggest that there is no finality to the path, that it is a lifelong process of learning and transformation. It is not possible to say a man is "cured" after so many years of following Aboriginal spirituality. If one were to follow the way of the pipe faithfully, one would probably not return to prison. This is very clear, since the criminal lifestyle is fundamentally incompatible with Aboriginal spirituality.[4] But attempting to evaluate effectiveness at some arbitrarily defined point in this process often results in scientific pronouncements that the treatment has been either inconclusive or a failure. Given the lifelong commitment required of Aboriginal spirituality, the complex social environment of prison with its many temptations, the many problems that inmates have, the general lack of knowledge about Aboriginal spirituality of most entering inmates, and the relatively short sentences being served, it is possible that any measurement of behavioural and attitudinal changes among followers would be inconclusive at best. "Success," as science understands it, is not an appropriate concept to be applied to Aboriginal spirituality.

One spiritual leader clearly articulated the problems he encounters when asked, in effect, to mediate between the Aboriginal and non-Aboriginal perspectives on "success":

> So I see many successes, although the institution doesn't see that because it's got to be evaluated. It's got to be this scale, where they fit on the scale. And that's one of my biggest struggles. They're always asking for an evaluation. How do you evaluate? This is how we evaluate in the Indian world. How is this guy behaving? What's he thinking? How's he dealing with each situation that comes up? I can't sit here and say that this guy has been successful in my program and from now on, he's going to be able to deal with whatever situation comes up. No, no. In what way? To whose values?

Individual inmates change in different ways and at a different pace. Another Elder stresses this point:

We're not Creators here, we're only simple human beings. So are the inmates, they're only simple human beings too. Some are more prepared to change than others, some take longer to change. You know, that's okay. I still see them as a success. As long as they keep coming and seeking the knowledge and seeking the help, seeking the understanding, then that's very successful, I think.

Despite the incongruity, some Elders are still asked to assess the risks of recidivism. This is difficult for them to do because this is neither their primary goal nor how they measure "success." An Elder explained the problems he has when asked to comment on the likelihood an individual may re-offend:

Now in an assessment, I have to say that as long as this fellow continues with what he's been doing here, if he stays in contact with the Elder, if he continues to go to ceremonies, if he continues to learn his culture and whatever it is that he's been doing here, then I believe that he will not return to these institutions. And some guys do. Some guys actually go out and do that. They just find the motivation to find the Elders. Some don't, they get out and they choose not to. It's their choice; I no longer have any control over them. I'm not saying that because this guy has met A, B and C, that he's a low risk to re-offend, or that because this guy hasn't met B, he should be denied [parole]. I'm not saying that.

Clearly, the concept of "success" within the context of Aboriginal spirituality and healing differs from that of the correctional system. This form of "success" is not easily defined, and there is no consensus among the Elders about what it means. Most Elders see rehabilitation as a lifelong process that only begins in prison; they are not surprised with backsliding. Some accept recidivism as a possible measure, but most are content to simply witness a change in the attitude and behaviour of the inmate. Below, an Elder describes how he gauges progress and discusses the positive relationship between involvement in Aboriginal spirituality and other prison programs:

By his attitude. I've seen guys come in here with scarred up knuckles because they get so frustrated. They start hitting the bars in their cells. And you start talking to them. A few weeks down the road you say, "Oh, you still fighting the doors?" [a reference to injured knuckles]

"No," he'll say.

Or else a guy says, "Oh, these fucking guards, these screws are fucking me around. They're doing this, they're doing that." And you start talking to them and next time when you're standing there and the guard opens the cell door, they'll say, "Thank you sir."

You can usually tell by the way a person approaches even other inmates. You can usually tell by their speech; they don't use so much profanity [in] the way they approach each other and the way they approach liaison officers.

When I first start dealing with these guys in terms of traditional counselling, they'd come in here and I'd say, "By golly. I have to see quite a few people today. Can you see [another counsellor]."

"I don't want to see him," he'd say. "He's a fucking dick-head." And then three or four weeks down the road, he'll say, "Well I can see him if you want."

This is what the [prison officials] don't understand or don't see. Or else when somebody comes up to you with a piece of paper and says, "This is my release plan. I'm going to see if I can get a hearing" and on that release plan you see some of the things that you've spoken to this guy about. That's a sign of progress.

Or somebody comes up here and says, "I don't want to go to school." Three or four weeks down the road, he asks, "Is there anytime I can see you, either maybe at dinner time or after school." They don't want to interrupt the classes because they know it's important now.

"Oh, I've got myself back into Anger Management," they say. Or else "I've signed up for Cog[nitive] Skills." Whereas a guy comes up to you before and says, "Anger Management pisses me off. I'm not going there anymore." But [later] he's saying "I signed up for Cog Skills. I'm going back to Anger Management. I go to AA four times a week instead of the once now. As a matter of fact, I'm heading one of the AA Meetings. I'm the chairman." Those types of things. Or else someone that can get up and make some sort of a speech or a commitment of himself to the group during Native Awareness night or during the healing circle. "From here on in, this is what I want to do. I want to be a little bit more kinder to people around me. All people." And the next thing you see them chatting in the door with guards that they've been calling down when they first started here.

That's how I evaluate them.

However, this Elder, like others, has doubts about his ability to mediate between the two systems:

> But what is it when I take that and write it down and give it to a professional? Is there a lot of things that I'm missing? Is there a lot of things about these individuals that I don't see or is my interaction with them everyday kind of blinding me about the negative things that other people see about them? I don't know. When you start dealing with the positive things of a person and you take them so far, I don't want to take them back to where I started from, because I think I've gained this guy's strength enough so that he can start providing some comfort for himself in here.

The narratives of transformation presented in this book would be seen as "anecdotal" evidence by the correctional system, useful perhaps, but hardly "scientific." Unlike the medical model, in which knowledge about treatment is thought of in terms of measurements of efficacy (through use of quantitative analysis and statistics), Aboriginal healing traditions incorporate different, broader, and more humanistic understandings of efficacy. Measurement, quantification and statistical analysis are not a part of these traditions. The European intellectual tradition and the scientific method are distinct from Aboriginal intellectual traditions and ways of knowing; only with great caution might they be employed in attempting to assess the efficacy of Aboriginal spirituality. As Dow (1986b:139) suggests, the "myth" which underlies particular systems of symbolic healing, a kind of cultural blueprint, "is as 'true' as science. It is simply based on another system of knowledge: knowledge of experience." These systems must be allowed to articulate or, if necessary, generate their own understandings of "success," and their own methodologies for measuring it. For Aboriginal spirituality in prisons, this has not yet been done.

The answer to the question, "does Aboriginal spirituality *work?*" must be situated within the context of how the Elders see inmates' problems in the first place, and how Aboriginal spirituality then deals with them. As this book has amply demonstrated, while offenders are recognized as having alcohol and drug abuse problems, as well as behavioural problems, these are defined by the Elders in much broader terms. The Elders speak not of "personality disorders" but of a lack of respect; they speak not of "schizophrenia" but of "bad medicine."[5] They view the individual's problems as rooted in historical processes which resulted in the loss of culture and spirituality for Aboriginal people. Forensic psychology seeks to change the individual, arguing that while historic, social and cultural factors may be important in understanding an individual, they are not relevant to treatment because the individual can do nothing about them. The Elders, in contrast, seek to reconnect the individual with his cultural and spiritual past, healing both the individual and his people. An understanding of historical factors plays an essential role in this.

In the process of symbolic healing, the individual's emotions, thoughts, and behaviours are interpreted in terms of historical processes of loss of culture and spirituality. Through the use of healing symbols, the individual is brought to understand his own predicament in terms of these historical forces, and in so doing comes to see the possibility for change. Behavioural change comes through an understanding and acceptance of the symbols of Aboriginal spirituality, providing both an explanation for how he came to be in prison and a plan for life that will show him how to be a good person. But the symbols are particularized to each individual in a unique way; a given symbol likely exists within fairly broad parameters of possible meaning, and may mean somewhat different things to different individuals. Even the Elders and healers have developed particular, somewhat unique, philosophies and understandings of the symbols. Given these facts, it is hard to conceive of a generalized evaluation tool or approach that would be appropriate to this form of healing.

Aboriginal Spirituality Within the Context of Oppression

It is within the context of oppression that Aboriginal spirituality as a form of symbolic healing is particularly attractive to Aboriginal inmates. Non-Aboriginal society is cast as being responsible for the processes of deculturalization and despiritualization that have affected Aboriginal people, and these forces are played out at the institutional and individual levels. Aboriginal inmates see themselves as being incarcerated by the same non-Aboriginal society that now says it wants to help through prison rehabilitation programs. But mainstream prison treatment can be seen to further the process of oppression through what Allan Wade (1995:201) describes as "psycho-colonization," that is "the inward movement of colonization, extended against the mind and spirit of the violated individual." Through this discourse, Wade suggests, "Aboriginal persons are seen as deficient

(damaged, disordered, dysfunctional, etc.) because they were violated and displaced. A therapy conducted along these lines consoli-
dates and enforces a subordinate victim status for the person attending
therapy, no matter how gently it is applied." Furthermore, it is based
upon a "White" middle-class standard which is implicitly
assimilationist and prone to creating failures. And any attempt to
simply apply biomedical understandings of therapeutic "success" and
deploy scientific methods of evaluation would be nothing more than
further psychocolonization.

French social philosopher Michel Foucault some years ago suggested
that the development of medical science was inextricably linked to
discourses of dominance and oppression (Foucault 1973). Following
along these lines, Wade argues persuasively that there is no such thing
as "politically or culturally neutral" therapy, adding that oppressed
people invariably react to and resist their oppression. Michael Taussig
(1987) writes that indigenous healing systems in general persist because they represent a form of political resistance to colonialism, and
Arthur Kleinman (1988:123) suggests that "Movements of social
change — reform, revolution, and reactionary revanchism — have
not infrequently enhanced their legitimacy by invoking therapeutic
metaphors." Kleinman (1988:129) also notes that healing systems
sometimes "offer interpretations that challenge orthodox political
definitions of reality." Indeed, Amanda Porterfield (1990:152) describes contemporary Aboriginal spirituality as a "countercultural
movement whose proponents [define] themselves against the cultural
system of American [and Canadian] society." Past religious and healing movements such as the Ghost Dance in the west demonstrate
that spirituality has played, and continues to play, an important role
in the resistance of Aboriginal peoples to colonialism.

We can easily recognize a political and racial dimension to Aboriginal spirituality within prison. While non-Aboriginal inmates and
staff may be welcome to participate and learn, Aboriginal spirituality remains, in effect, the legacy of the Aboriginal people. Aboriginal
inmates are seeking to repossess an aspect of their lives and heritages
that was once discouraged and even criminalized. Their re-
spiritualization is a highly effective rehabilitative measure that also
serves to define and energize their resistance. This is done constructively, however, since the teachings promote understanding, forgiveness, racial harmony, and nonviolence. It allows offenders to deal
with the collective trauma that has befallen their people at the same
time as it offers them a new life. It also gives them a highly visible
and significant method of opposing the prison system and the

criminalization of their people in a way that institutions must grudgingly accept. In effect, it empowers the ultimate disenfranchised group, Aboriginal prison inmates. It is a form of reaction and resistance to oppression.

Viewed in this way, Aboriginal spirituality as a form of symbolic healing can be understood within the discourse of oppression, liberation, and cultural repatriation. This form of healing speaks not only to the individual's affective or emotional state, but also to the whole of his existence as understood in cultural as well as historical terms. It offers him a contemporary identity that is a reaction to oppression but which is anchored in a belief in a better time gone by, supported by age-old traditions which are recast as answers to contemporary problems.

In some instances, the reasons why men become initially involved with Aboriginal programming in prison are related more to these political aspects than to a perceived need for spiritual instruction or healing. Csordas (1983) makes this point clear: healing is not always the reason for involvement in religious groups, but often becomes a goal after the individual has first been socialized and educated into the complexities of the new philosophical worldview. Some inmates initially become involved with spirituality for political reasons; that is, they wish to demonstrate Aboriginal solidarity, to separate and insulate themselves from the "White" majority in prisons, or to use the rhetoric of freedom of religion to bully prison administrators. Within the framework of Aboriginal spirituality, these are the wrong reasons. Not surprisingly, however, these individuals often become devout followers of the spiritual path.

Of course other inmates may seek out Elders for help with specific, healing-related problems, such as bad medicine or suicidal thoughts, but for most healing is a byproduct of the process of re-spiritualization. Inmates do not normally present themselves to the Elders with a disease or disorder, and only sometimes with a specific psychological or somatic complaint. Prison therapy programs are often very problem-specific; there is Alcoholics Anonymous, Narcotics Anonymous, Anger Management, and so on. Aboriginal spirituality, in contrast, is more holistic in orientation. Specific problems are handled within the context of a more general healing process because these specific problems are seen not as the problems *per se*, but rather as *symptoms* of the real problem: the loss of culture and spirituality as a consequence of colonialism and oppression.

The fight to have their spirituality recognized in Canadian prisons has been a long one for Aboriginal people. One wonders if the participants in the Kent incident anticipated that their struggle for spiritual freedom would eventually grow into the movement that it has become. However, to simply stop at the recognition of Aboriginal spirituality as "religion" is to greatly misunderstand its true nature. The conclusion that flows logically from this study is that, for many Aboriginal inmates, Aboriginal spirituality is the single most important avenue for change within their lives. Not only does the spiritual path provide its own intrinsic therapy, it also helps Aboriginal offenders develop a more positive attitude toward other prison programs.

Aboriginal spirituality seems to speak to something within Aboriginal offenders. Since the experience is so personal, what Aboriginal spirituality does for the men cannot be easily "observed" in the empirical sense. Furthermore, since Aboriginal spirituality is a part of Aboriginal cultures, most non-Aboriginal people cannot really expect to fully understand it. The attraction of Aboriginal spirituality seems to stem from the many years of colonization and oppression, and it offers a positive identity and a plan for living that is more rewarding than what many men have been experiencing. There is no biological imperative at work here; some Aboriginal men reject the spiritual path, and some non-Aboriginal men have also become involved. Many Aboriginal men know little or nothing of their language and culture, and therefore their "return" to the Aboriginal way must be viewed in a broader, historical sense as a return to the ways of their people. Education is the key, and therefore it is theoretically possible for anyone to participate. It is the recovery of their repressed heritage that renders Aboriginal spirituality most attractive to Aboriginal men.

This is not to argue that Aboriginal spirituality works in the same way for each offender; indeed, the hallmark of symbolic healing is that it is particularized to each individual (McCreery 1979; Dow 1986a). What is unique to our understanding of symbolic healing, however, is the importance of spiritual education and the way in which this form of individual healing is congruent with and supportive of collective political aims and cultural goals. The identities that emerge from encounters with Aboriginal spirituality in prison are hardly uniform, but insofar as inmates accept the Elders' interpretations of both their past and their future, all are, in effect, on the same path. Aboriginal offenders, as with all Aboriginal people, must be viewed in the first instance as having a multiplicity of cultural identities, with varying orientations to Aboriginal and Euro-Canadian cultures.

Yet all can find something meaningful in Aboriginal spirituality. It touches them in a way quite unlike any other prison programming.

Across Canada, one hears stories of Aboriginal prison programming being suffocated by under-funding. In terms of Elders and spiritual leaders, all institutions are understaffed, and these individuals underpaid and under-appreciated. Unnecessary roadblocks are put in the path of the Elders and the inmates: sweat lodge ceremonies are scheduled around other programming; the resources to acquire wood and rocks run out; searches of sacred materials still occurs; and inmates are harassed when they seek to practise their spirituality. The stress that results often leads to a high turnover among Elders and spiritual leaders.

Yet, despite these problems, men are finding the spiritual path and are being healed. Even some correctional workers and parole board members are learning to accept Aboriginal spirituality as an alternative to mainstream correctional treatment. More Aboriginally-controlled half-way houses are allowing inmates to be released into environments that foster their continual healing through spirituality.

I opened this final chapter with the words of one warden regarding an Elder: "How do I justify in writing what he does? I know what he does, but I can't explain it." I believe that we are in a better position to understand *why* Aboriginal spirituality works than we are to understand *how* it works. Certainly the Elders and offenders involved know that Aboriginal spirituality "works" as a form of therapy, although their explanations for why and how it works may not be compatible with scientific understandings. The point that I have tried to make in this book, however, is that the understandings of the Elders in particular are paramount to our comprehension of Aboriginal spirituality as a form of therapy. Like all therapies, it is not a magic bullet; it does not "work" for everyone. But it is the best chance for many Aboriginal inmates to deal with the trauma of their past and the stresses of their prison existence, and to define a new life course. It could be many years before Aboriginal spirituality as a form of symbolic healing can be proven effective according to the scientific intellectual tradition, if, indeed, this is possible at all. For some bureaucrats within the correctional system and some psychologists and other "scientists," to accept that Aboriginal spirituality is therapeutic, in the absence of scientific "proof," is to take a leap of faith. These individuals should be reminded that it is *not* a leap of faith for the Elders, the spiritual leaders, and the Aboriginal inmates. The Way of the Pipe *is* a way of transformation and healing.

NOTES

1   My discussion here should not been seen as an anti-science rant; the gains in knowledge acquired through the scientific method are acknowledged. However, it is essential that we also accept the gains in knowledge acquired by other intellectual traditions. Science is not the only legitimate lens through which the world must be viewed.

2   Personal communication with Pamela Downe, March 1996.

3   This aspect of traditional healing has not been given much attention in the literature, but seems essential to our understanding of how these approaches to healing work.

4   Men may find their way back to prison in a variety of ways. One such individual missed a curfew at his half-way house because he was late returning from an Aboriginal ceremony. This was a violation of his parole conditions, and he was returned to prison. It is difficult to think of him as a recidivist.

5   In using these terms, I am not implying that they describe the same phenomenon, i.e., that schizophrenia is the same as "bad medicine." I simply wish to stress the fundamental differences between the two healing traditions in all areas.

The Story Continues...

*I guess it goes back to... the residential schools.
I lost my language. I became White, even
though I was red outside. I lost my identity,
I lost my culture, I lost total respect for myself.
Now that I know who I am, it's taken forty-
seven years to learn to fly, learning who I am
and learning to respect myself. Because I am
doing things for the first time that I feel are
right. And I guess it was the Elder that made
that eagle fly. He took the time to explain one
day who he was, what they represented, what
they stood for. I have to be proud of who I am.
It's more like I'm that eagle and I'm now just
starting to gain the strength in my wings. I'm
getting strength, I'm getting stronger in my
spiritual and cultural beliefs. I'm not ready to
fly, but I am flexing my wings. It's going to take
a lot for me to fly, but the only way I can keep
learning is by going to the Elders and listening
and asking rather than sitting back... and
people telling me what to do, where to do it,
how to do it.*

*So it's going to take a long time, but I guess
when I do fly, when I'm soaring around, I'll
really be proud too and I'll pass on the knowledge
that I've gained because I think that's what
the Creator wants me to do. I've been greedy
all my life, but now I got something that I got
for free that I can pass on with dignity and*

sincerity. Other people are not going to question my identity anymore. It will be done with respect. I guess I'm respecting myself.

There's still some work to do... there's still a lot of work to do on the hatred and the animosity against the people that looked after me. But I can look at it now and probably understand why they did it. And it's something that I have to let go because I know from that eagle, if I keep carrying all these problems, all these things that I've been carrying around all my life, I'll never get off the ground. I have to let go. Maybe a couple of years from now, you'll probably see me soaring. I'll be flying up there with more knowledge than I ever had before, and I'm just sorry that I didn't do it before. I guess I was still in the chicken coop, still going through the motions like everybody else. I was being told, when, how, why, by whom. That was basically it. I now address my problems more sincerely, especially with the staff here that work for us or are trying to work for us. But I think they have to be educated themselves. I think they're like the eagle in the chicken coop.

There's a bond that's already been established between the Elder and I. I used to be afraid of Elders. With this Elder, he puts me on an equal footing. We talk like as if we've known each other for a long, long time. He doesn't say, "You must do this, or you must do that." He gives me a lot of latitude and there's no lecture. There's no instant solution. There's no time limit. It's my own pace. I'm not running any more, I'm learning, especially my culture. I'm learning to crawl again. I'm like a little baby learning to crawl and then when I learn more, I'll be able to walk and when I learn more and more I'll be able to run. So I'm reverting back to a very early infant stage. I'm proud. I can talk about it freely. I always thought of myself as different, like I was dirty and different from other males, because of what happened to me

*as a kid. And if I did tell people about what
happened when I was a kid, they thought I
was lying and making up stories. Because all
through my life, that's the way it has been. So
I've always resented people in authority. I'm
always challenging them. But now I show a lot
of humility. I'm still very submissive. Now I
talk to people because I do have a problem. If
I don't have the answers myself, then I'm always
seeking answers.*

*I'm looking forward to the sweat on Saturday.
I know I'm going to pay severely. My life has
always been walking on thorns and hot stones
anyway... I've learned to live in pain, but it's
the pain that I feel that's going to be very
beneficial to me because... I always go in the
sweat with an open mind. I've learned how to
pray. I don't just pray for things anymore, I
pray for other people. I got out of the "I" or
"me," it's now others that I pray for. I pray for
everything, be thankful for what's mine, not
because it has a right to be, just give thanks.*

*It's a lot of work and I feel great. A lot has
been happening and it's like if things move in
the right direction, then that's my destiny, that's
my circle that's working. I think that's my
contribution. Things are going okay. That's it...*

References

ACHTERBERG, JEANNE
1985   *Imagery in Healing: Shamanism and Modern Medicine.* Boston: New Science Library.

ADAIR, J., K. DEUSCHLE, AND C. BARNETT
1988   *The People's Health: Anthropology and Medicine in a Navajo Community.* Albuquerque: University of New Mexico Press.

AMERICAN PSYCHIATRIC ASSOCIATION
1994   *Diagnostic and Statistical Manual of Mental Disorders.* Fourth Edition. Washington, DC: American Psychiatric Association.

ANDERSON, ROBERT
1991   "The Efficacy of Ethnomedicine: Research Methods in Trouble." *Medical Anthropology* 13 (1-2): 1-17.

ANDREWS, D.A., I. ZINGER, R. HOGE, J. BONTA, P. GENDREAU, & F. CULLEN
1990   "Does Correctional Treatment Work? A Clinically Relevant and Psychologically Informed Meta-Analysis." *Criminology* 28(3): 369-426.

BECKER, HOWARD
1967   "Whose Side Are We On?" *Social Problems* 14: 239-247.

BENNET, GLIN
1987   *The Wound and the Doctor: Healing, Technology and Power in Modern Medicine.* London: Secker and Warburg.

BROWNER, C., B. ORTIZ DE MONTELLANO, AND A. RUBEL
1988   A Methodology for Cross-Cultural Ethnomedical Research. *Current Anthropology* 29(5): 681-700.

CANADA. SOLICITOR GENERAL. MINISTRY SECRETARIAT.
1988a   "Correctional Issues Affecting Native Peoples." *Correctional Law Review Working Paper No. 7*, Feb. 1988. Canada. Solicitor General.
1988b   *Final Report.* Task Force on Aboriginal Peoples in Federal Corrections. Ottawa: Supply and Services.

CAWSEY, R.A., CHAIR
1992   *Justice on Trial.* Report of the Task Force on the Criminal Justice System and its Impact on the Indian and Metis People of Alberta. Edmonton.

COUTURE, JOSEPH E.
1994   *Aboriginal Behavioral Trauma: Towards a Taxonomy.* Saskatoon: Corrections Canada.

CSORDAS, THOMAS J.
1983   "The Rhetoric of Transformation in Ritual Healing." *Culture, Medicine and Psychiatry* 7: 333-375.

DOW, JAMES
1986a   "Universal Aspects of Symbolic Healing: A Theoretical Synthesis." *American Anthropologist* 88: 56-69.
1986b   *The Shaman's Touch: Otomi Indian Symbolic Healing.* Salt Lake City: University of Utah Press.

DURAN, EDUARDO, AND BONNIE DURAN
1995   *Native American Postcolonial Psychology.* Albany: State University of New York Press.

EHRENWALD, JAN
1966   *Psychotherapy: Myth and Method; An Integrative Approach.* New York: Grune and Stratton.

EKSTEDT, J.W., AND C.T. GRIFFITHS
1988   *Corrections in Canada: Policy and Practice.* 2nd edition. Toronto: Butterworths.

ELIADE, MIRCEA
1964   *Shamanism: Archaic Techniques of Ecstasy.* Princeton: Princeton University Press.

ERIKSON, KAI T.
1976   *Everything in its Path: Destruction of Community in the Buffalo Creek Flood.* New York: Simon and Shuster.

FINKLER, KAJA
1985   *Spiritualist Healers in Mexico: Successes and Failures of Alternative Therapeutics.* South Hadley, Mass.: Bergen and Garvey.

FOUCAULT, MICHEL
1973   *The Birth of the Clinic.* London: Oxford University Press.

FRASER, IRENE
1992   *The National Parole Board: Addressing the Needs of Aboriginal Offenders.* Ottawa: National Parole Board.

GARRO, LINDA
1990   "Continuity and Change: The Interpretation of Illness in an Anishinaabe Community." *Culture, Medicine and Psychiatry* 4: 417-454.

GLIK, DEBORAH
1988   "Symbolic, Ritual and Social Dynamics of Spiritual Healing." *Social Science and Medicine* 27(11): 1197-1206.

GRIFFITHS, CURT T., AND SIMON VERDUN-JONES
1989   *Canadian Criminal Justice.* Toronto: Butterworths.

GROBSMITH, ELIZABETH
1989   "The Impact of Litigation on the Religious Revitalization of Native American Inmates in the Nebraska Department of Corrections." *Plains Anthropology* 34-124 (1): 135-147.

GROBSMITH, E., AND J. DAM
1990   "The Revolving Door: Substance Abuse Treatment and Criminal Sanctions for Native American Offenders." *Journal of Substance Abuse* 2: 405-425.

HALIFAX, JOAN
1979   *Shamanic Voices: A Survey of Visionary Narratives.* New York: E.P. Dutton.

HALL, R.
1986   "Alcohol Treatment in American Indian Populations: An Indigenous Treatment Modality Compared with Traditional Approaches." *Annals of the New York Academy of Sciences* 472: 168-178.

HAMILTON, A.C., AND C.M. SINCLAIR
1991   *Report of the Aboriginal Justice Inquiry of Manitoba.* Winnipeg: Queen's Printer.

HERMAN, JUDITH LEWIS
1992   *Trauma and Recovery.* New York: Basic Books.

HULTKRANTZ, AKE
1992   *Shamanic Healing and Ritual Drama: Health and Medicine in Native North American Religious Traditions.* New York: Crossroad.

JACKSON, MICHAEL
1989   "Locking Up Natives in Canada." *University of British Columbia Law Review* 23(2): 215-300.

KALWEIT, HOLGAR
1992   *Shamans, Healers, and Medicine Men.* Boston: Shambhala.

KIRMAYER, LAURENCE
1993   "Healing and the Invention of Metaphor: The Effectiveness of
        Symbols Revisited." *Culture, Medicine and Psychiatry* 17: 161-195.

KLEINMAN, ARTHUR
1988   *Rethinking Psychiatry: From Cultural Category to Personal
        Experience.* New York: The Free Press.

KUNITZ, S.J.
1989   *Disease Change and the Role of Medicine: The Navajo
        Experience.* Berkeley: University of California Press.

LÉVI-STRAUSS, CLAUDE
1967   *Structural Anthropology.* New York: Basic Books.

LINN, PATRICIA
1992   *Report of the Saskatchewan Indian Justice Review Committee.* Regina.

LITTLEWOOD, ROLAND, AND SIMON DEIN
1995   "The Effectiveness of Words: Religion and Healing Among the
        Lubavitch of Stamford Hill." *Culture, Medicine and Psychiatry*
        19(3): 339-383.

MATTHIESSEN, PETER
1983   *In the Spirit of Crazy Horse.* New York: Viking.

McCASKILL, DON
1985   *Patterns of Criminality among Native Offenders in Manitoba:
        A Longitudinal Analysis.* Saskatoon: Dept. of Solicitor General,
        Correctional Service of Canada, Prairie Region.

McCREERY, JOHN L.
1979   "Potential and Effective Meaning in Therapeutic Ritual."
        Culture, Medicine and Psychiatry 3: 53-72.

MOERMAN, DANIEL E.
1979   "Anthropology of Symbolic Healing." *Current Anthropology*
        20(10): 59-66.
1983   "Physiology and Symbols: The Anthropological Implications of
        the Placebo Effect." In *The Anthropology of Medicine: From
        Culture to Method.* L. Romanucci-Ross, D. Moerman, L. Tancredi,
        eds., pp.156-171. South Hadley, Mass.: Bergen and Garvey.

NESS, ROBERT C.
1980   "The Impact of Indigenous Healing Activity: An Empirical Study
        of Two Fundamentalist Churches." *Social Science and Medicine*
        14(B): 167-180.

PETTIPAS, KATHERINE
1994   *Severing the Ties that Bind: Government Repression of
        Indigenous Religious Ceremonies on the Prairies.* Winnipeg:
        University of Manitoba Press.

PORTERFIELD, AMANDA
1990   "American Indian Spirituality as a Countercultural Movement."
        In *Religion in Native North America*, C. Vecsey, ed., pp. 152-
        164. Moscow, Idaho: University of Idaho Press.

REASONS, CHARLES
1975   *Native Offenders and Correctional Policy.* Unpublished manuscript.

SANDNER, DONALD
1979   *Navajo Symbols of Healing.* Rochester, Vermont: Healing Arts Press.

SINCLAIR, MURRAY
1990   *Dealing with the Aboriginal Offender.* Presentation to New
        Provincial Court Judges. Val Morin, Quebec, 5 April, 1990.

SKULTANS, VIEDA
1976   "Empathy and Healing: Aspects of Spiritualist Ritual." In *Social
        Anthropology and Medicine*, J.B. Loudon, ed., pp.190-222.
        London: Academic Press.

SWARTZ, LISE
1988   "Healing Properties of the Sweatlodge Ceremony." In *Health
        Care Issues in the Canadian North*, D. Young, ed., pp.102-107.
        Edmonton: Boreal Institute for Northern Studies.

TAUSSIG, MICHAEL
1987   *Shamanism, Colonialism and the Wild Man: A Study in Terror and
        Healing.* Chicago: University of Chicago Press.

WADE, ALLAN
1995   "Resistance Knowledges: Therapy with Aboriginal Persons Who
        Have Experienced Violence." In *A Persistent Spirit: Towards
        Understanding Aboriginal Health in British Columbia*, P. Stephenson,
        S. Elliott, L. Foster and J. Harris, eds., pp.167-206. Canadian
        Western Geographical Series Vol.31, University of Victoria.

WALDRAM, JAMES B., D. ANN HERRING, T. KUE YOUNG
1995   *Aboriginal Health in Canada: Historical, Cultural and Epide-
        miological Perspectives.* Toronto: University of Toronto Press.

WEIBEL-ORLANDO, JOAN
1989   "Hooked on Healing: Anthropologists, Alcohol and Intervention."
        Human Organization 48(2):148-155.

WILBUSH, JOEL
1988   "Placebo Effects Associated with Sweatlodge Therapy." In
        Health Care Issues in the Canadian North, D. Young, ed.,
        pp.95-101. Edmonton: Boreal Institute for Northern Studies.

YOUNG, ALLAN
1995   *The Harmony of Illusions: Inventing Post-Traumatic Stress
        Disorder.* Princeton: Princeton University Press.

Index